I0810058

IMAGES
*of America*

# LOCATION FILMING IN THE ALABAMA HILLS

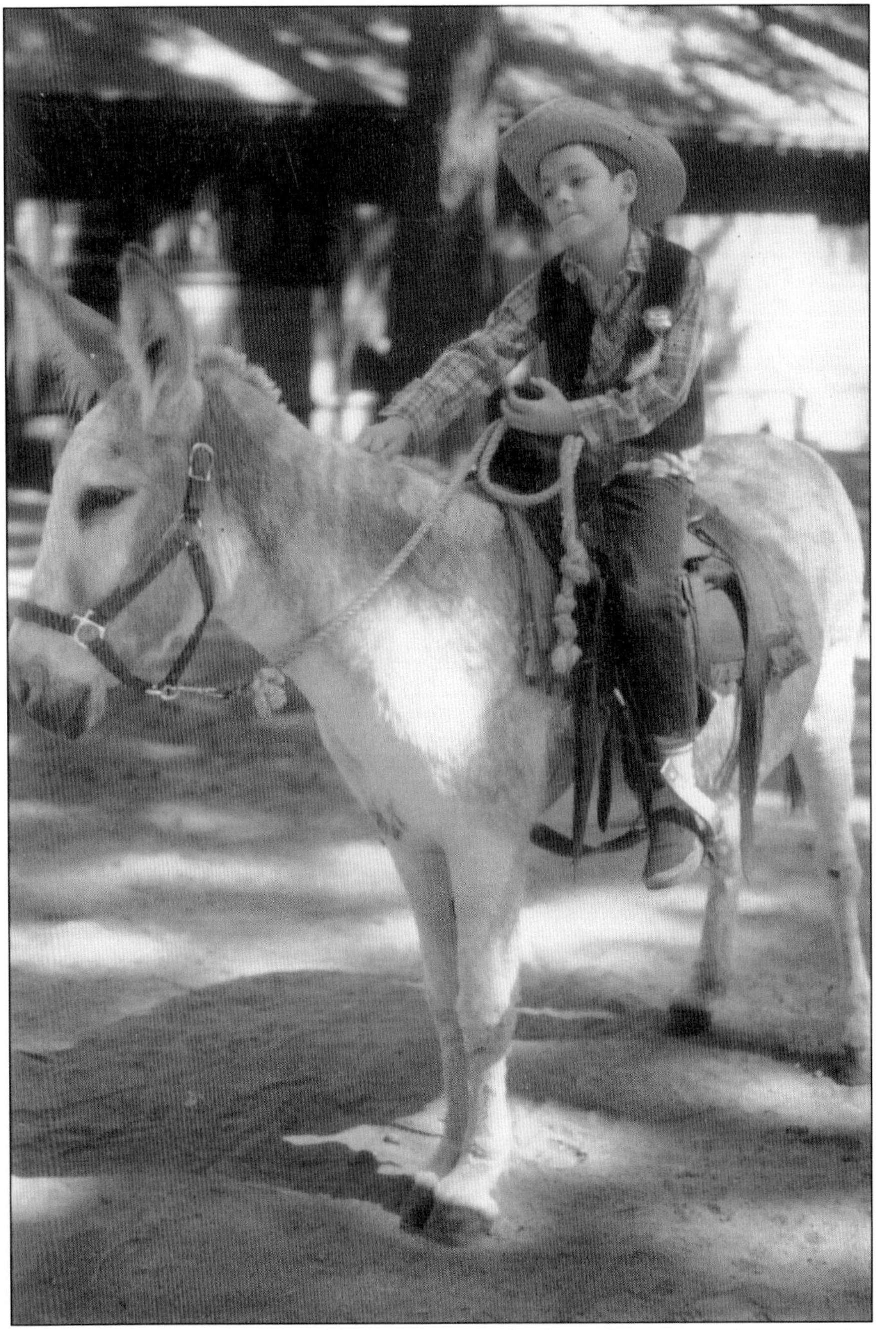

The Alabama Hills provide a wonderful place to pretend to be in the movies, chasing the bad guys, saving the damsel in distress, charging up the hill, or even riding a horse or a mule. Shown here is the author in 1981 at eight years old, along with his friend Brandy. (Author's collection.)

**On the Cover:** This scene shows Anne Baxter aiming a Winchester lever-action rifle from atop an Alabama Hills filming location for *Yellow Sky* (1948), a 20th Century Fox production. (Courtesy of Melissa Galt.)

IMAGES
*of America*

# LOCATION FILMING IN THE ALABAMA HILLS

Charles Michael Morfin

ARCADIA
PUBLISHING

ISBN 978-1-4671-3131-5

Published by Arcadia Publishing
Charleston, South Carolina

Printed in the United States of America

Library of Congress Control Number: 2013947988

For all general information, please contact Arcadia Publishing:
Telephone 843-853-2070
Fax 843-853-0044
E-mail sales@arcadiapublishing.com
For customer service and orders:
Toll-Free 1-888-313-2665

Visit us on the Internet at www.arcadiapublishing.com

*To my beautiful "pretties," Doughgirl, with whom I found many locations . . . my grandparents, who taught me life is learned through film . . . the entire movie industry and the timeless efforts that goes into making movies . . . editors such as Jared Nelson and publishers such as Jeff Ruetsche at Arcadia Publishing, who grant the first opportunity and a dream come true for authors with a passion to write. Lastly, I humbly dedicate this work to a talented, hard-working actress from Brooklyn. She cherished filming, was always on time to set, and was born by the name of Ruby Stevens. She now rests in peace forever among the beauty of the Alabama Hills.*

# Contents

# ACKNOWLEDGMENTS

I would to like thank the numerous people who helped make this book to a reality. The late, great Dave Holland and his knowledge of movies fueled my passion, as did Michael Holland and Melody Holland-Ogburn, who embraced my story. Thanks to Robert Sigman, who supported me through this venture, and my editor, Jared Nelson, who was patient and who along with Arcadia gave me the opportunity. Thanks to my parents, my grandparents, my great-aunt and -uncle Ann and John Gillanders, my brother David M. Morfin and pets Akira, Ichiro, Doughgirl, Ernies, Koda, and Simba. Thanks to my beloved friend Jeff Finney and his brother Jerry Finney, who stayed up late, often to talk about films. Thanks also to Carrie-Anne Christian, whom I will always love unconditionally. Thanks to the people of Lone Pine who shared their stories, Kathleen from the Lone Pine Chamber of Commerce, the friendly staff at Margie's Merry-Go-Round, Jake's Saloon, and the entire staff at the Dow Villa Hotel. I wish to personally thank Melissa Galt-Baxter; Manuel Ruiz; the California Highway Patrol and Ofc. Bryan Duncan; Elaine Delaney and Marty from Aberdeen; John Girodo and Sue Slutzky from Hollywood Heritage; Margot Gerber Barry and staff at the Egyptian Theatre; American Cinematheque; Jamie and staff at the Pig 'n Whistle; Stan and Lynn Fedderly; Vince and Chao at the Formosa Café; Stephen Blackheart at Edendale 56; Eric Heisner; Joe Haney; Jim Phillips-Arbuckle; Mrs. Bates from the Hopalong Cassidy Museum; Cattle Headquarters; Art's Camera; Jim Hastings; Jay Dee Witney; Mike Johnson; Lone Pine Film Festival members and founder Kerry Powell; Chris Langley; and the entire Lone Pine Film History Museum staff, including Judyth, Jackie, Karen, and Susan. Thank you to Maureen Holmes, Lydell Romero, and Leon Boyer of the Inyo County Sheriff's Office for the local town stories. Thanks to the Los Angeles Department of Water and Power, the Bureau of Land Management, Inyo County, and the Forest Service folks with Smokey the Bear. Lastly, thanks to the Native Americans and their stories, which were often written on rocks, thus becoming the first books of the Alabama Hills.

Unless otherwise noted, all images are courtesy of the author's collection.

# INTRODUCTION

Location filming has always intrigued the moviegoer. When sitting at home or at a theater, one might say, "Where is that place?" One might wonder, "Where is that giant boulder my favorite actor is standing on?" For some, it becomes a destination—they want to visit and see firsthand where all that movie magic took place. And that place is often the Alabama Hills.

Like director Ridley Scott said while filming *Gladiator* (2000), there was no other location in the world that could give them that grandeur, "not even Malta." That is what has made and continues to make the Alabama Hills such a popular filming location. During *Gladiator*, it served as the Spanish Alps. The hills became India in 1939's epic *Gunga Din*, and in Edmond O'Brien and Ida Lupino's 1953 film *The Hitch-Hiker*, they served as Mexico.

The Alabama Hills lie under the majestic and jaw-dropping landscape of the Eastern High Sierras in the Owens Valley. As the afternoon sun slowly sets behind Mount Whitney, the ancient rock formations of the hills change colors and provide breathtaking beauty to fortuitous observers. This scenery resembles the Gobi and Sahara Deserts, Africa, India, Spain, Peru, Argentina, Arizona, Utah, Colorado, Alaska, Mexico, California, and even other planets.

The Alabama Hills are still used as a movie location for directors and is administered by the Bureau of Land Management. They are also a recreational area where visitors can go fishing, rock climbing, and camping and where artists come to sketch or paint spectacular scenery.

This was a very sacred place to the native Paiute, who lived in the area for hundreds of years. They have left evidence of their lives throughout the Owens Valley region. Petroglyphs, bedrock mortars, burial grounds, and obsidian used for tools and weapons can be seen.

Trapper Joseph Reddiford Walker is credited with being the first white explorer in the area. Then, in 1864, Clarence King named Mount Whitney, the highest mountain in the contiguous United States, after his boss, Josiah Dwight Whitney, of the California State Geological Survey.

Clarence King climbed Mount Whitney in 1871, setting the pace for future climbers in the area. Norman Clyde climbed Whitney in 1930 and was commonly referred to by others as the "pack who walked like a man" because of his ability to carry heavy gear without apparent effort. Clyde ascended more peaks in the Eastern High Sierras than any other climber.

In the early part of the 20th century, climbers and visitors came back to Los Angeles with pictures and stories of these magical Alabama Hills. A movie crew decided to look into the place, and in 1920, Hollywood shot its first movie there. The rest is history.

As viewers of film, readers might remember the Alabama Hills because of Hoppy's laugh, Roy Rogers's horse, John Wayne's voice, Errol Flynn's moustache, the Lone Ranger's mask, Gene's singing, or perhaps even the cowboy rope tricks and stunts of Tom Mix or Monty Montana. Visitors to the Alabama Hills can attend the Lone Pine Film Festival, held annually on Columbus Day weekend since 1990, to experience the glory of films shot at this historic location.

Throughout these pages, readers will venture through time, viewing images that endure on film and others that have rarely been seen. Some visit the Alabama Hills because of their appreciation for movie-making and to connect with actors of old by standing in the exact spot the stars stood. Others may create permanent footprints by shooting new films to preserve memories of their own.

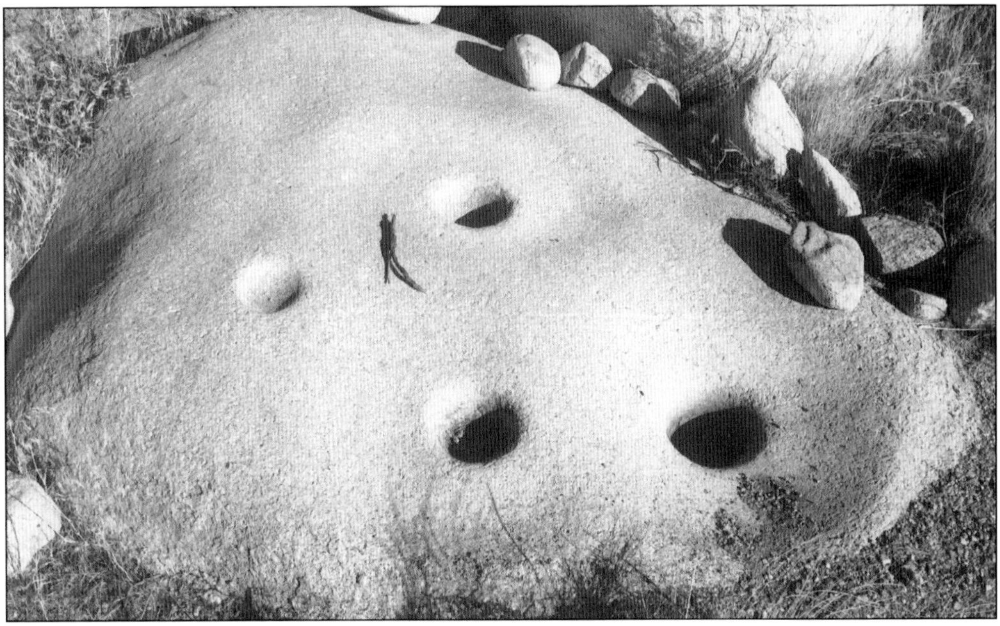

The Native Americans were the first group of people to live in the Alabama Hills and Eastern Sierras. Shown here is a bedrock mortar where holes were formed as a result of grinding acorns and other materials to make powders used for medicine, food, and any other survival necessities. This bedrock mortar was located where a Native American village once stood. Near here is the site of a massacre against Native Americans at the hands of white settlers.

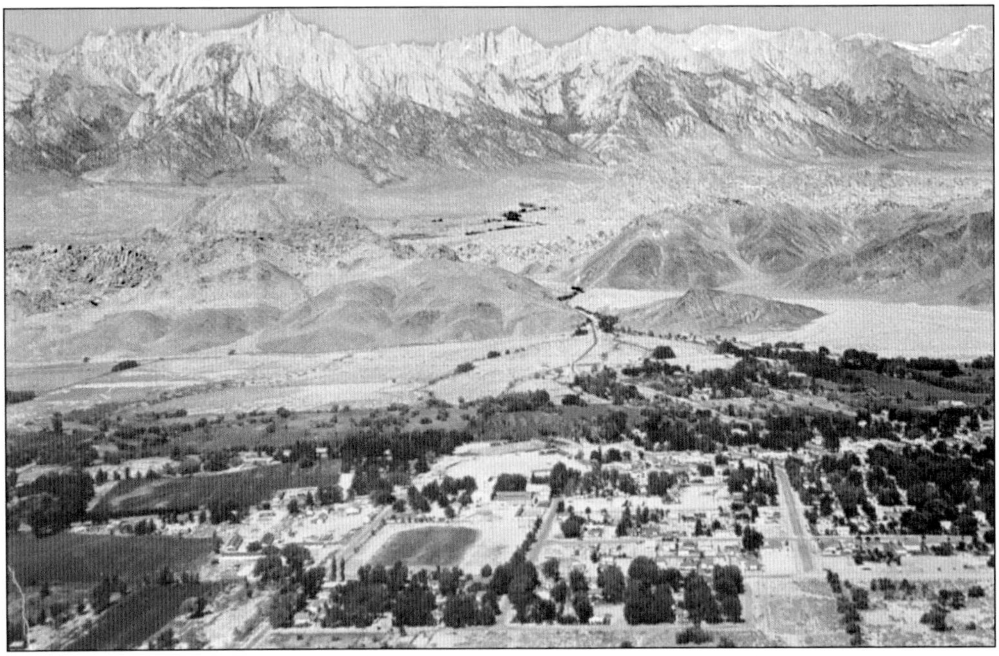

This postcard from the early to mid-20th century shows the city of Lone Pine, California, at the intersection of US Highways 6 and 395. This was the gateway to the Alabama Hills and to the movie industry that has created hundreds of films here. The picturesque, 14,496-foot-high Mount Whitney looms among the Sierra Nevada in the background.

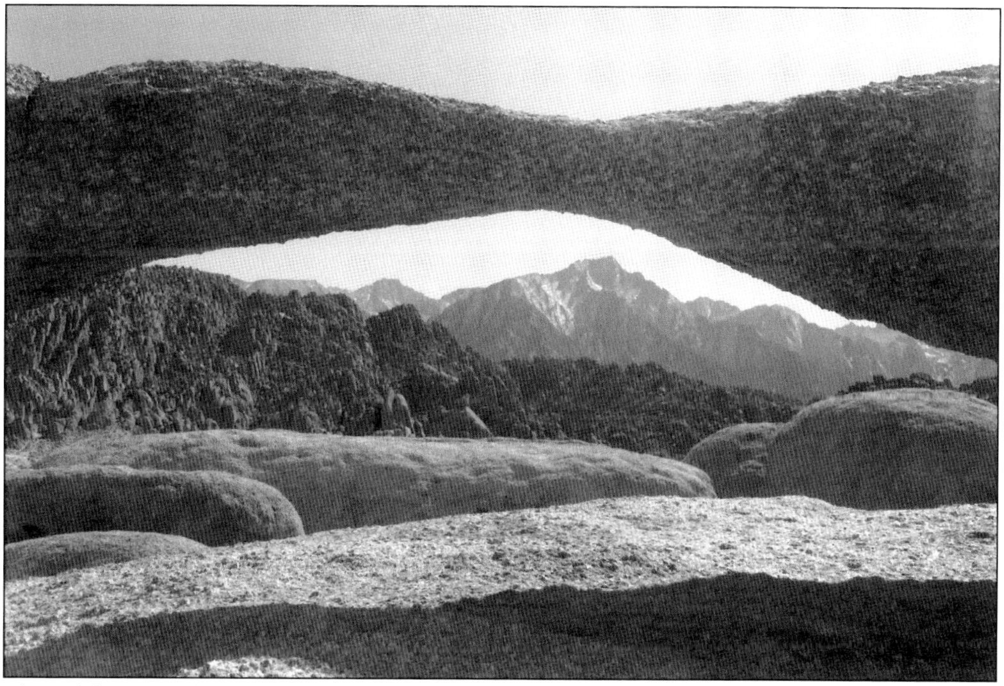

The Alabama Hills are among the earth's oldest geological areas. The rocks in the hills have forged astonishing shapes that look like sculptures. These sculptures are natural rock formations that may look like a walrus, an eagle, or even a bat. There are many picturesque arches that can be discovered. The arches of the Alabama Hills bring artists from around the world. They can also be seen in films shot in the hills, such as the recent *Lone Ranger* (2013).

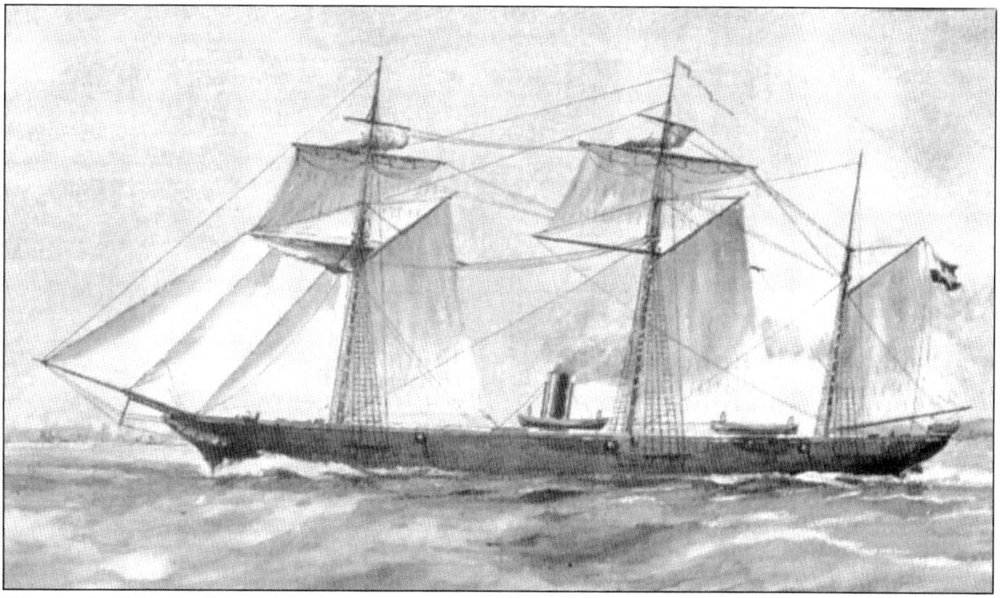

The CSS *Alabama*, for which the Alabama Hills were named, saw service around the world during the American Civil War. It operated successfully overseas but never docked in a Confederate port. It was sunk in 1864 by the USS *Kearsarge* off the coast of Cherbourg, France. (Courtesy of Library of Congress.)

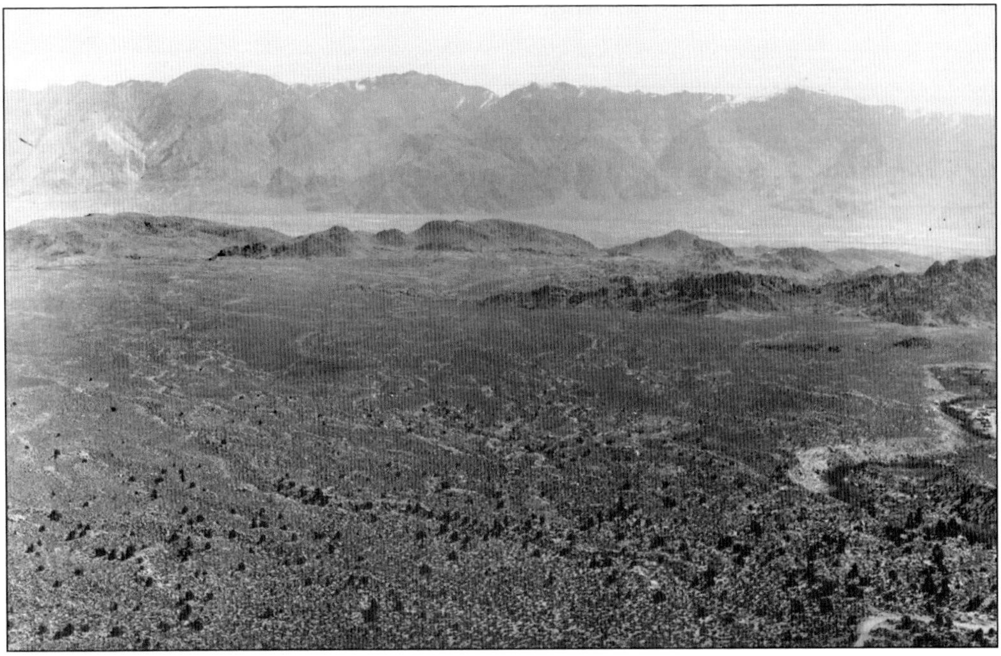

Above is a view of the Alabama Hills in the 1930s. Frontier scenic space is plentiful, resulting in an ideal filming location for epics and Westerns. The image below shows a location from *Brigham Young* (1940) from atop Whitney Portal Road, with Owens Lake (a common film and commercial location) in the background. Republic Studios, Paramount Studios, RKO Pictures, Universal Pictures, MGM, 20th Century Fox, Warner Bros. Studios, Columbia Pictures, and more have filmed in the Alabama Hills.

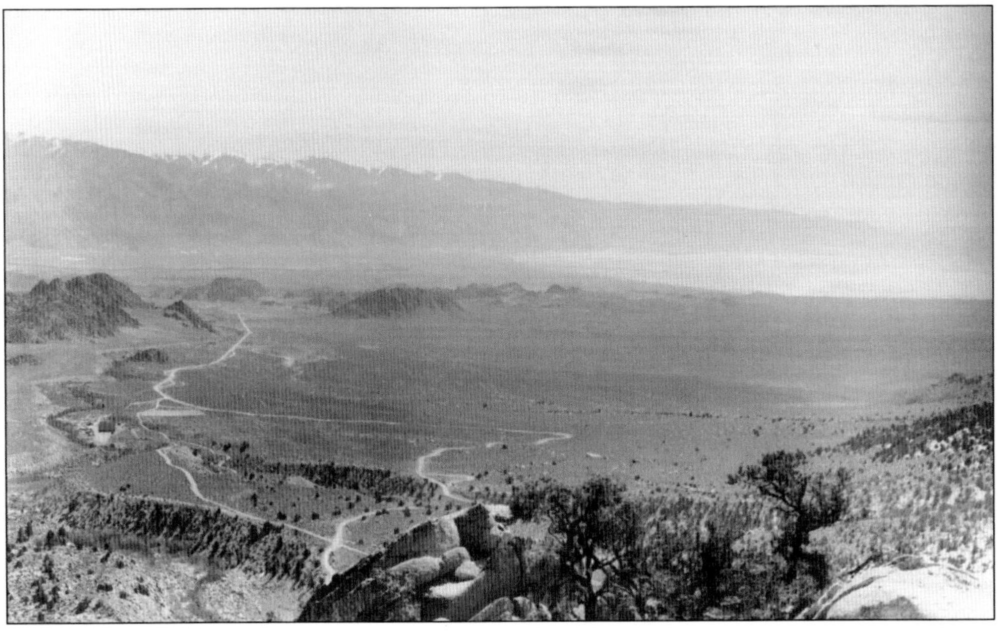

# *One*

# EARLY DAYS

The first recorded movie filmed in the Alabama Hills area was *The Round Up* (1920), starring the famous comedian Roscoe Conkling "Fatty" Arbuckle. A year later, Arbuckle was involved in a scandal at the St. Francis Hotel in San Francisco. Arbuckle was taken to trial and his reputation ruined, though he was eventually acquitted. He introduced Charlie Chaplin and Bob Hope to Hollywood, and soon after died of heart failure.

*The Round Up* and many other early films were the result of an influential local named Russ Spainhower. Russ Spainhower was a facilitator to countless projects in the Alabama Hills and for decades served as a point of contact for location managers scouting the area. He provided cattle, wagons, lodging, local residents as extras, or anything else needed for filming. He is buried next to his wife in the Independence Cemetery in Independence, California.

Early filming locations also exist near Tuttle Creek Road and the town of Lone Pine. These locations can be seen in early silent movies, including four directed by William Wellman. Wellman directed *Wings* (1927) with Clara Bow and received the first Academy Award for Best Picture in the Blossom Room at the Hotel Roosevelt on Hollywood Boulevard.

The actor William Boyd lived on Tuttle Creek Road in the "Hoppy Cabin," once a country club, during much of the period that he made films in the area. In his early years as Hopalong Cassidy, Boyd also lived at 2010 Vine Street, which is located near the famous intersection of Hollywood and Vine.

A movie crew once had lunch in the middle of Tuttle Creek Road. For those seeking to explore the area, Thundercloud Road, Sunset Road, and Indian Springs Road are sites of other film locations lying right off Tuttle Creek Road.

Just as the silent films were quiet, take a moment of silence to gaze upon the splendor of movie making beginnings and the beautiful High Sierras. Appreciation is owed to the filmmakers, actors, crew, and everyone involved who shaped our love of film.

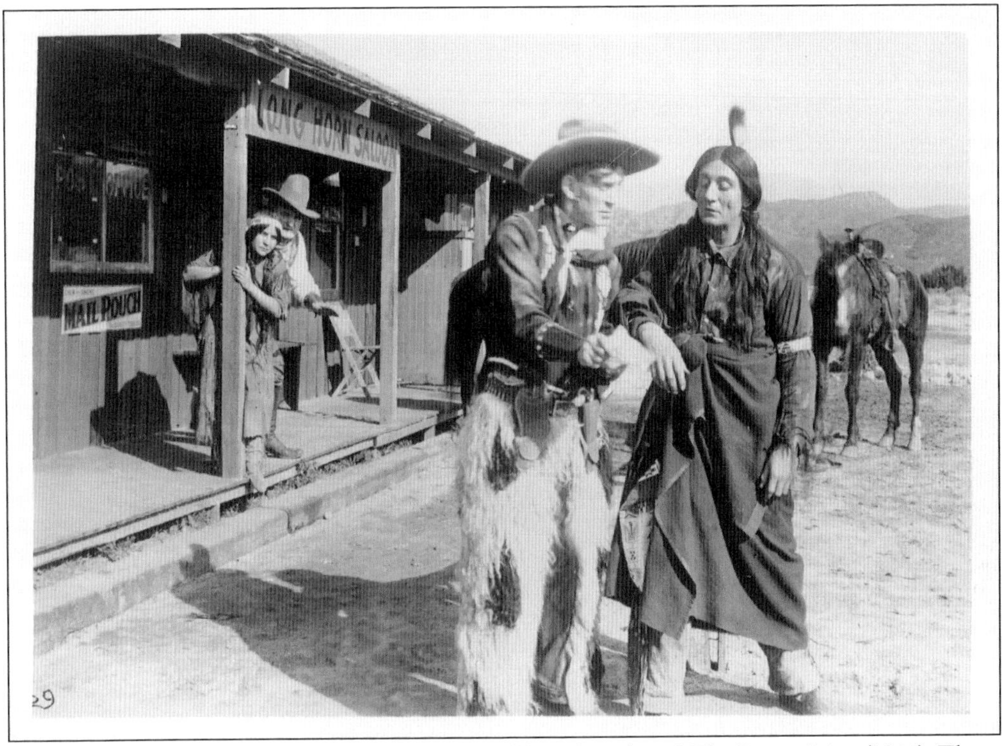


Early Western films included *The Great Train Robbery* (1903) and *The Squaw Man* (1914). These helped set the pace for the first film to be shot in the Alabama Hills. Here is a scene from *The Squaw Man*, shot on the corner of Sunset and Cahuenga Boulevards in Hollywood, California.

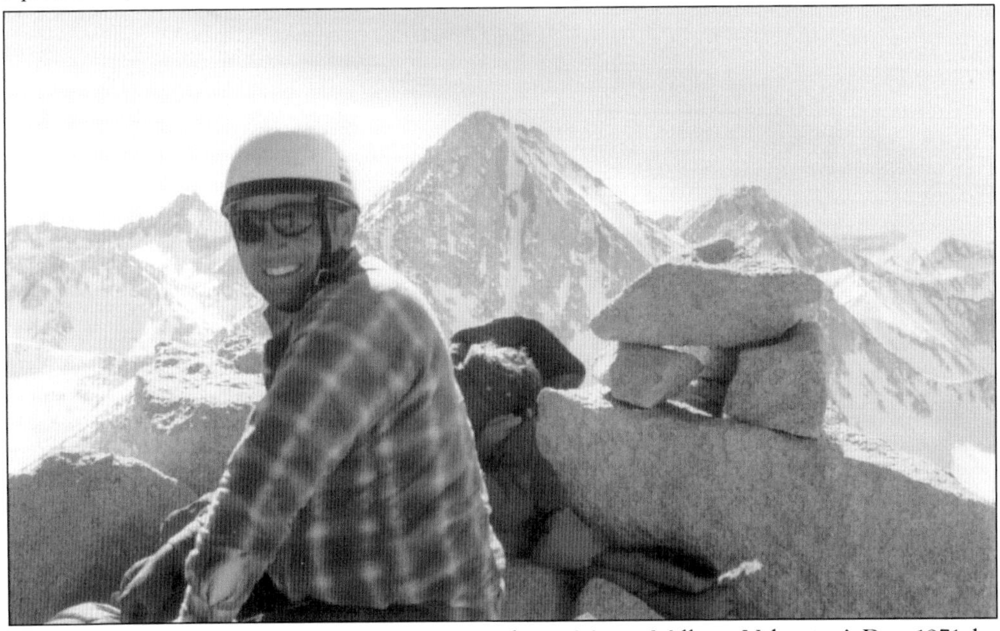

The author's father, Charles Morfin Jr., is pictured atop Mount Mills on Valentine's Day, 1971; he was the first to make a winter ascent of the mountain in the Rock Creek Lake area near where an early film, *The Golden Princess* (1925), took place.

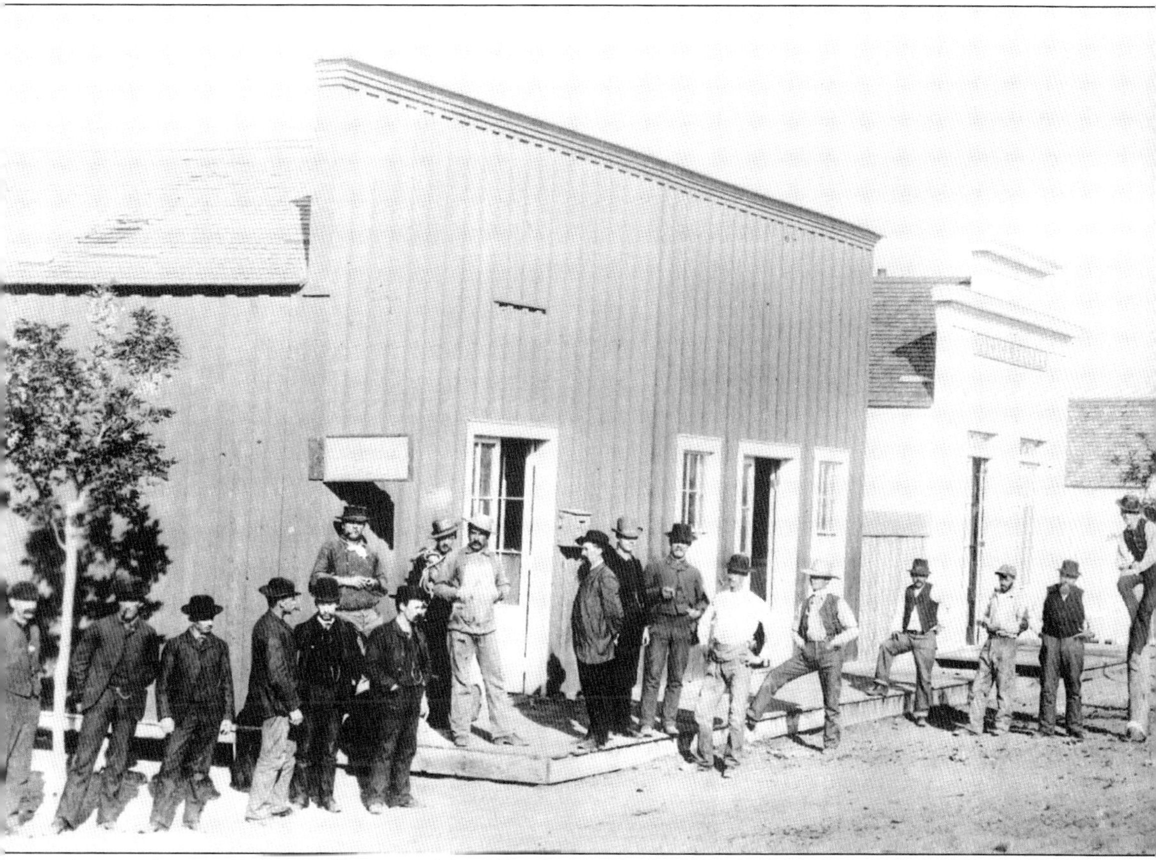

A typical mining town of the 1880s thrived in the region near the Alabama Hills. This photograph of Keeler shows some of its merchants. People such as these named the Alabama Hills after the Confederate ironclad.

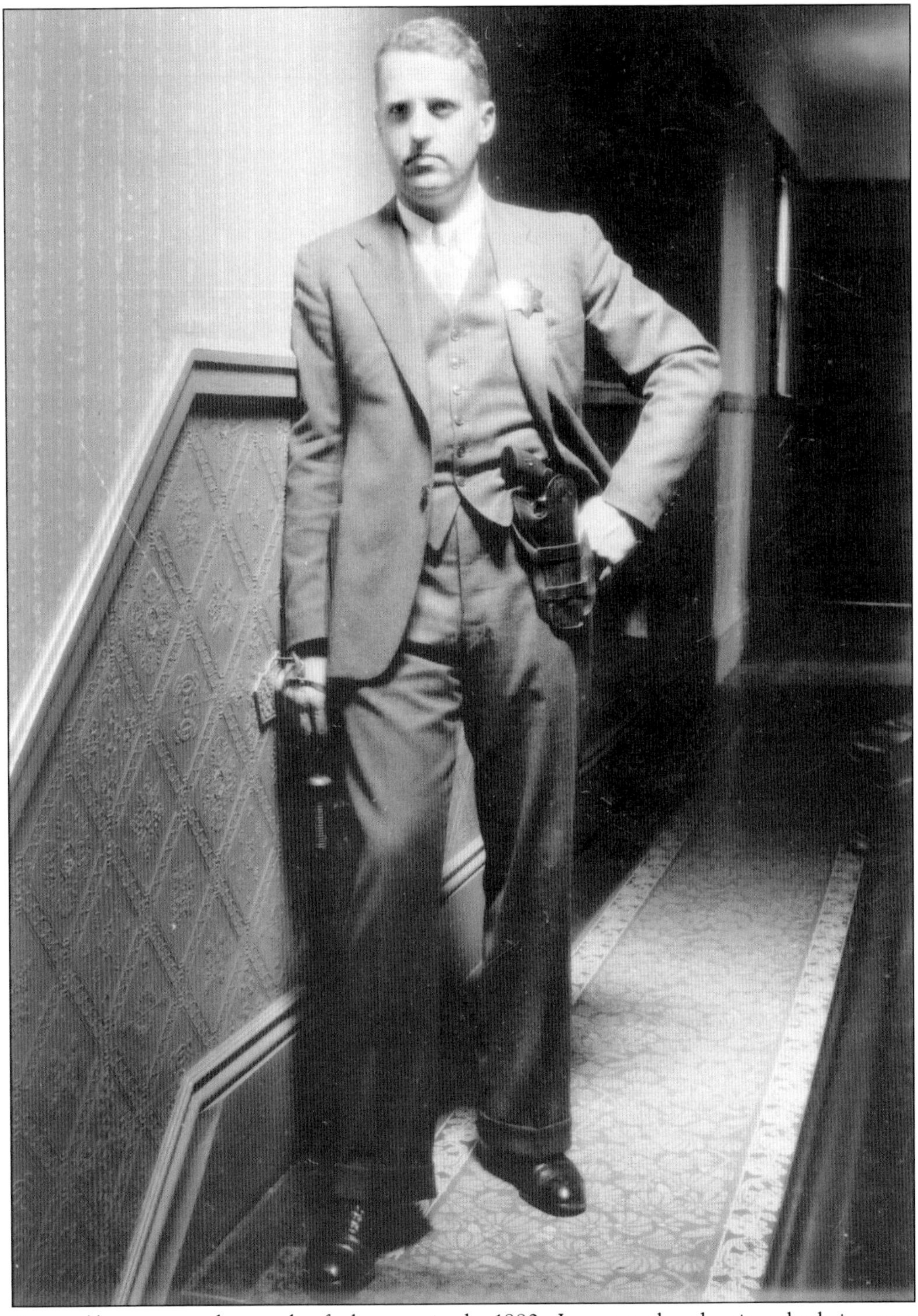

Pictured here is a good example of a lawman in the 1880s. Lawmen played a pivotal role in many movies that were filmed in the area. They were also involved in historic events in the Eastern Sierras, such as when convicts escaped in 1880 near a filming location in Mammoth. The area is now known as Convict Lake.

Buffalo Bill Cody was known for his Wild West shows, where people could see real cowboys and Indians performing skits and stunts depicting events in the Old West. It was these performances that led to screenplays of Westerns and early Hollywood filmmaking.

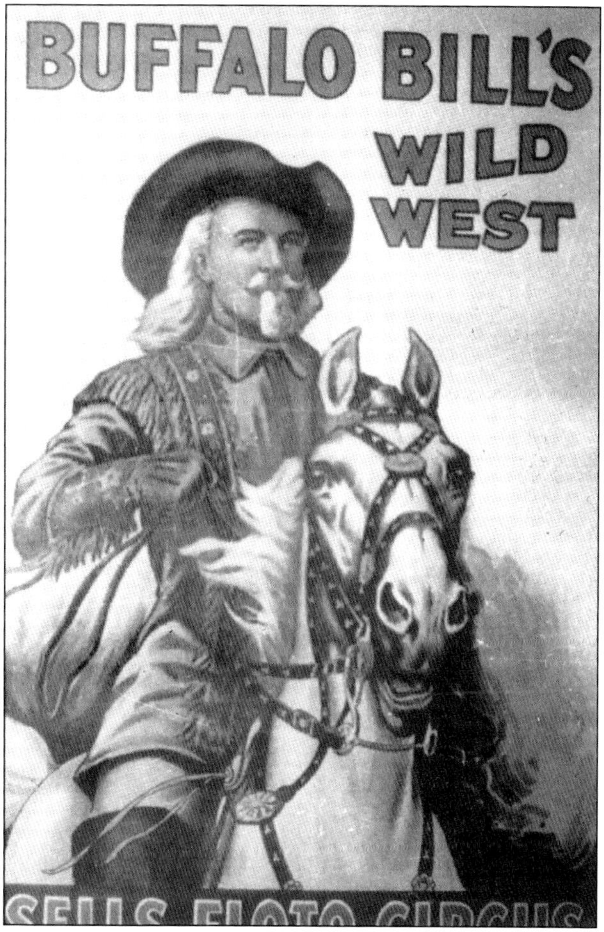


This image of an early Western film crew, taken before Alabama Hills became a popular filming location, shows the various equipment and people that make movies. The filming crew was (and still is) very important in providing success.

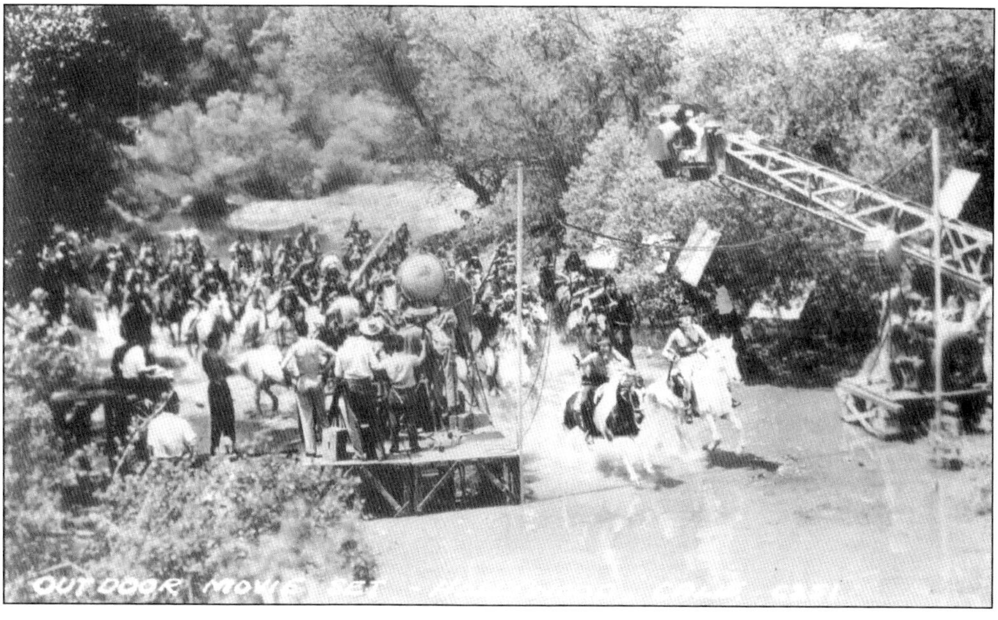

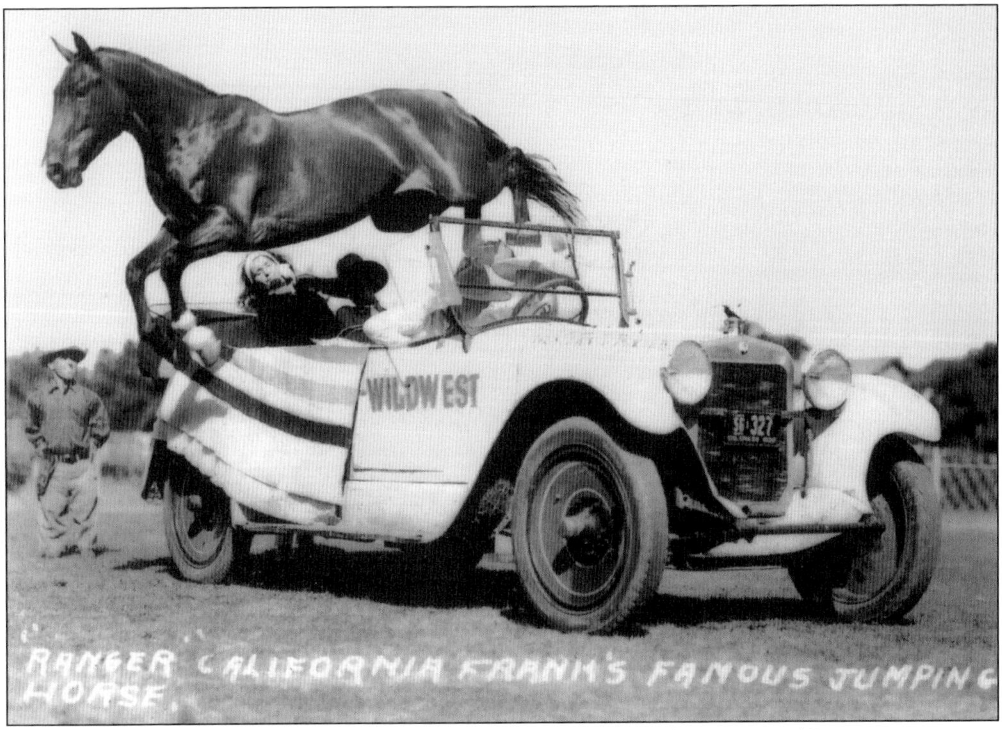


Stunts at Wild West shows were performed using horses. Here, a horse named Ranger is jumping over a car. In *Trail to San Antone* with Gene Autry and Peggy Stewart and *Hands Across the Border* with Roy Rogers, similar scenes were recreated. Watching Wild West shows was a preview to the future of watching movies.

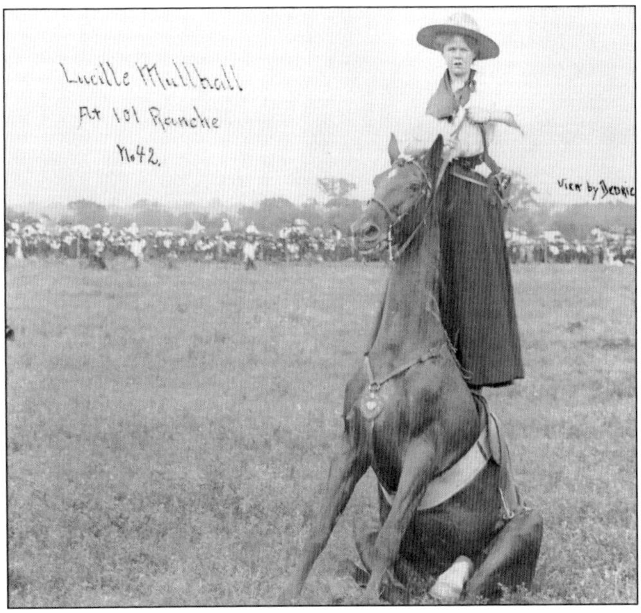


Performing here in 1909 for the Miller 101 Ranch Show is Lucille Mullhall, the "Rodeo Queen." Wild West shows like this piqued the nation's interest in early Westerns. Jack Hoxie and Tom Mix were regular performers at these live shows, and they became big stars of early Hollywood Westerns. Indeed, many of their films would be shot in the Alabama Hills—like Hoxie's *The Back Trail* (1924), *A Six Shootin' Romance* (1926), and *Rough and Ready* (1927) and Mix's *Just Tony* (1922), *Riders of the Purple Sage* (1925), and *Flaming Guns* (1932). (Courtesy of Library of Congress.)

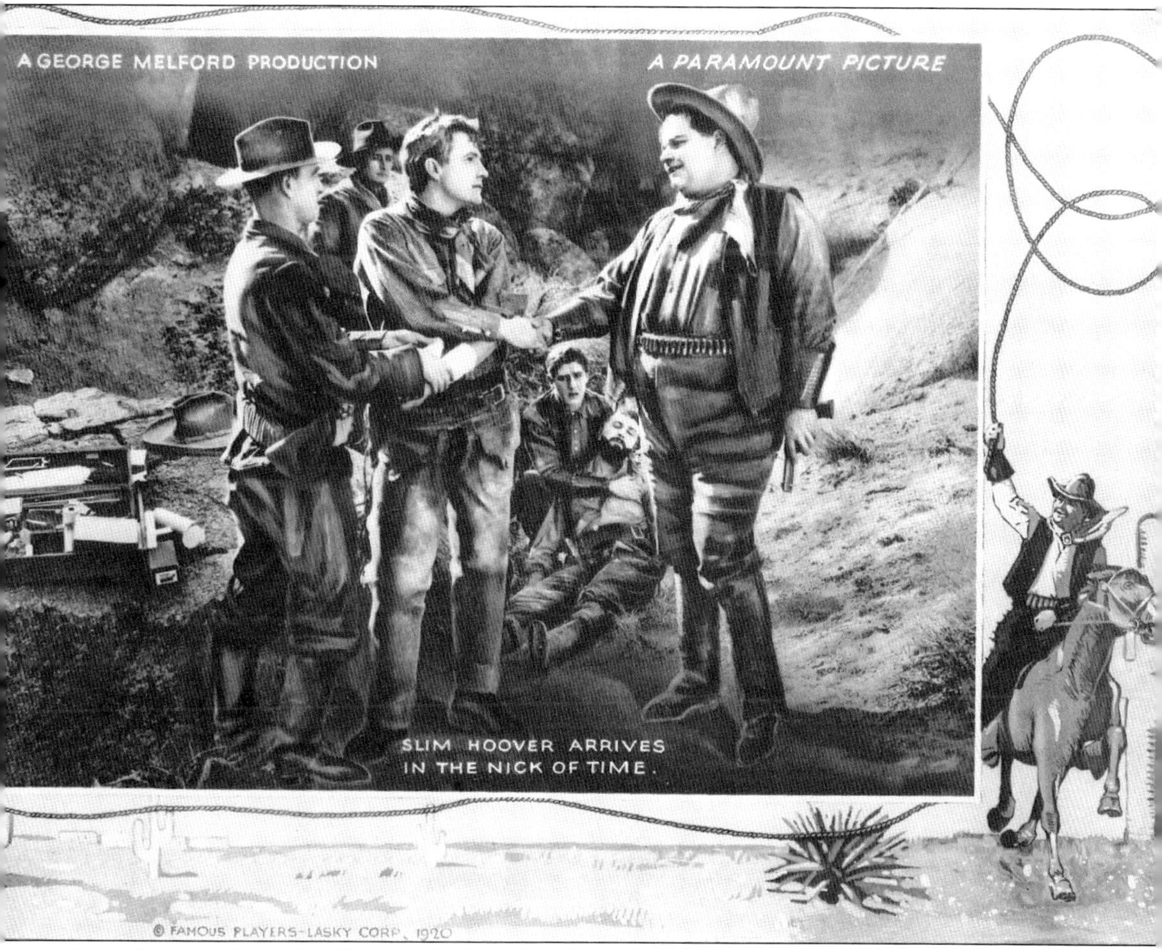


According to a letter by Clarence Badger, the short film *Water, Water Everywhere*, released in early 1920, was shot near the Alabama Hills. Will Rogers said it was a Western in which he starred, but the film is lost. The screenplay was written by Robert F. Hall. It is still speculated that Badger's film may have brought Hollywood to the Alabama Hills. However, the first accepted feature film (lasting 60 minutes or longer) shot in the Alabama Hills was *The Round Up*, released in late 1920 and directed by George Melford. *The Round Up* was Roscoe "Fatty" Arbuckle's first feature film. The rare lobby card shown is an example of early advertising. This was a result of the influence of Broadway shows, Old Wild West shows, carnivals, the 101 Ranch Shows by the Miller Brothers, and early silent Westerns starring William S. Hart. Many of the early Westerns were screened at the Million Dollar Theater, which was the first theater built by Sid Grauman, in 1917, in Los Angeles. Located downtown, one can still gaze upon the sculpted bison heads outside of the theater.

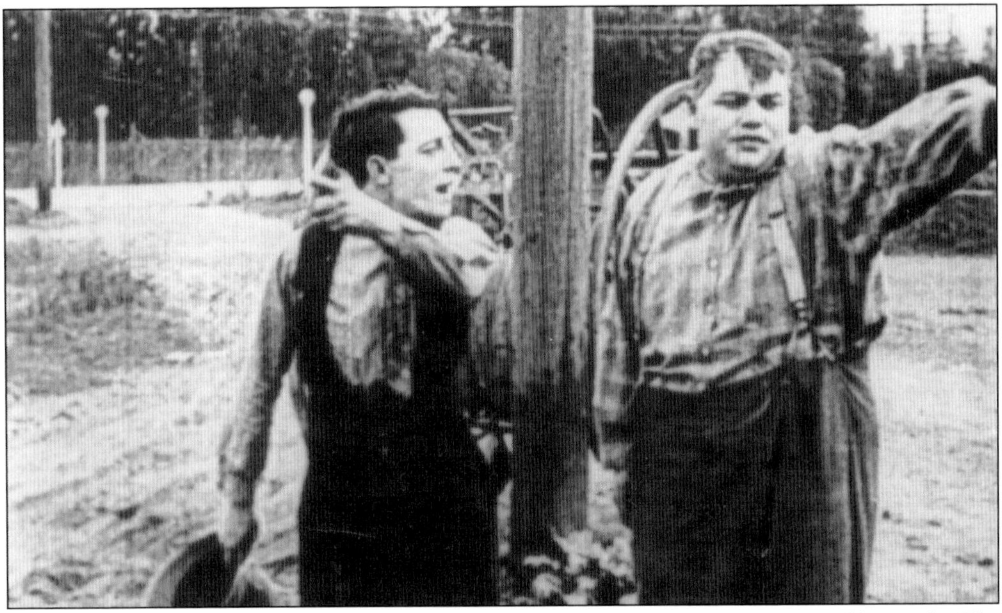

This is a movie still showing Arbuckle (right) and friend Buster Keaton. During filming for *The Round Up* (1920), Keaton appeared as an unbilled extra on set as a favor. Early filming took place along and near Tuttle Creek Road and the southern and eastern parts of the Alabama Hills. These sites include Skull Rock, Ruiz Hills, and the famous Anchor Ranch, located near Highway 395 near the town of Lone Pine.

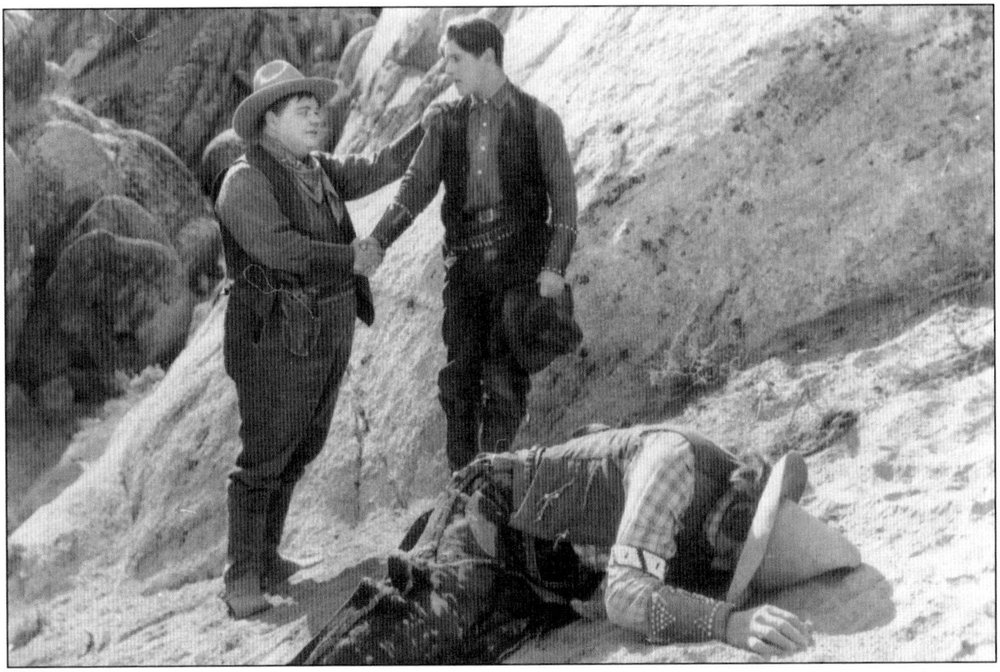

This rare movie still from *The Round Up* shows Roscoe Arbuckle as Slim Hoover. This was Arbuckle's first feature film as well as the first feature film to be shot in the Alabama Hills near Lone Pine, California. The cast and crew stayed at the Lone Pine Hotel, which is now the chamber of commerce.

This is a luggage tag from the St. Francis Hotel in San Francisco, California. It was here that a year after the filming of *The Round Up*, a scandal that started in room 1219 involving the death of actress Virginia Rappe resulted in a trial and ruined Arbuckle's reputation. He was acquitted, but his career was destroyed. He later died of heart failure and was cremated. Virginia Rappe is buried at Hollywood Forever Cemetery in Hollywood, California.

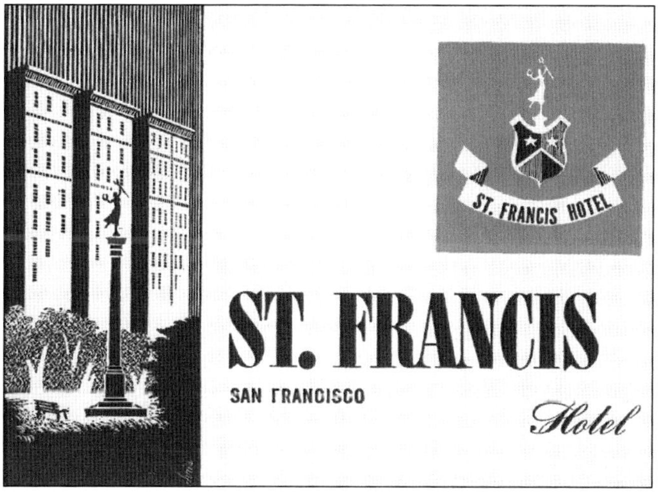


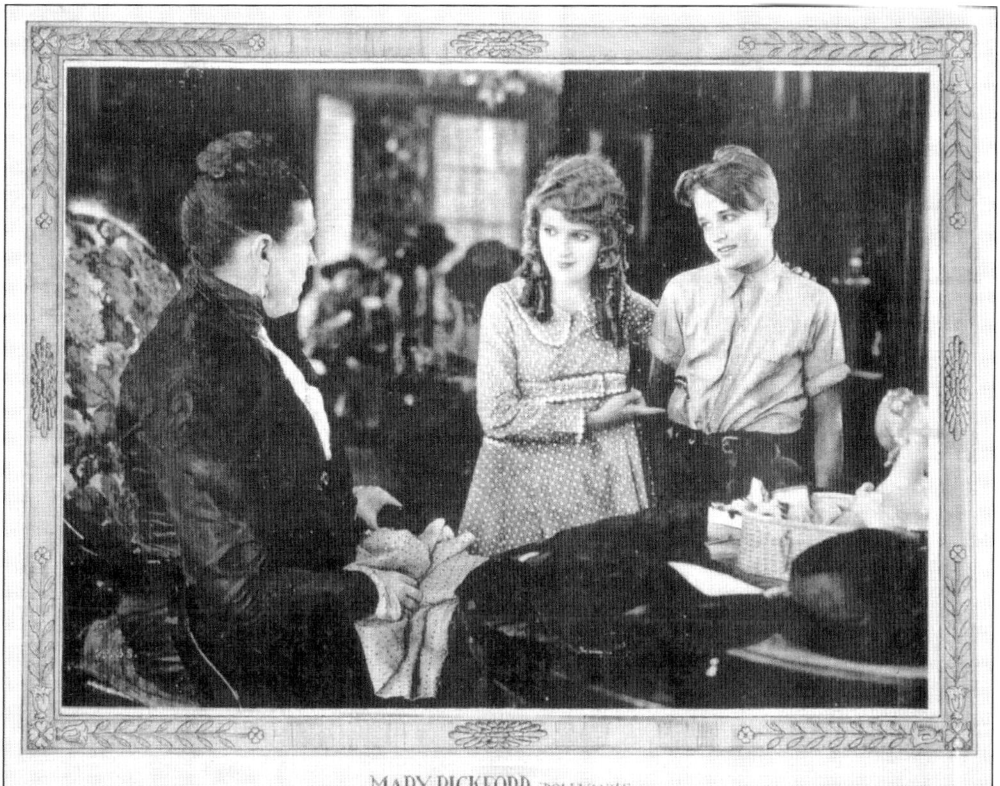


This lobby card shows famous actress Mary Pickford in *Pollyanna* (1920), another early film shot in Lone Pine and Independence. Pickford was most famous for her marriage to the swashbuckling Douglas Fairbanks Sr., with whom she owned the Roosevelt Hotel in Hollywood, California.

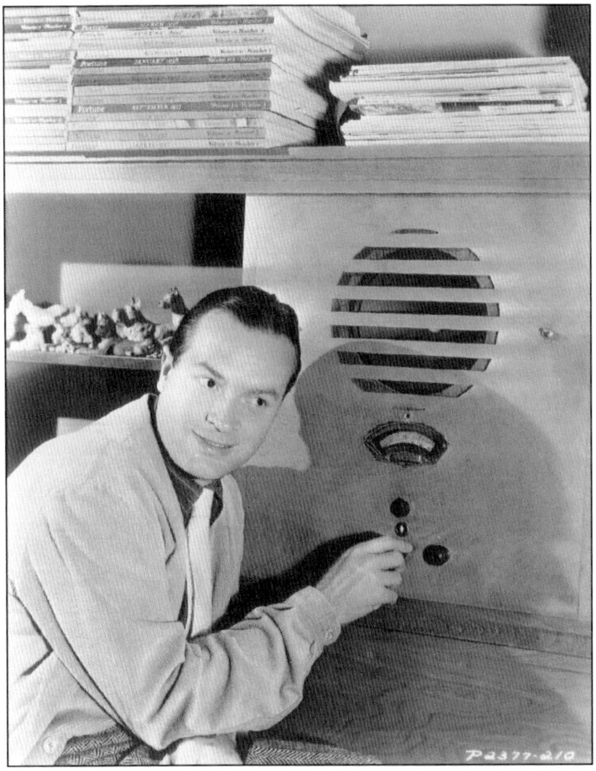

Bob Hope was famous for his charm and wonderful entertainment throughout show business. Roscoe "Fatty" Arbuckle introduced both Bob Hope and Charlie Chaplin to Hollywood.

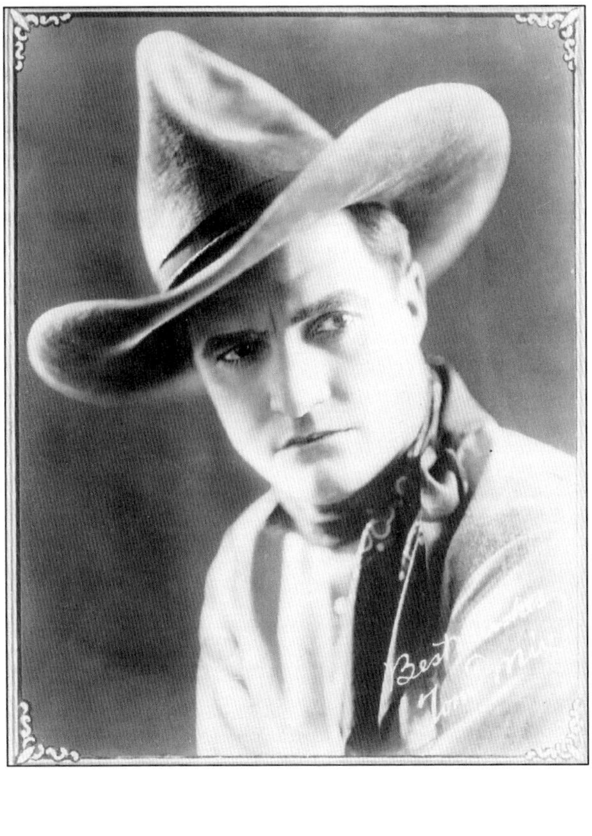

Tom Mix made the famous *Riders of the Purple Sage* in 1925 in the Ruiz Hills area of the Alabama Hills. Mix starred in 291 films, was a veteran of Teddy Roosevelt's Rough Riders in the Spanish-American War, and worked mostly out of his Mixville studio. Mixville was a Western town at the present intersection of Glendale Boulevard and Rowena Avenue in Silverlake, California, built by William Selig in 1915 and sold to William Fox in 1916. Near Mixville, Mix hung out at Tam O'Shanter and Edendale 56 Firehouse, where he played poker and gathered people together for pancake breakfasts, carrying these traditions with him when filming up in Lone Pine. He served as a pallbearer at Wyatt Earp's funeral, took part in radio productions, and had a horse named Tony the Wonder Horse. Mix is buried at Forest Lawn Cemetery in Glendale, California.

Fred Humes was another famous actor of the silent era. In addition to appearing in Westerns, he was a gorilla in *Lorraine of the Lions* (1925) and *Circus Rookies* (1928). Fred Humes starred in a silent film, *The Arizona Cyclone* (1928), near the Anchor Ranch, which was owned by a real cowboy and rancher named Russ Spainhower.

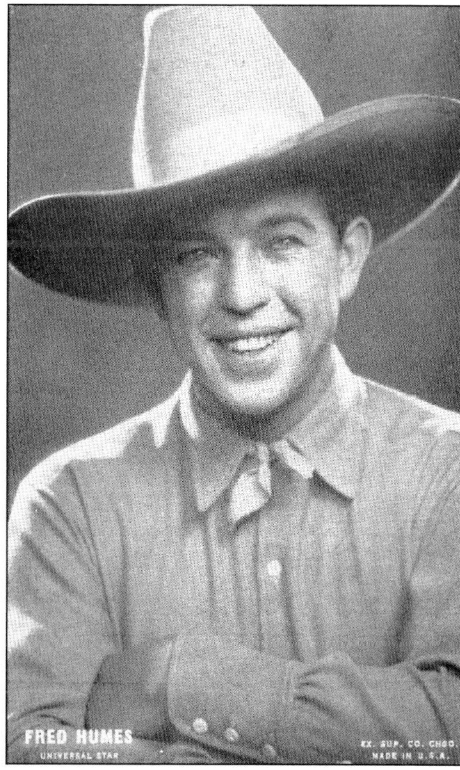


Jack Hoxie and Dixie Starr were the first big-name duo entertainers, before the likes of Roy Rogers and Dale Evans. Jack and Dixie performed in the Miller 101 Ranch Wild West Shows for crowds in the early days of carnivals and rodeos.

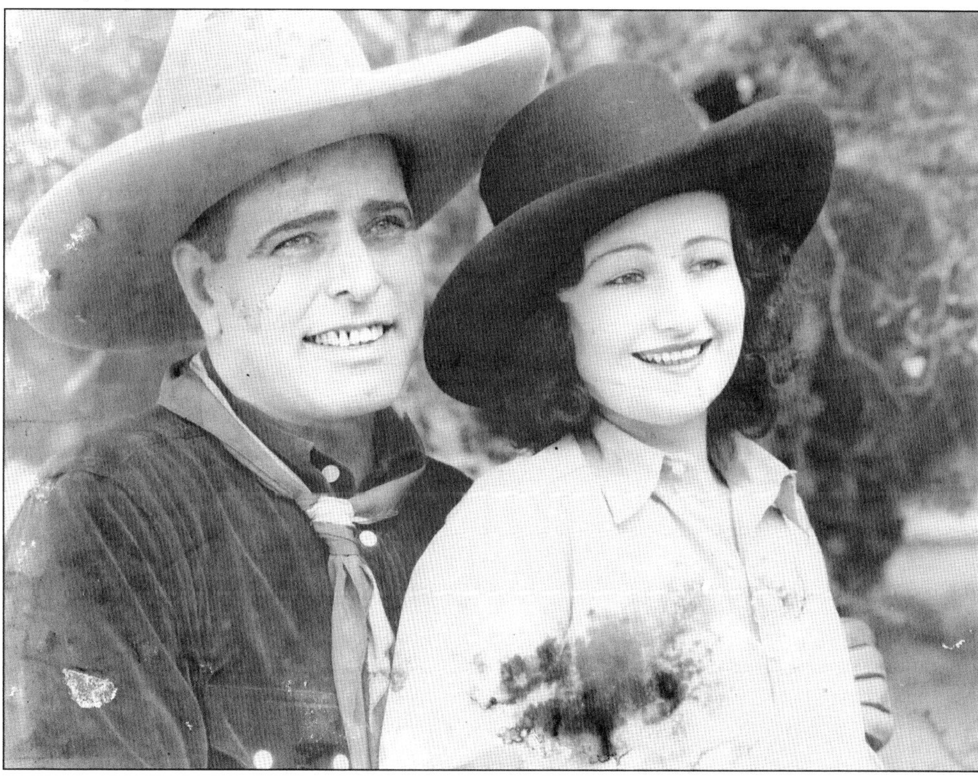

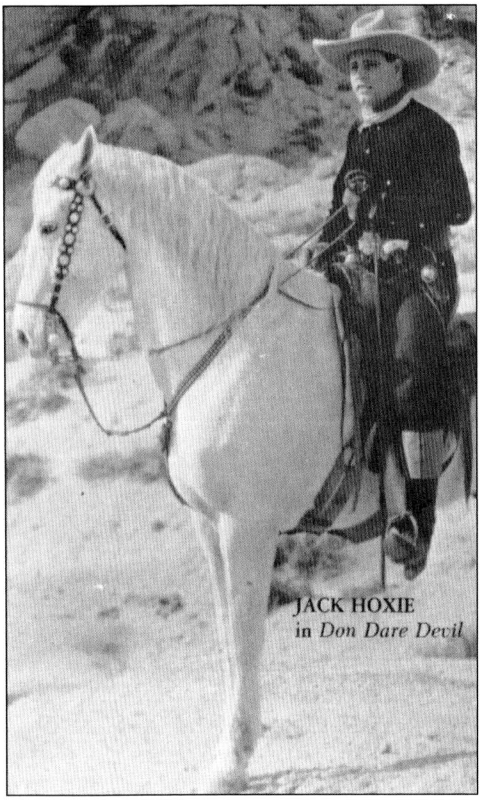


Jack Hoxie made more pictures in the Alabama Hills than any other silent actor of the day. He and his horse White Fury are shown here in *Don Dare Devil* (1925), which was filmed in the Ruiz Hills area. He also had a horse named Scout.

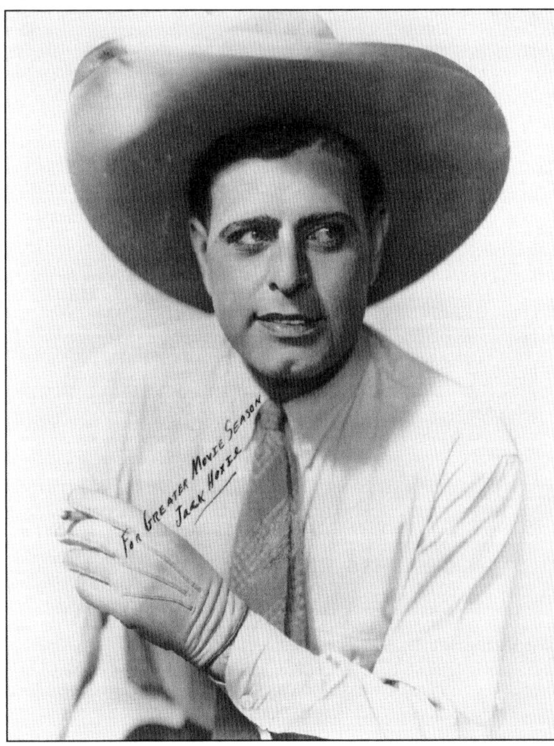


Jack Hoxie can also be seen in numerous other films, including *Back Trail* (1924), also filmed in the Ruiz Hills area. Jack Hoxie, like Tom Mix, was one of the more famous cowboys of the early era and is buried at Willowbar Cemetery in Keyes, Oklahoma.

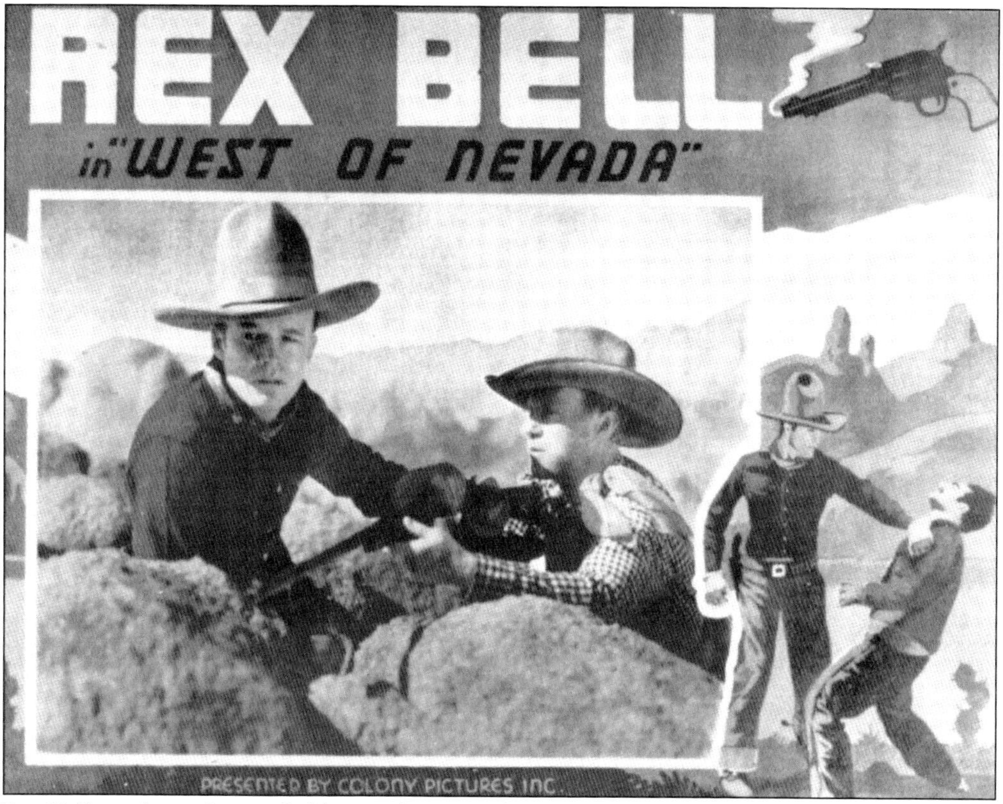

Rex Bell was born George Beldam and was in silent Westerns in the 1920s. In 1931, he married the famous Clara Bow. He made six epics for the Alexander brothers. *West of Nevada* (1936), the second in this series, was filmed in the Alabama Hills.

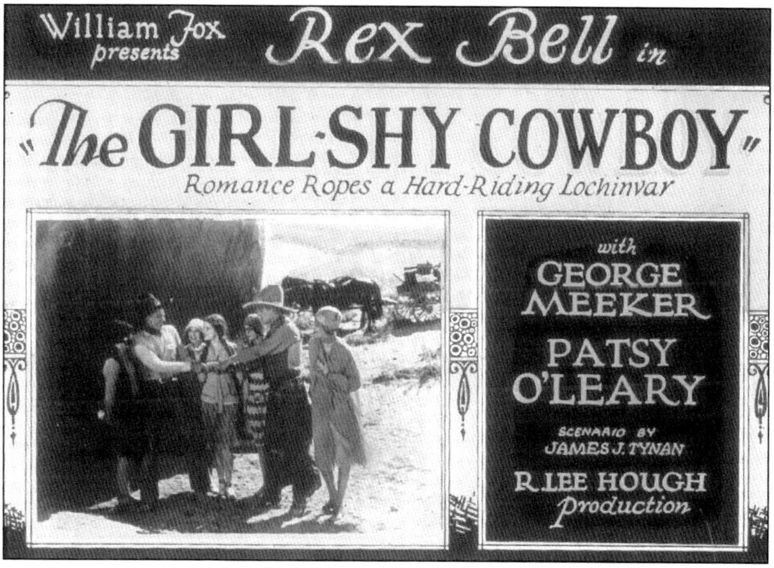

Under William Fox, Rex Bell starred in *The Girl-Shy Cowboy* (1928). This is a glass slide that typically was used in silent theaters as an advertisement, lobby card, or preview for movies to come.

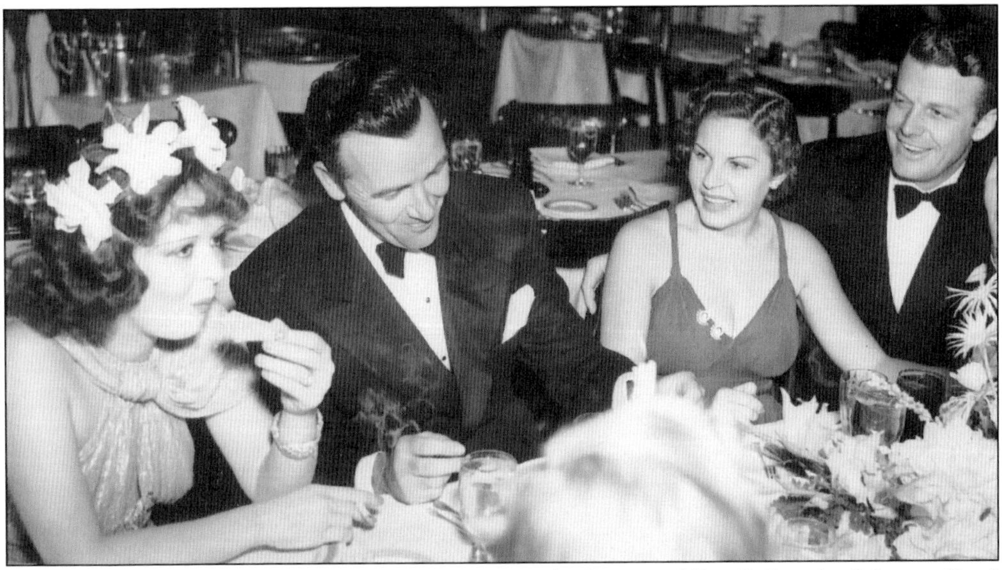

From left to right are Clara Bow, Preston Foster, Martha Raye, and Rex Bell at the Biltmore Bowl in the Biltmore Hotel in Los Angeles in 1937. All except Clara Bow starred in movies filmed in the Alabama Hills. Clara Bow, however, often went to visit her husband, Rex Bell, when he was filming there and became familiar with the area.

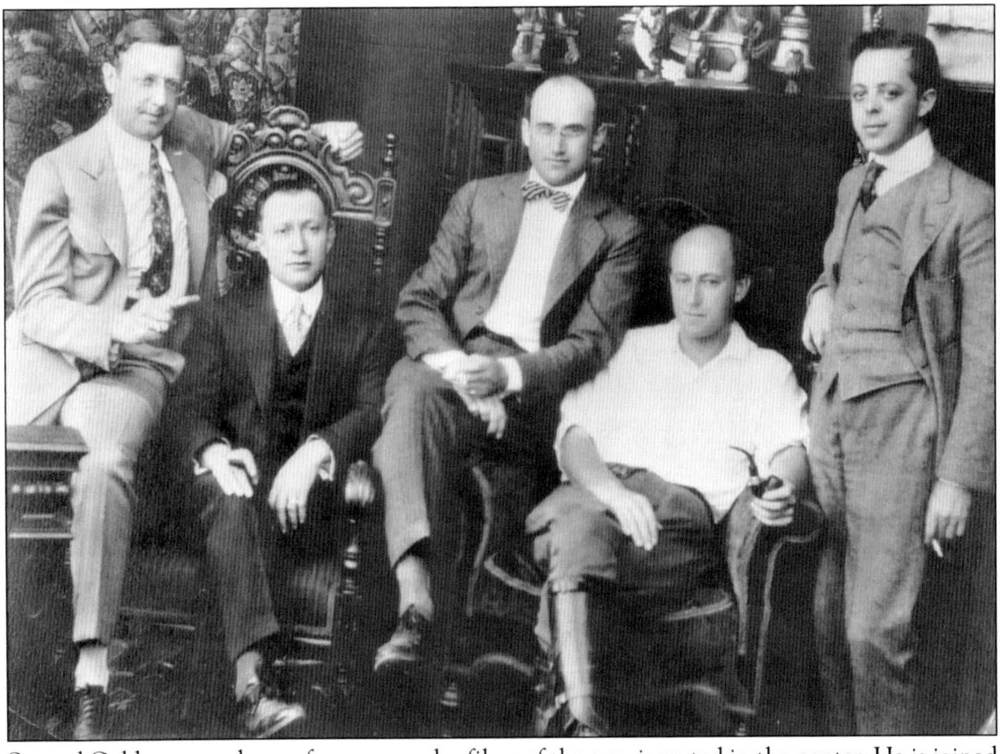

Samuel Goldwyn, producer of many popular films of the age, is seated in the center. He is joined by early Hollywood moguls Cecil B. DeMille (second from right), Jesse Lasky (left), and Adolph Zukor (second from left). These legendary figures of movie history and their efforts echo through movie studios even today.

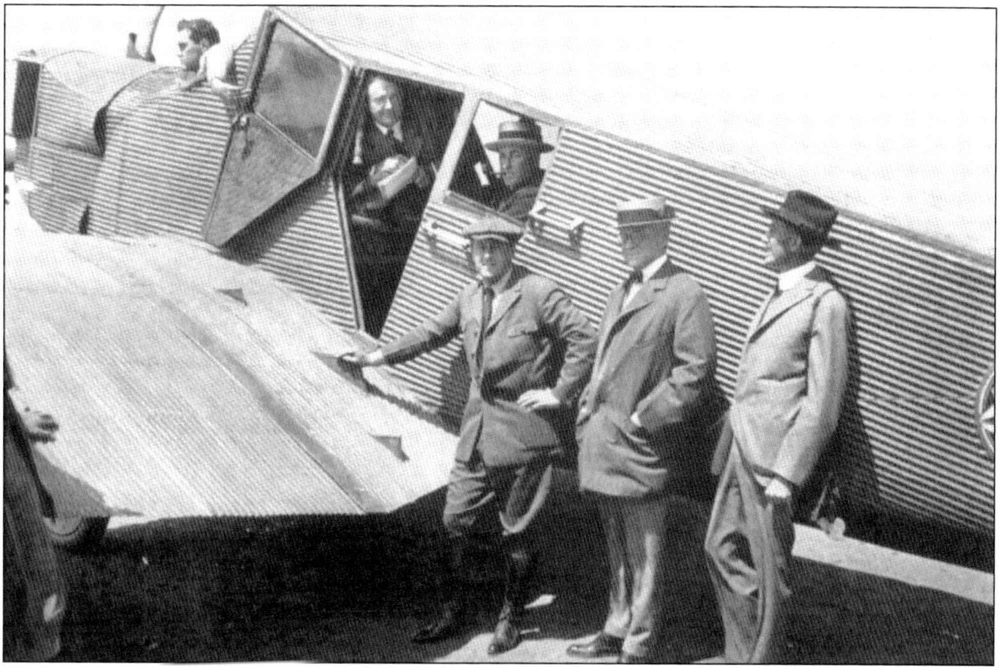

Cecil B. DeMille is shown here (center) in a rare picture of the Junkers airplane he took when location filming. His film *Samson and Delilah* (1949) was shot in the Alabama Hills, and he was involved in the early movie making of Hollywood. The Hollywood Heritage Museum barn has wonderful exhibits about Cecil B. DeMille and many other famous names of the early film era displayed on-site.

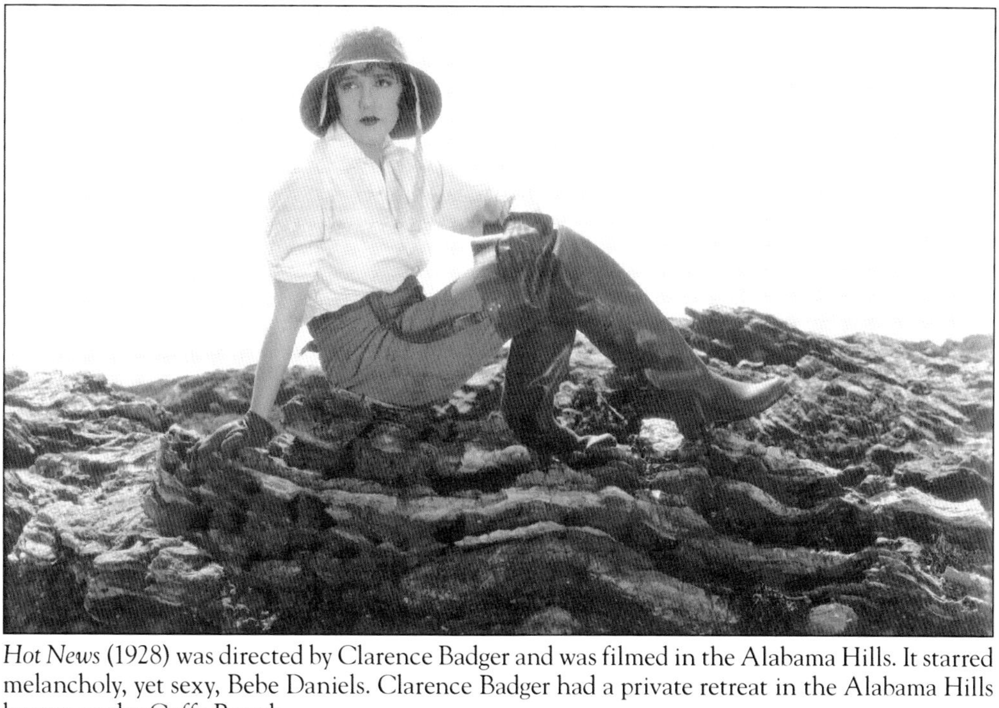

*Hot News* (1928) was directed by Clarence Badger and was filmed in the Alabama Hills. It starred melancholy, yet sexy, Bebe Daniels. Clarence Badger had a private retreat in the Alabama Hills known as the Cuffe Ranch.

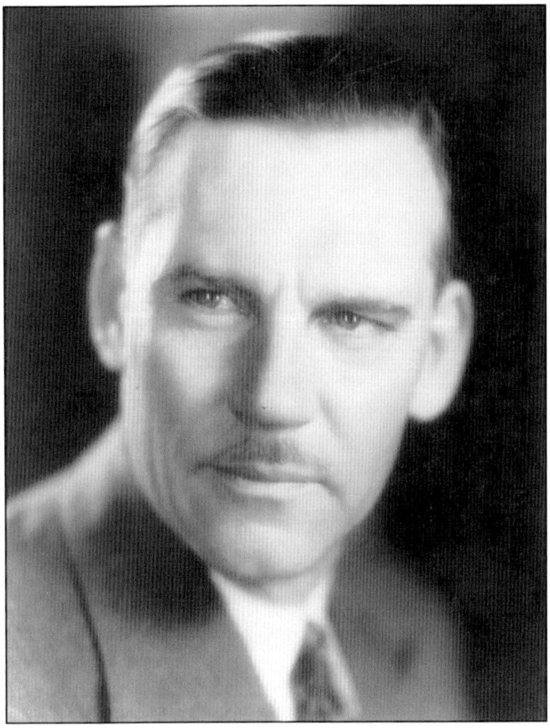

Walter Huston is shown here in *The Bad Man* (1930), which was based on a popular 1920 play of the same name. In this film, shot in the Alabama Hills and directed by Clarence Badger, Huston plays a bandit. This film is rare and can be viewed at the University of California, Los Angeles Film and Television Archive—a wonderful place for any film historian.

*Gun Gospel* (1927) is another rare film starring the famous Ken Maynard and his horse named Tarzan. *The Wagon Master* (1929), also starring Maynard, was the first cowboy film to feature a singing cowboy and the first film with sound shot in the Alabama Hills. This paved the way for other singing cowboys like Tex Ritter.

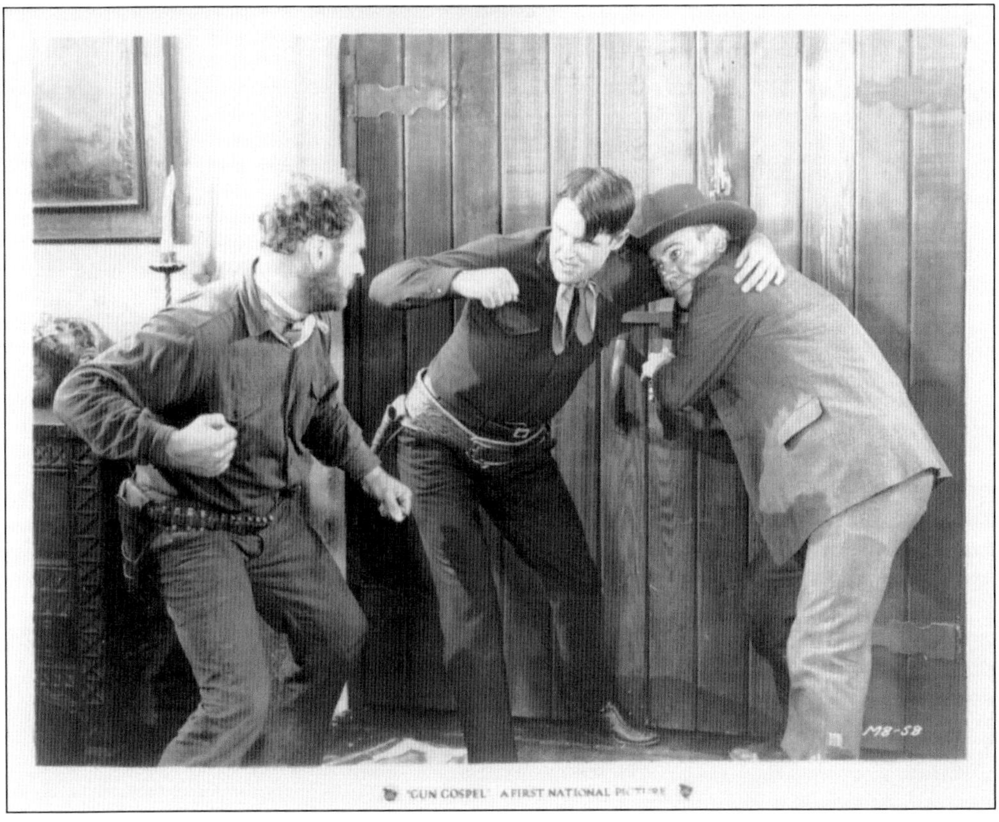

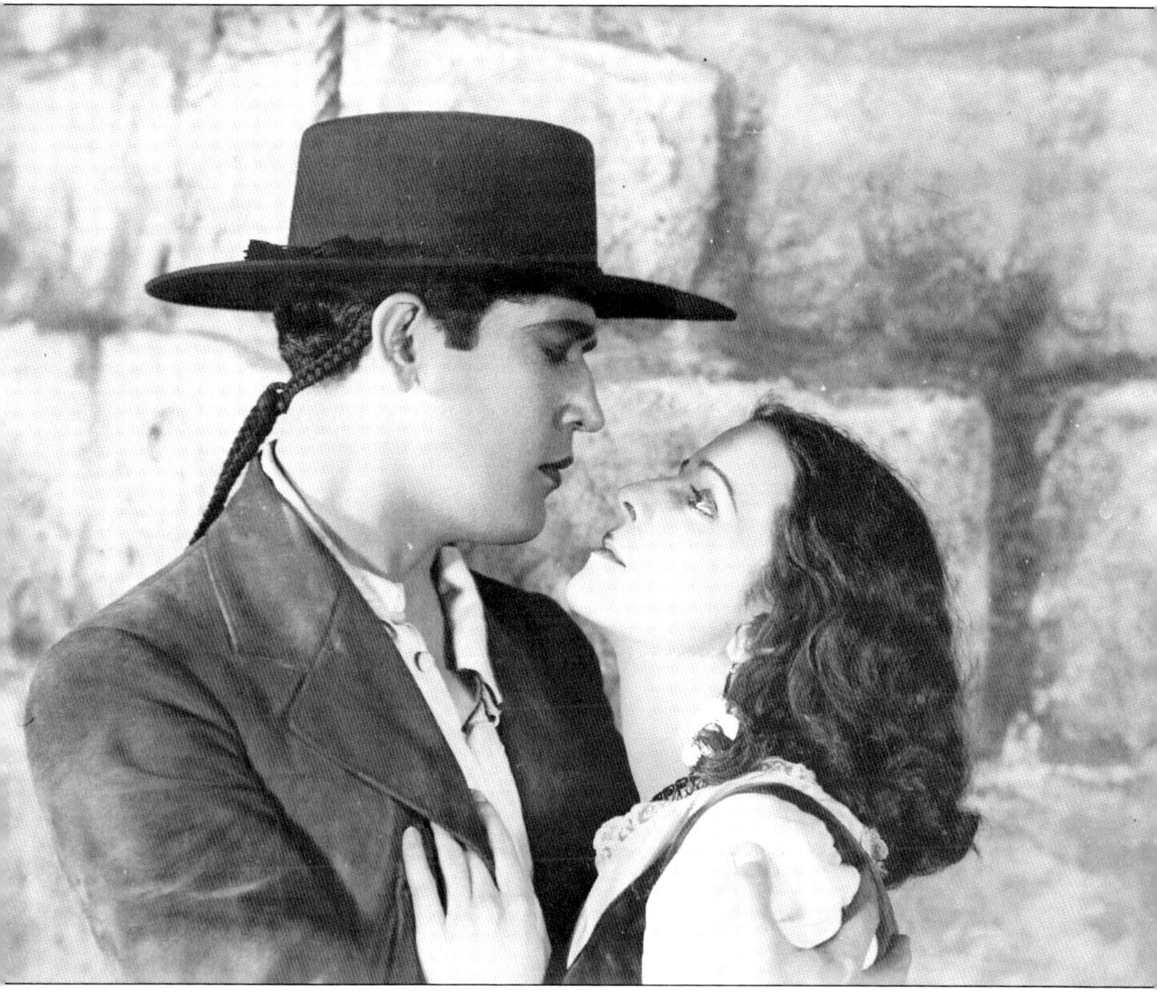

*One Mad Kiss* (1930), starring newcomer Don Jose Mojica and Mona Maris, was also a singing-cowboy movie. It had a swashbuckling Robin Hood–like theme, as Mojica's character robs from the rich to give to the poor. It was a Fox Movietone production. Mojica, shown here, had a superb lyric tenor voice, and Maris was an Argentine dancer of note.

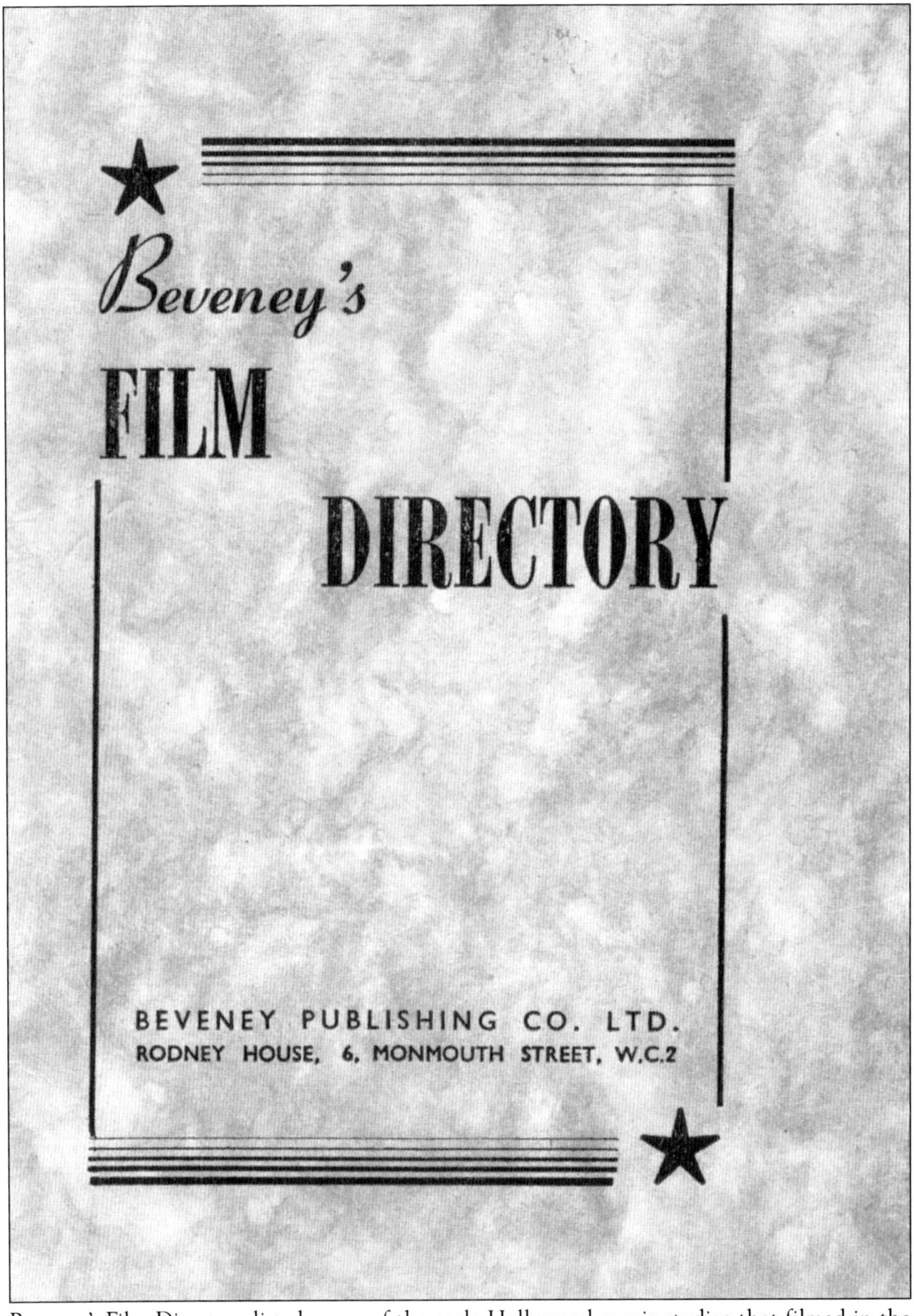


Beveney's Film Directory listed many of the early Hollywood movie studios that filmed in the Alabama Hills. Monogram Pictures, Movietone News, Paramount Pictures, Hal Roach Studios, Republic Pictures, and many others were included. Just about every major studio of Hollywood has filmed in the hills at one time or another throughout the last century.

# *Two*

# Serials and B Westerns

In the northern part of the Alabama Hills, there are two areas to explore: the northwest unnamed rocks near roads off Movie Road and the named northern rocks area northeast of Movie Road. These are the easiest movie locations to find, and rewarding once discovered.

The northwest area is where one can see the *Gunga Din* (1939) suspension bridge, which still has the concrete construction that once supported an elephant. Also in the northwest area are locations of various film stunts, a movie burial site, and locations of films including *Maverick*, with James Garner and Mel Gibson.

In the northeast area are the more notable sites of the B Westerns and serials. The locations are identified best by the rock formations that are easily spotted. This area has a dominant gravel path that can be easily walked while exploring various filming locations. Find the Lone Ranger Canyon, where a concert is held every June by organizers in Lone Pine.

Lone Ranger Canyon is where the Lone Ranger is ambushed and becomes a legend. A scene from Quentin Tarantino's 2012 film *Django Unchained* was filmed in the canyon. The film used props from early Western films, including *The Lone Ranger*. Walk a few feet up the gravel path eastward and one will discover the site where the first Republic Picture, *Westward Ho*, starring John Wayne, was filmed.

Ambush Rock, or "Hoppy Rocks," is located further along the path. It is named after Hopalong Cassidy, who evades the bad guys in the movie *Silent Conflict*. Gene Autry Rock, named for the famous B Western singing cowboy, is also near here, and can be seen in *Boots and Saddles* (1937), which he starred in. Continue up the path to the top and turn right to find Gary Cooper Rock. This landmark is prominent in Cooper's 1935 classic, *The Lives of a Bengal Lancer*.

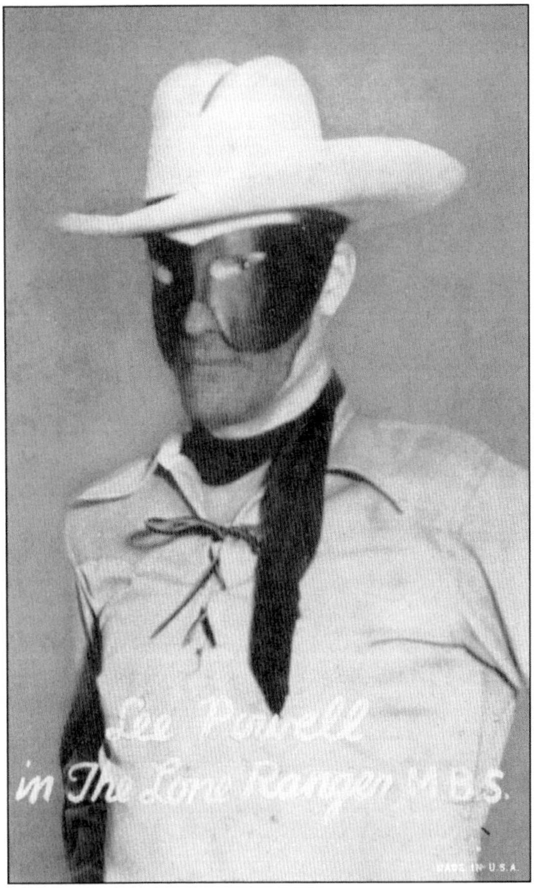


Lee Powell starred in the first Lone Ranger serial, directed by William Witney, in 1936. Lone Ranger Canyon, also known as "Ambush Canyon," remains one of the most visited filming locations in the Alabama Hills. Lee Powell served in World War II as a US Marine. He passed away in 1943 from drinking moonshine in the Pacific and is buried on the island of Saipan.

Here is a rare photograph of the first horse named Silver that the Lone Ranger rode. The Lone Ranger's sidekick was Tonto, his trusted friend who rode a horse named Scout. It is said that Silver still rides today when the *William Tell* Overture is played by an orchestra. Tonto's horse, Scout, is buried at the Los Angeles Pet Cemetery in California.

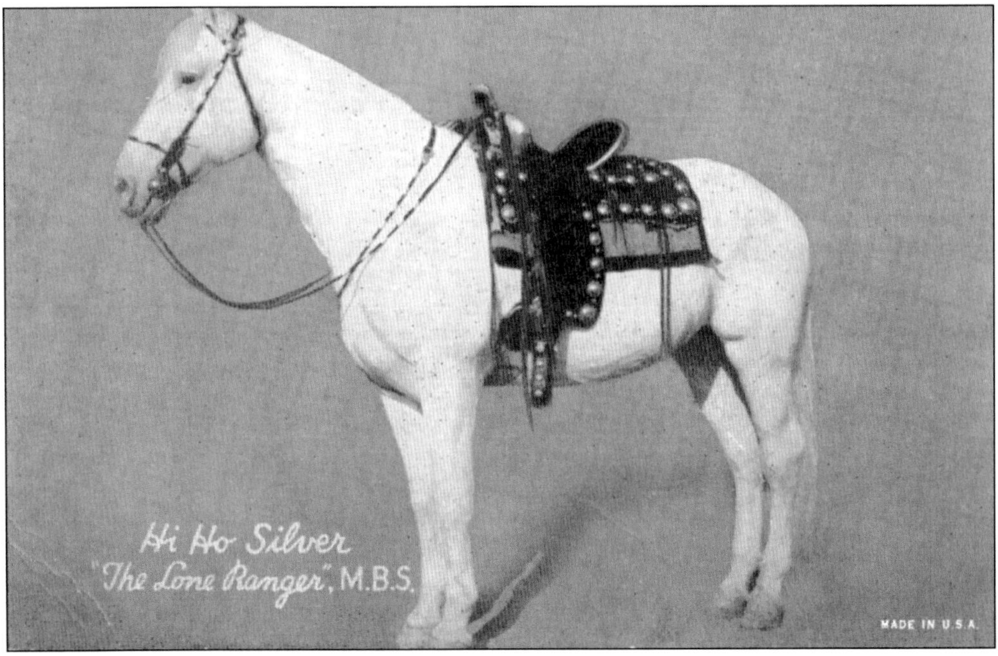

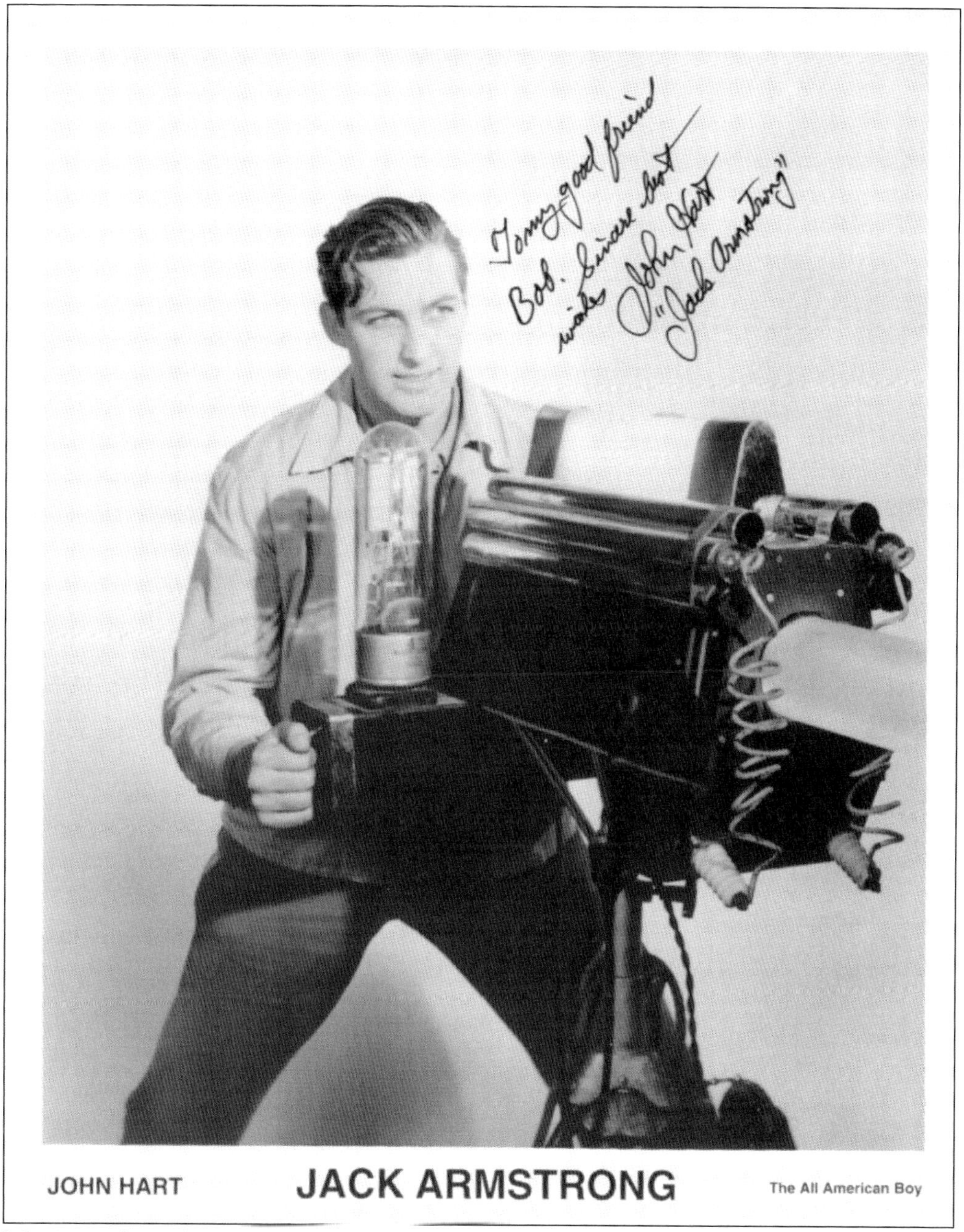


John Hart, shown here, also starred as the Lone Ranger, replacing Clayton Moore for two seasons. However, Hart is best remembered as the titular character in *Jack Armstrong, the All American Boy*, a famous serial of the time. Hart appeared as Hawkeye in the 1957 television series *Hawkeye and the Last of the Mohicans* and played Captain Africa in *Adventures of Captain Africa* (1955). His last role was as a news writer in *The Legend of the Lone Ranger* (1981).

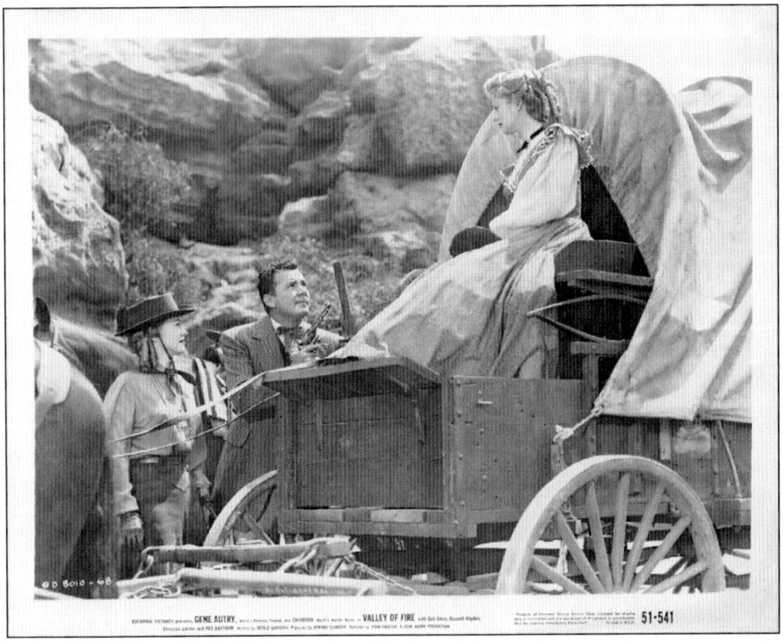


Shown here is Gail Davis in *The Valley of Fire*, produced by Gene Autry. Davis is best known for her work as Annie Oakley, a cowgirl who saved the West with a horse named Target. She starred alongside Roy Rogers, Gene Autry, and many other B Western legends.

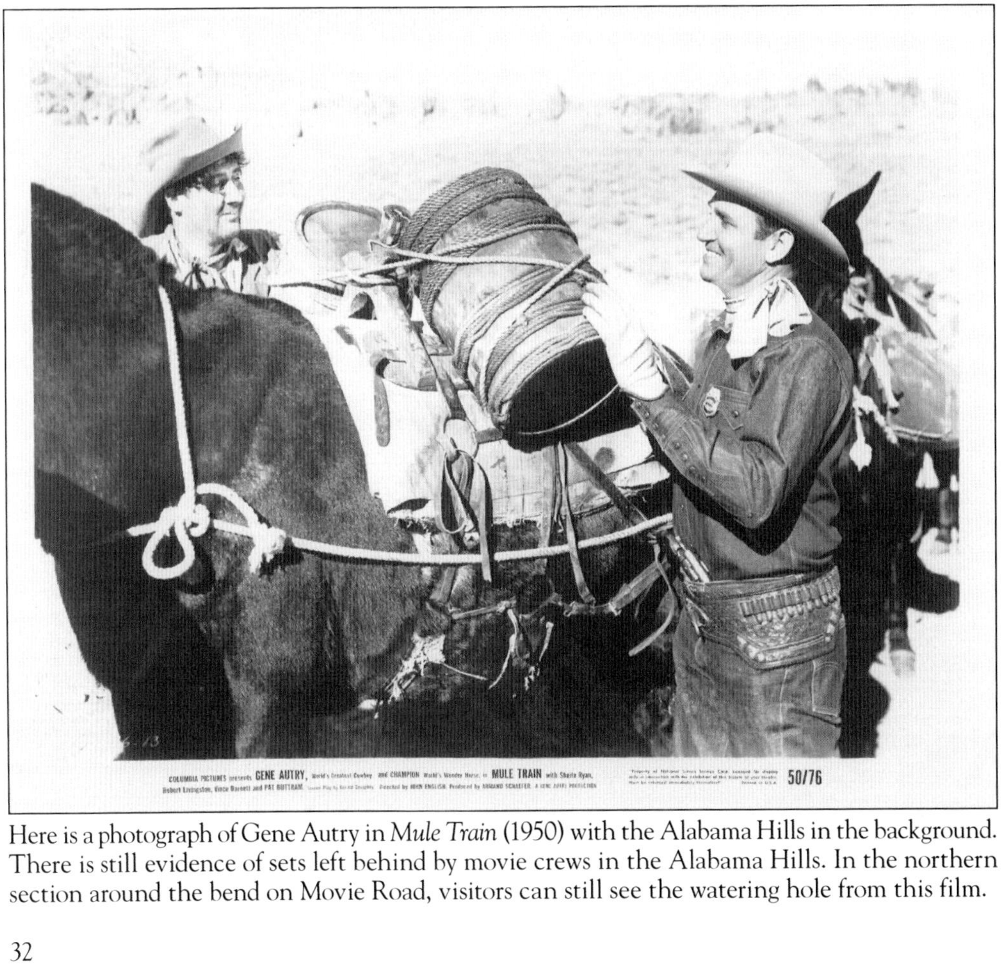


Here is a photograph of Gene Autry in *Mule Train* (1950) with the Alabama Hills in the background. There is still evidence of sets left behind by movie crews in the Alabama Hills. In the northern section around the bend on Movie Road, visitors can still see the watering hole from this film.

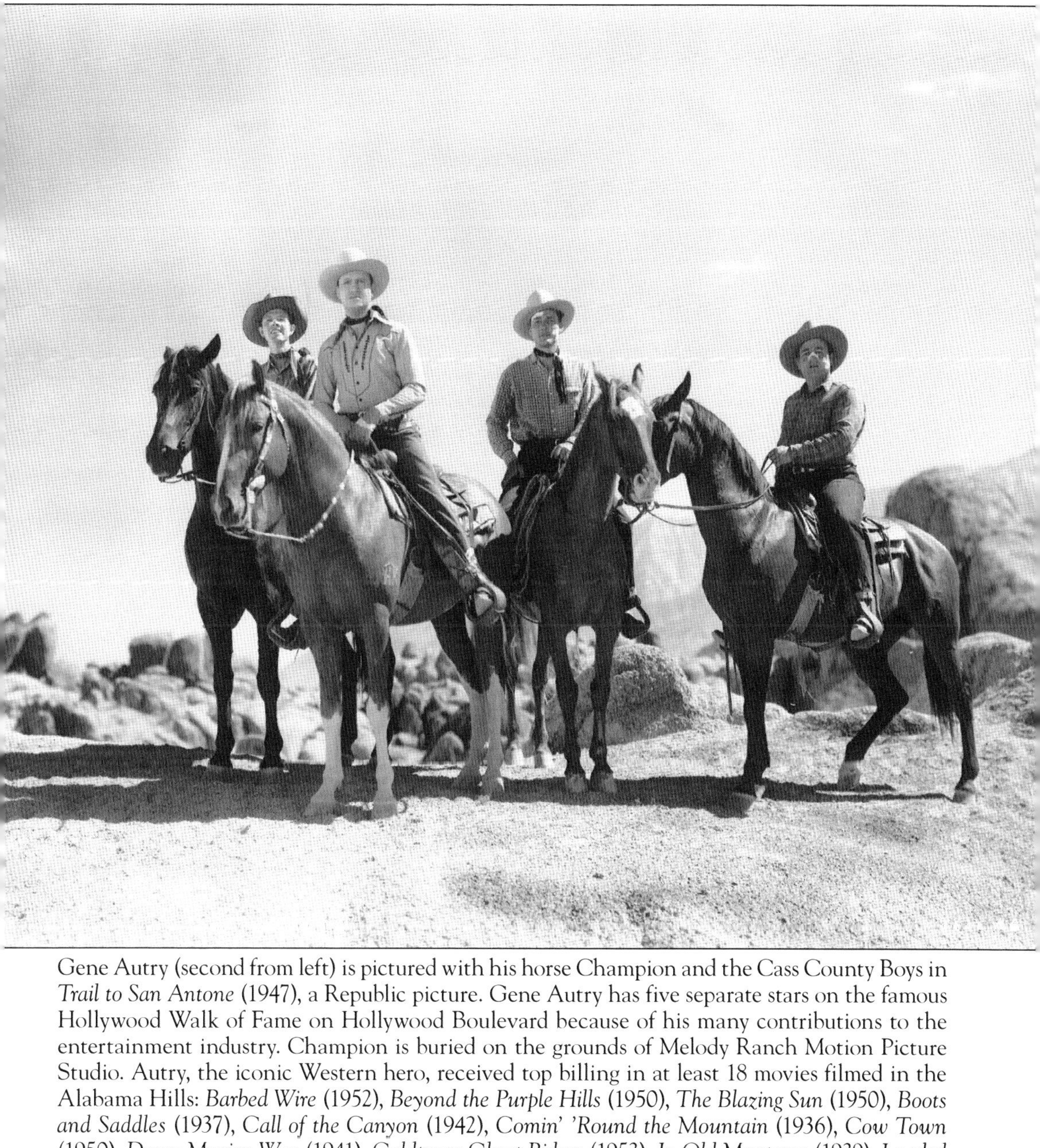

Gene Autry (second from left) is pictured with his horse Champion and the Cass County Boys in *Trail to San Antone* (1947), a Republic picture. Gene Autry has five separate stars on the famous Hollywood Walk of Fame on Hollywood Boulevard because of his many contributions to the entertainment industry. Champion is buried on the grounds of Melody Ranch Motion Picture Studio. Autry, the iconic Western hero, received top billing in at least 18 movies filmed in the Alabama Hills: *Barbed Wire* (1952), *Beyond the Purple Hills* (1950), *The Blazing Sun* (1950), *Boots and Saddles* (1937), *Call of the Canyon* (1942), *Comin' 'Round the Mountain* (1936), *Cow Town* (1950), *Down Mexico Way* (1941), *Goldtown Ghost Riders* (1953), *In Old Monterey* (1939), *Loaded Pistols* (1949), *Melody Ranch* (1940), *Mule Train* (1950), *Oh, Susanna!* (1936), *The Old Barn Dance* (1938), *Rootin' Tootin' Rhythm* (1937), *Trail to San Antone*, and *Valley of Fire* (1951).

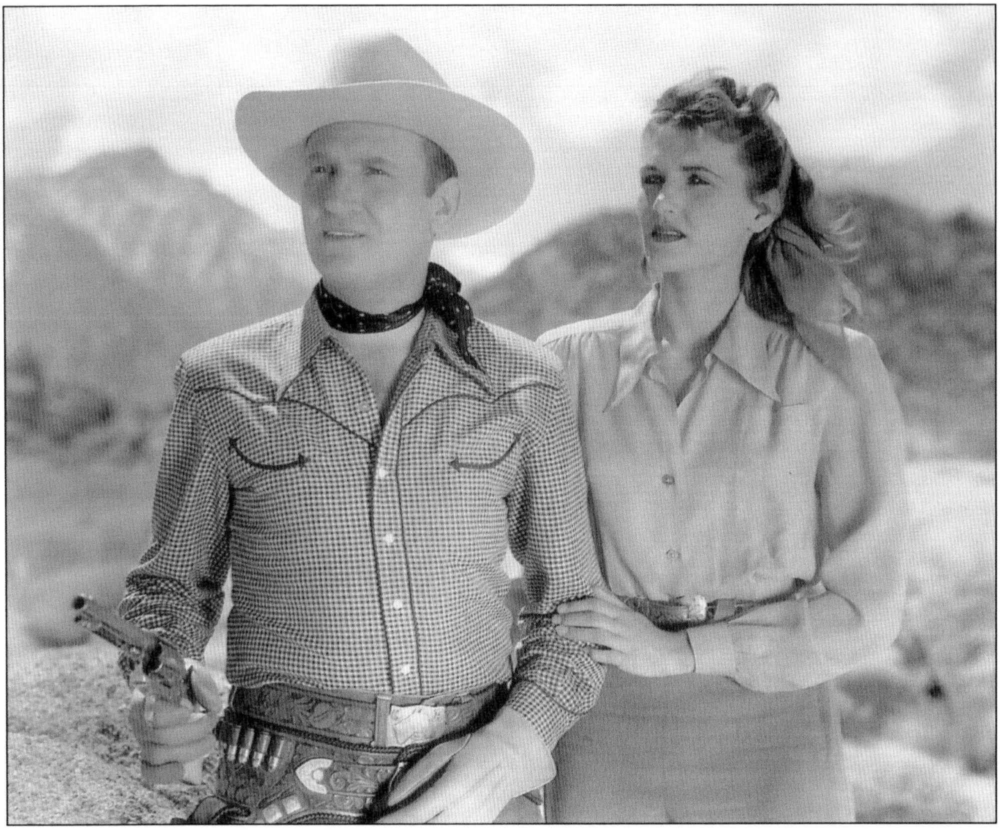

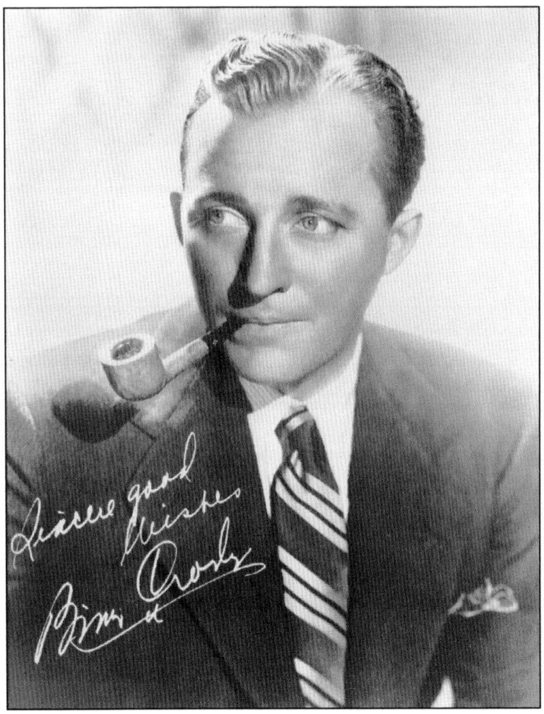

Here is a wonderful photograph of Gene Autry and Peggy Stewart, with Lone Pine Peak in the background. Autry had a rock in the hills named after him that can be seen in another film, *Boots and Saddles* (1937). Stewart, known as the queen of the B Westerns, is credited with working on many productions in a short amount of time—including no less than 27 films from 1945 through 1947.

Bing Crosby was involved in *Rhythm on the Range* (1936), in which he sings the famous song "I'm an Old Cowhand," written by Johnny Mercer. Crosby is remembered as a brilliant and dedicated singer.

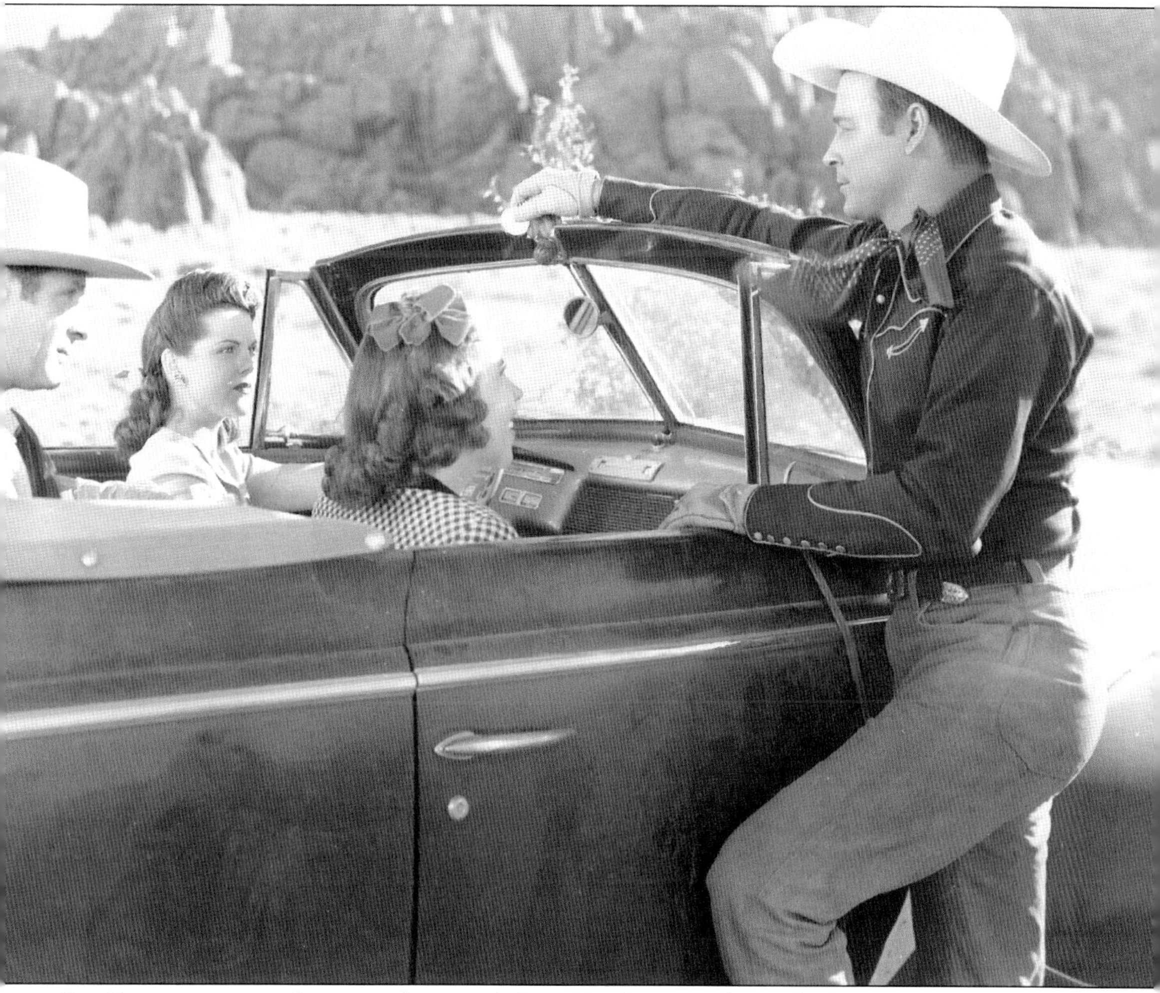

Roy Rogers is seen in this great photograph from *Hands Across the Border* (1944). This scene was filmed in the Alabama Hills. Like Autry, Rogers played many leading roles in productions filmed the Alabama Hills: *Hands Across the Border*, *Man from Music Mountain* (1943), *Saga of Death Valley* (1939), *Song of Texas* (1943), *Under Western Stars* (1938), and *Utah* (1945).

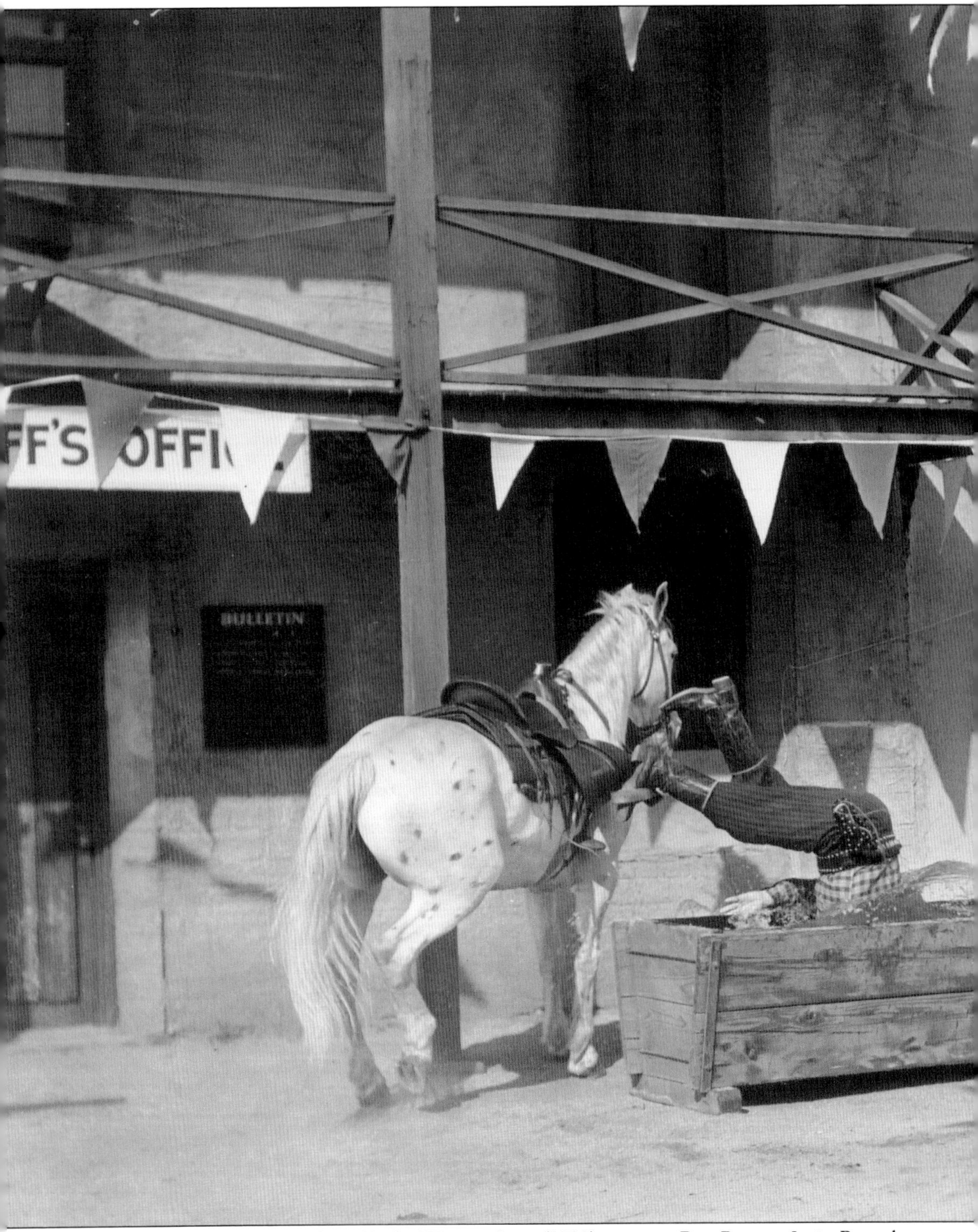


Here is a still action shot from *Under Western Stars* (1938), starring Roy Rogers. In it, Roy plays himself campaigning for a seat in the US Congress, hoping to draw the government's attention to the plight of farmers in the Dust Bowl of the 1930s. Note the banner. This scene was probably

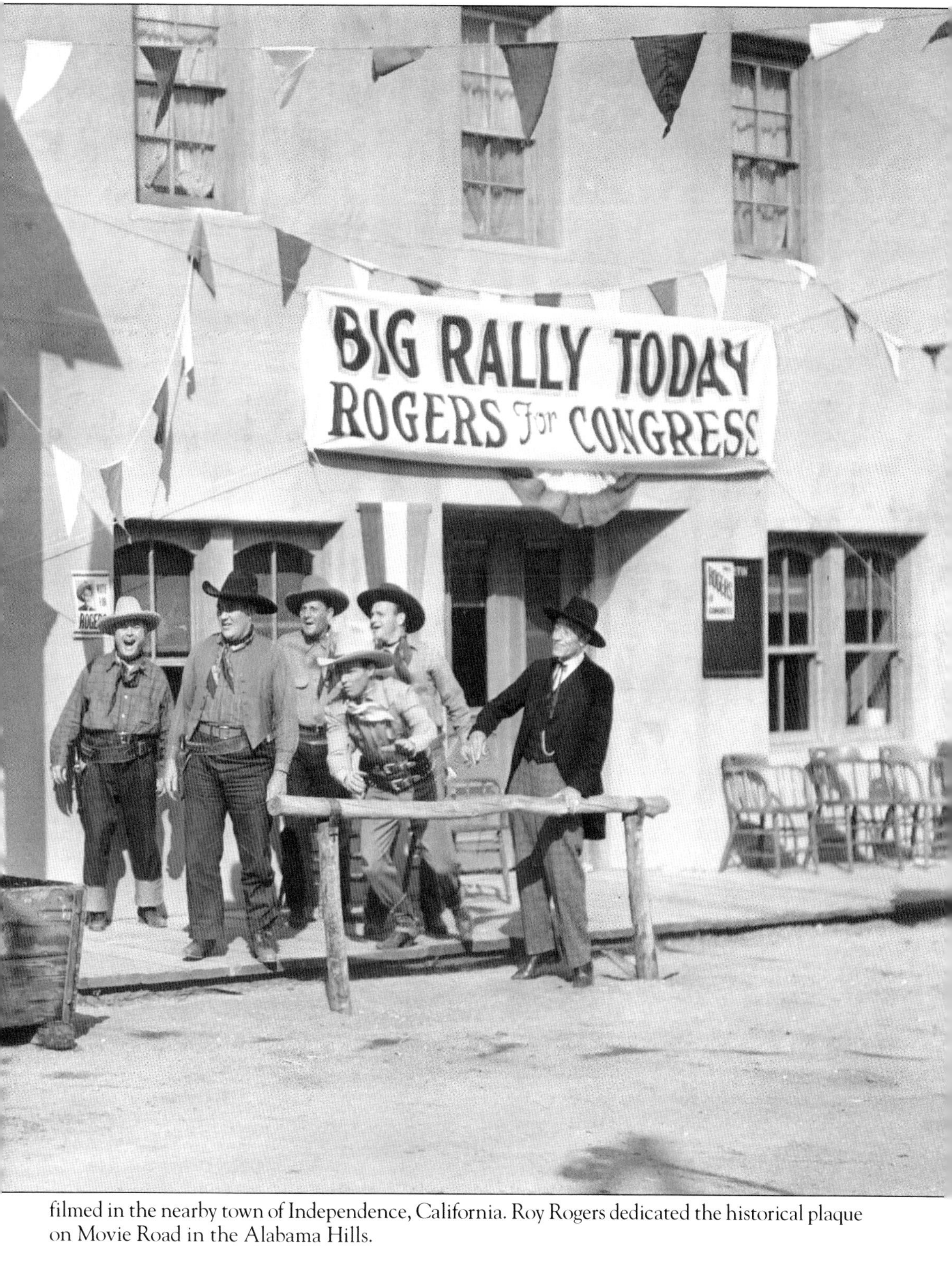


filmed in the nearby town of Independence, California. Roy Rogers dedicated the historical plaque on Movie Road in the Alabama Hills.

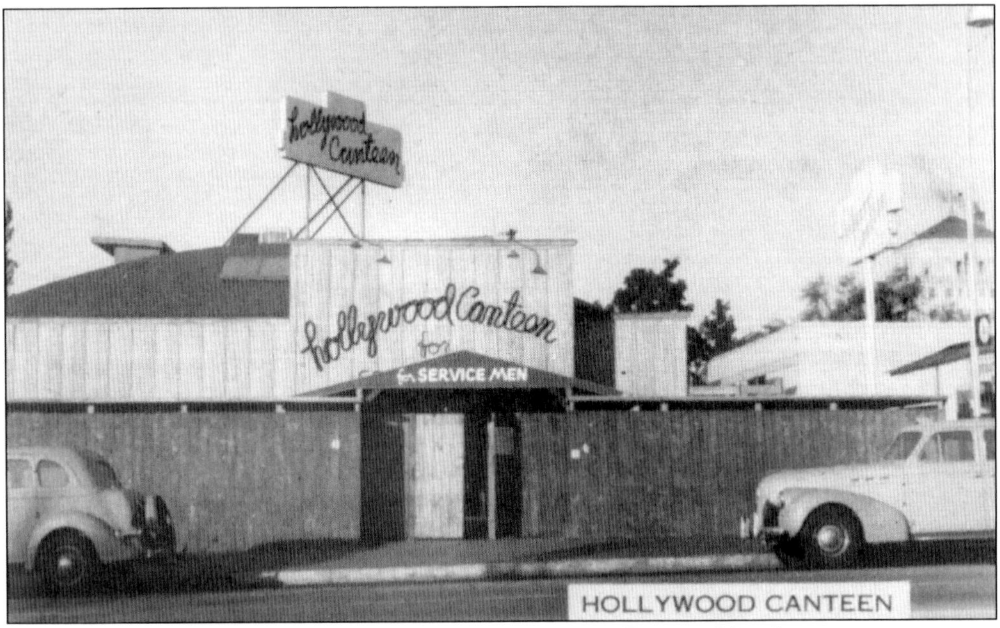


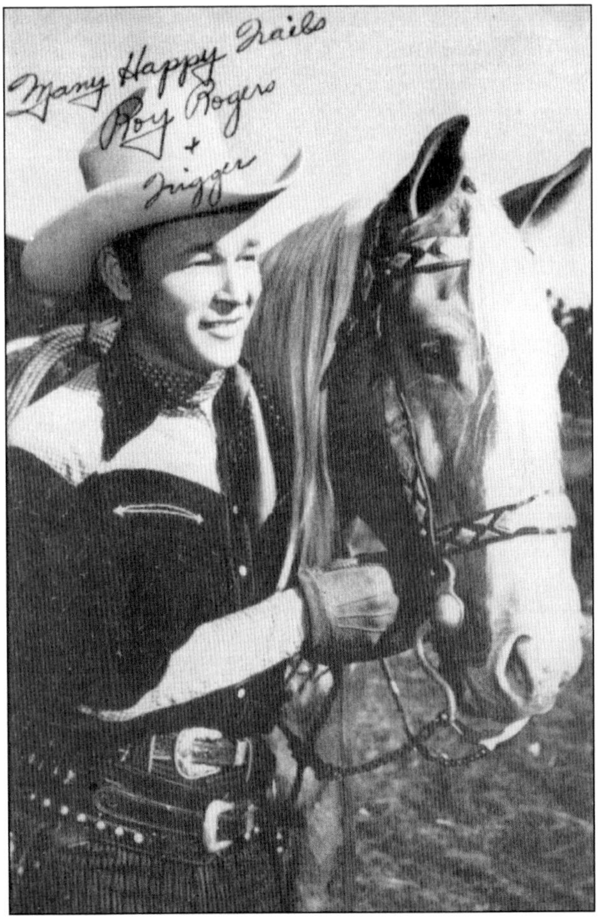


Roy would make appearances, along with his horse Trigger and dog Bullet, at the famous Hollywood Canteen for the troops during World War II. This was during his later days at Knott's Berry Farm in Buena Park, California. Bullet and Trigger are preserved via taxidermy and were stuffed and mounted on display for years at a now defunct museum; they were purchased for $265,500 by a Nebraska television network in 2010.

Roy Rogers was known as "King of the Cowboys." Dale Evans, his wife, was also a successful entertainer and Western star and was known as "Queen of the West." Her horse was named Buttercup. Roy and Dale are buried together at Sunset Hills Cemetery in Apple Valley, California.

This photograph shows an action scene in *Bar 20 Rides Again* (1935). The location is a cabin positioned along Tuttle Creek Road in the Alabama Hills. This was also the residence of actor William Boyd, who played Hopalong Cassidy in the famous serial. He also lived at 2010 Vine Street in Hollywood, not far from the famous intersection with Hollywood Boulevard. Later in life, Boyd lived in Palm Desert, California.

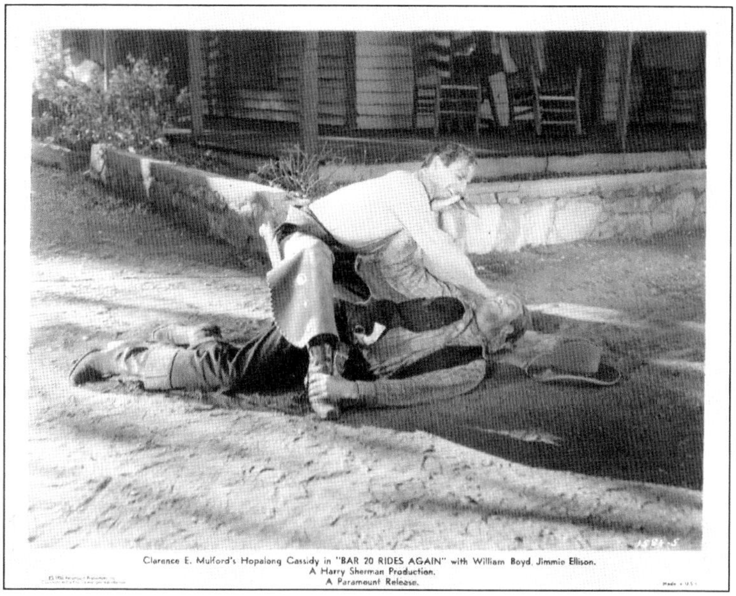


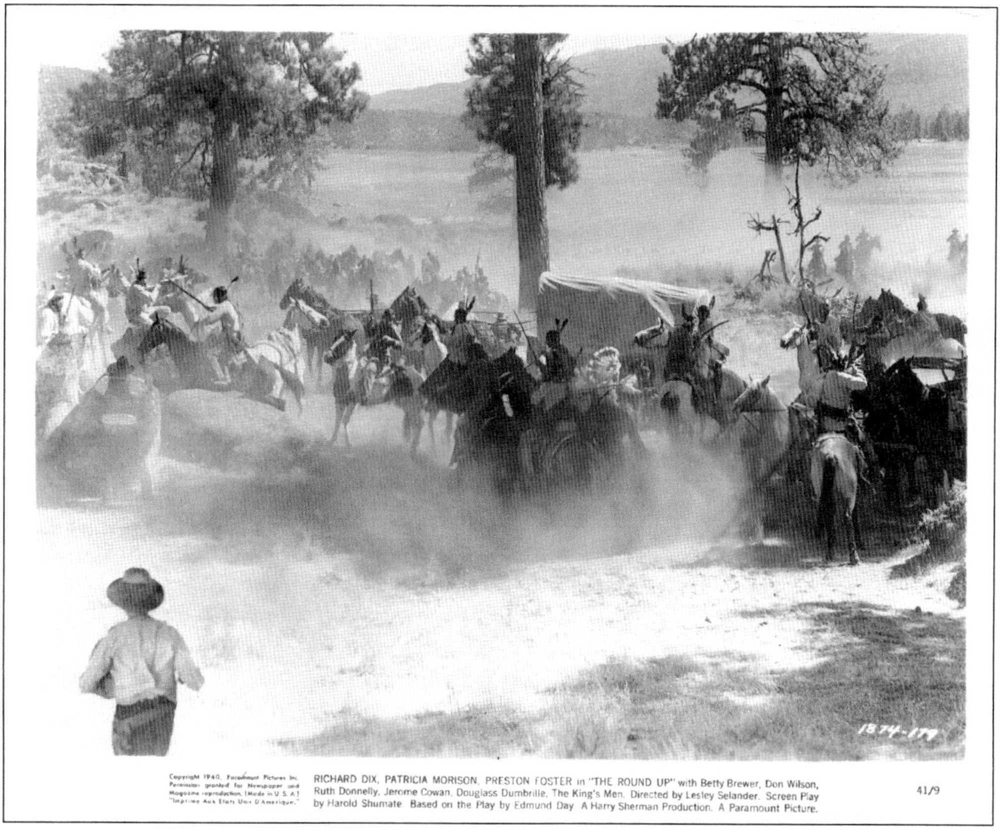


This photograph shows a battle scene from the 1940 remake of the 1920 film *The Round Up*. It was filmed in Lone Pine and Rock Creek Lake near Tom's Place, California. Richard Dix and Preston Foster made the trip to work in the Alabama Hills, as did producer Harry Sherman, who worked on over 50 episodes of the Hopalong Cassidy serial.

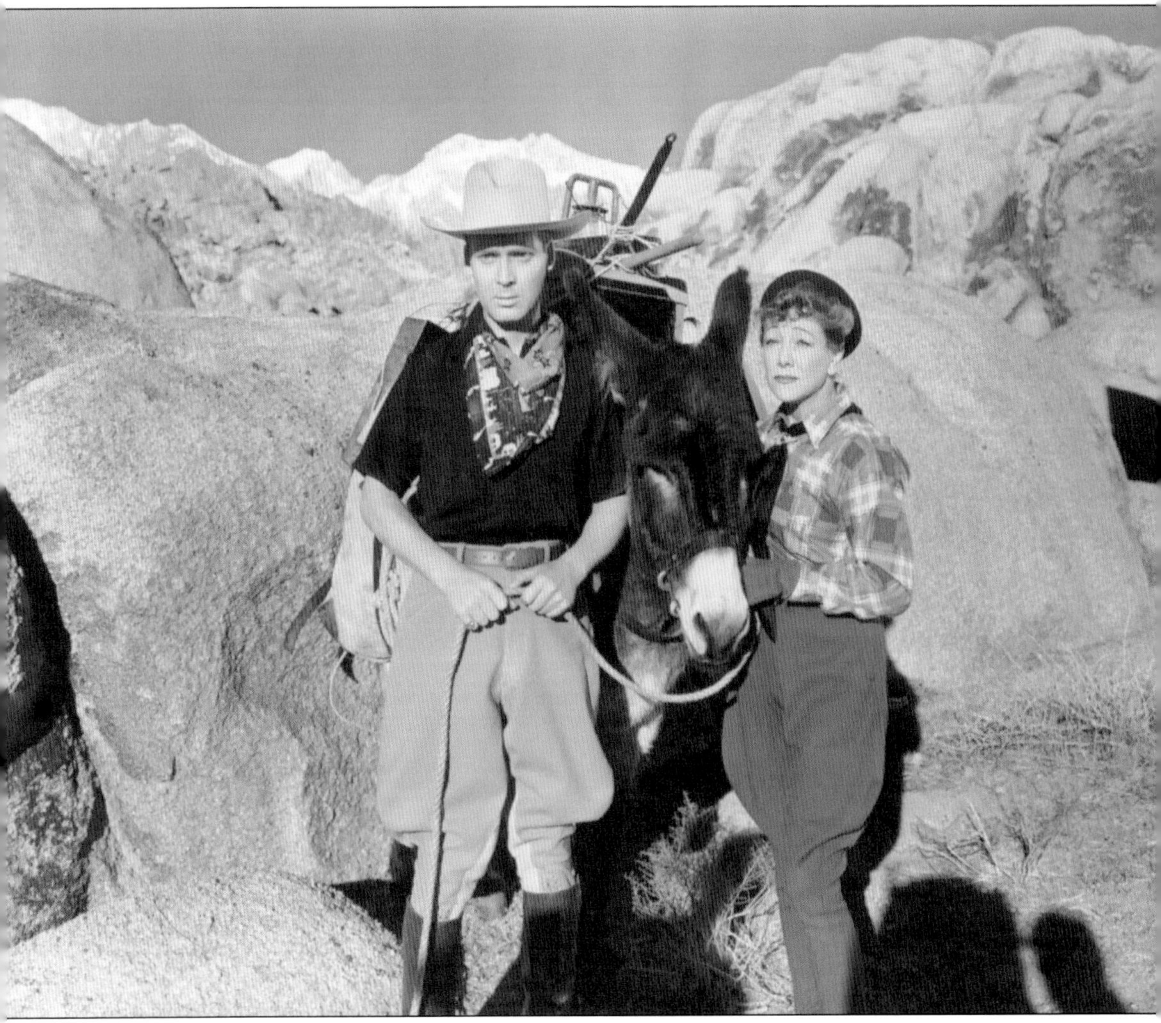

This is a photograph from *Dudes are Pretty People* (1943), starring Jimmy Rogers and Marjorie Woodworth. B Westerns such as these were the bread and butter of movie houses during the 1940s. This one was a Hal Roach Studio film from the creators of *Our Gang* (better known as *The Little Rascals*). At 43 minutes, it was the first of the studio's many so-called Western "streamliners," films that were longer than "shorts" but shorter than full-length features. The unmistakable terrain of the Alabama Hills provides a nice background.

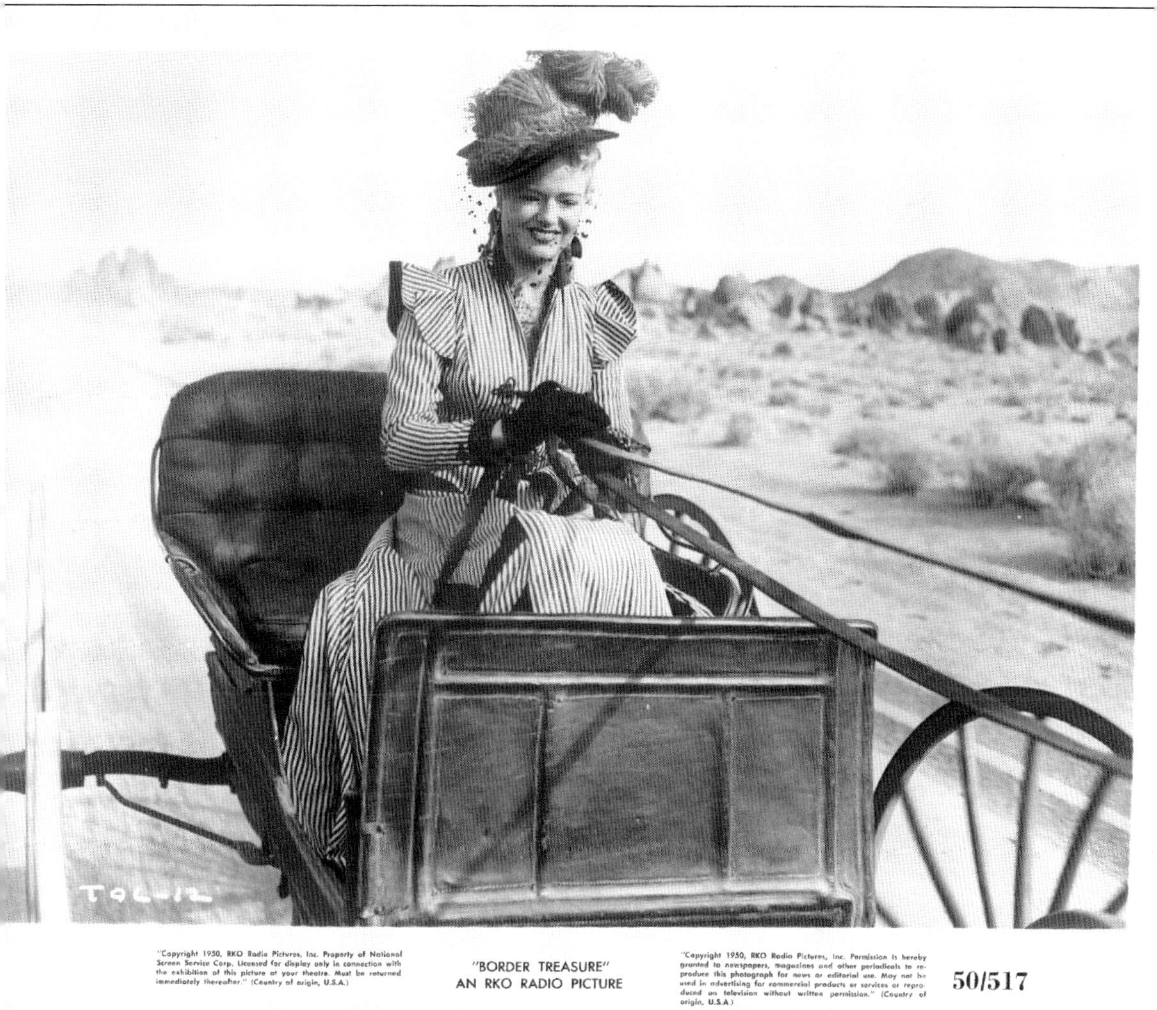


Jane Nigh, a redhead like Lucille Ball, was seen in many B Westerns and was a civilian defense worker during World War II. She starred in films for Monogram Pictures and 20th Century Fox, and this image shows her in the RKO Radio Picture *Border Treasure* (1950). This photograph shows her driving a wagon along Movie Road in the Alabama Hills.

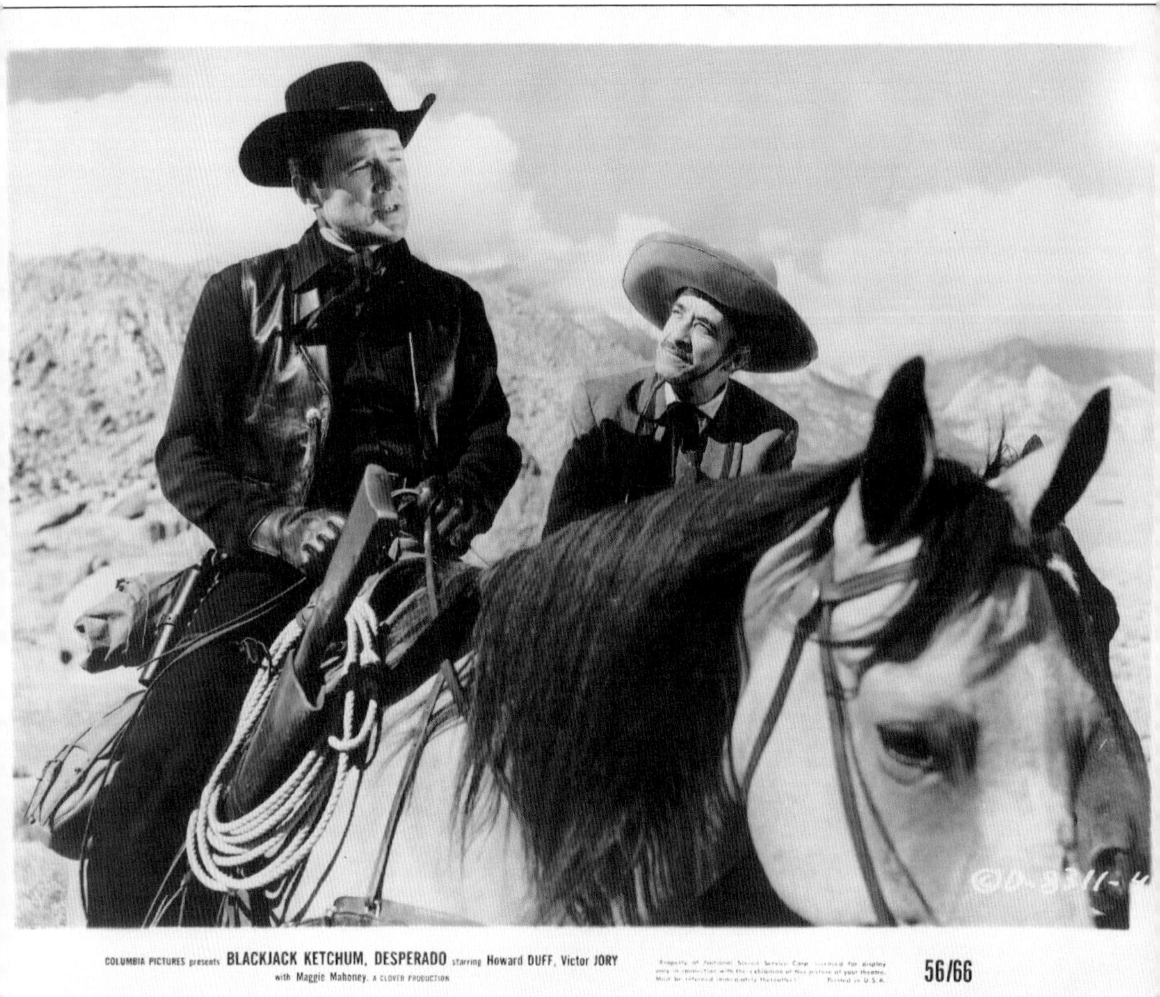


Howard Duff is seen riding in the Alabama Hills in *Blackjack Ketchum, Desperado* (1956). This film was from a novel written by Louis L'Amour. Howard Duff was married to Ida Lupino, who starred in *High Sierra* (1941); together, they were a power couple of the Hollywood elite during the 1950s.

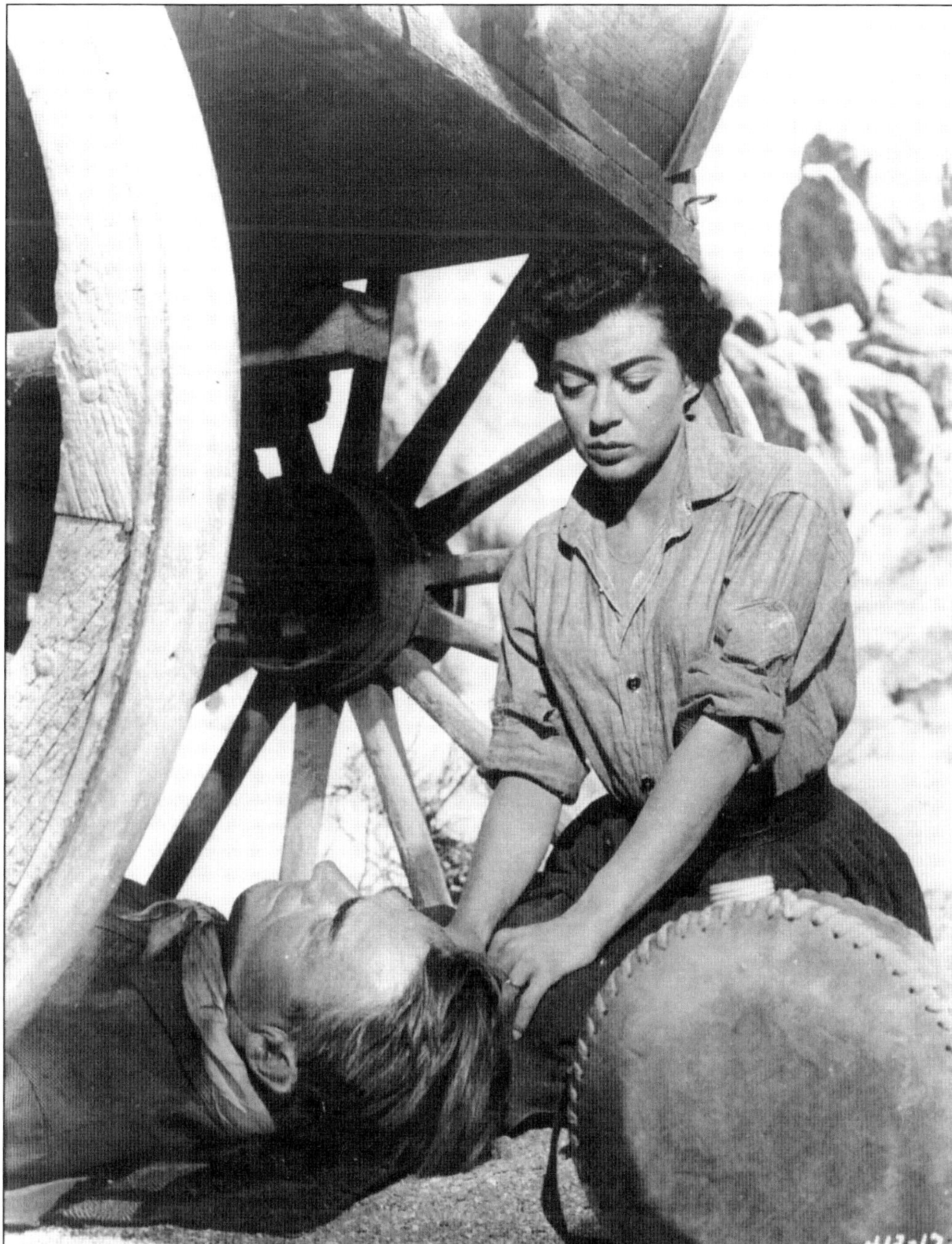


Gail Russell and Randolph Scott starred in *Seven Men from Now* (1956), which is regarded as one of the best motion pictures ever filmed in the Alabama Hills. Scott was a favorite among locals as well as his peers, and he loved riding in the Alabama Hills. He had a horse named Stardust, which he gave to a local rancher in Lone Pine.

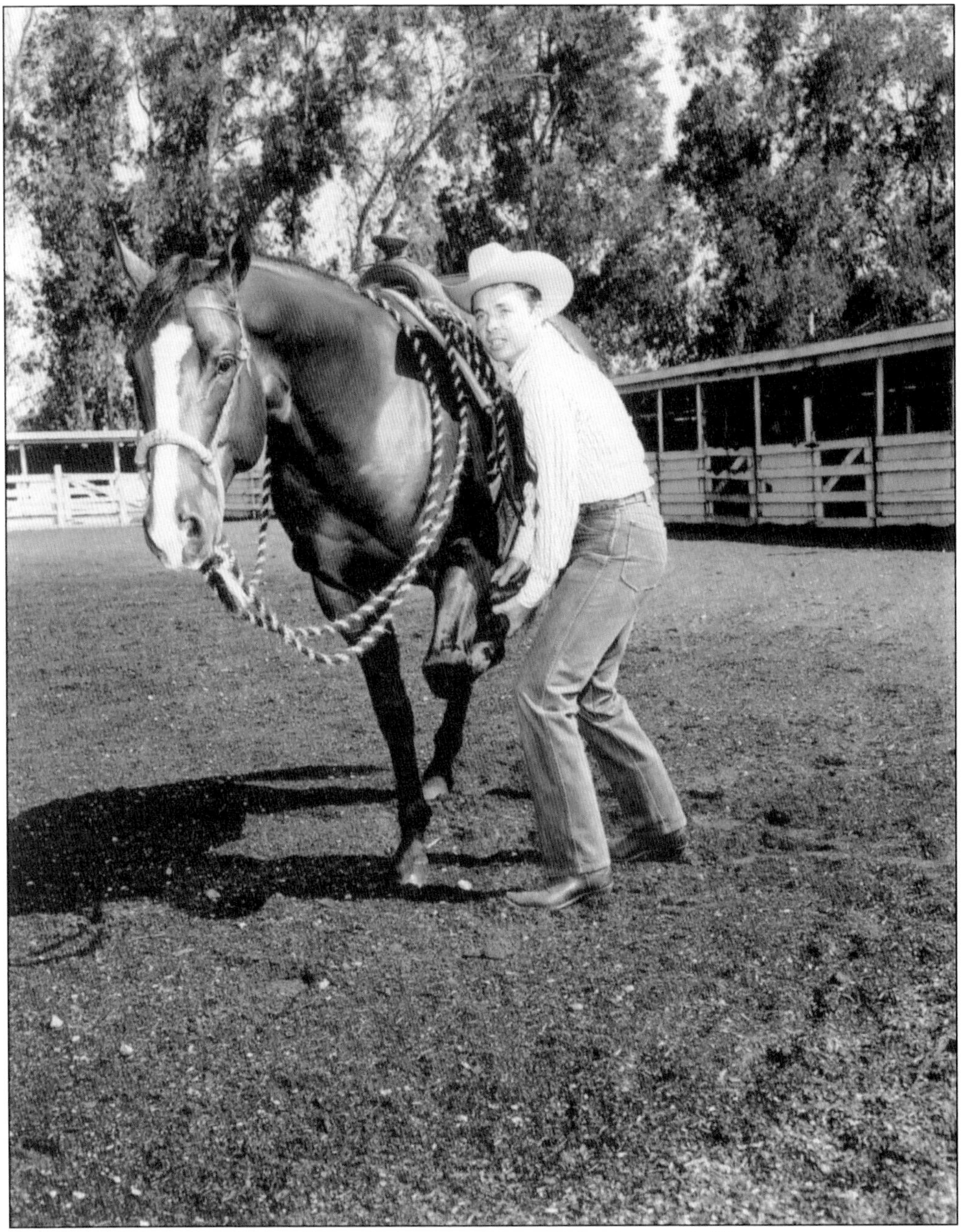

The most decorated soldier of World War II and last of the famous B Western stars was Audie Murphy, shown here getting ready to ride. He made over 40 movies, mostly Westerns. Films like *Hell Bent For Leather* (1960) and *Showdown* (1963) are among the most popular of him riding in the Alabama Hills. Murphy died at the age of 42 in a plane crash on May 28, 1971. He is buried near the Tomb of the Unknown Soldier in Arlington National Cemetery.

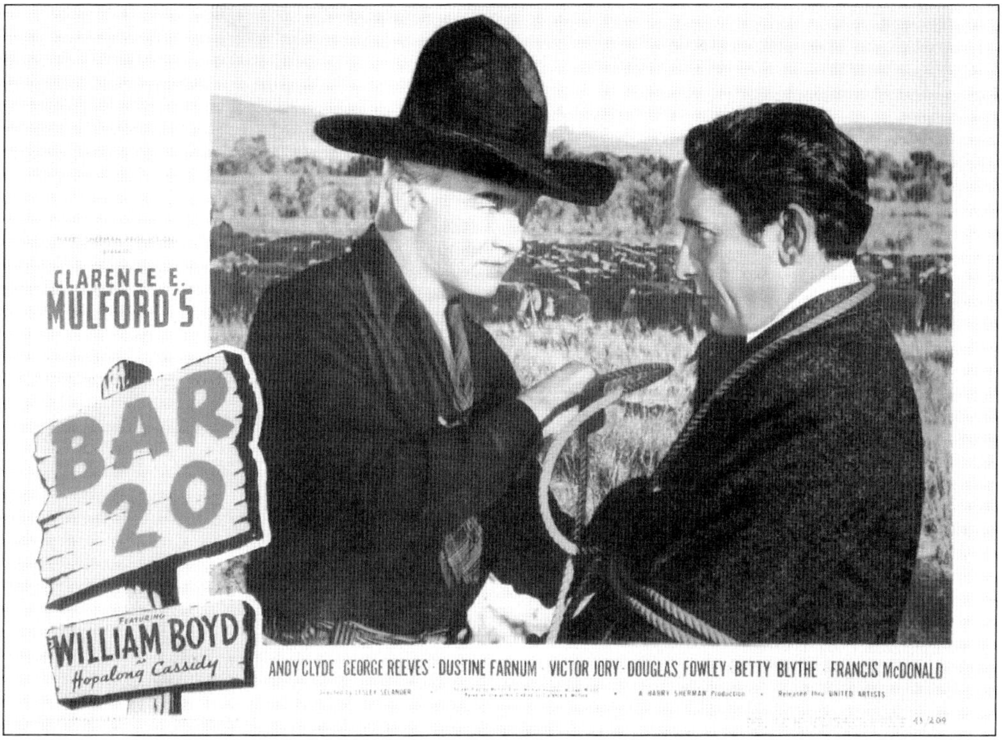


Pictured above is the lobby card for *Bar 20* (1943), which is widely considered one of the best in the Hopalong Cassidy serials. Below is the lobby card for *Hands Across the Border* (1944), the film in which Trigger is introduced for the first time.

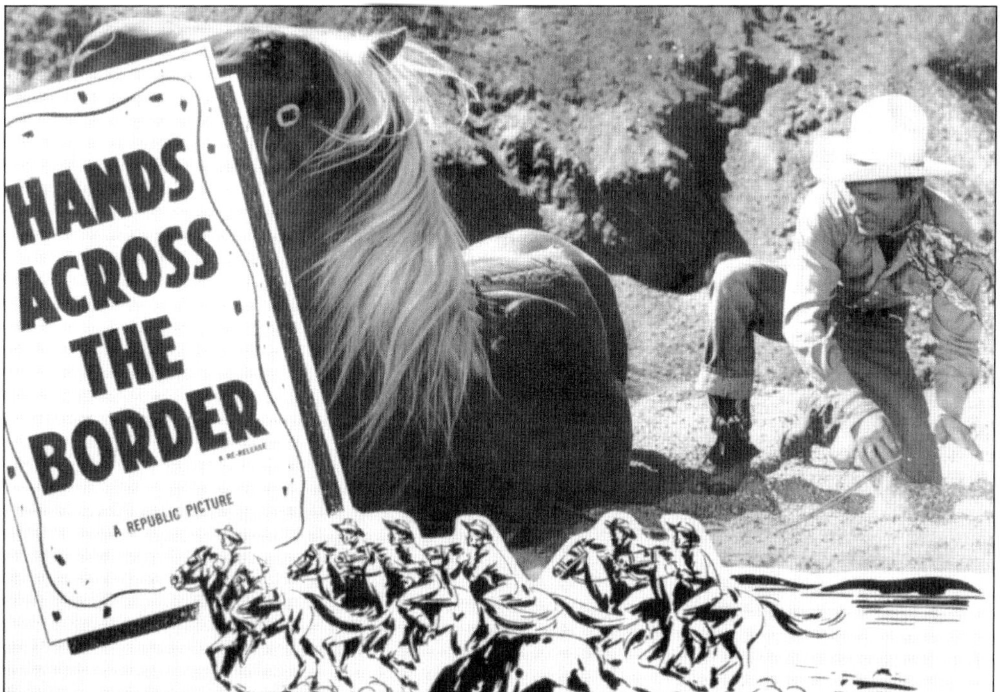

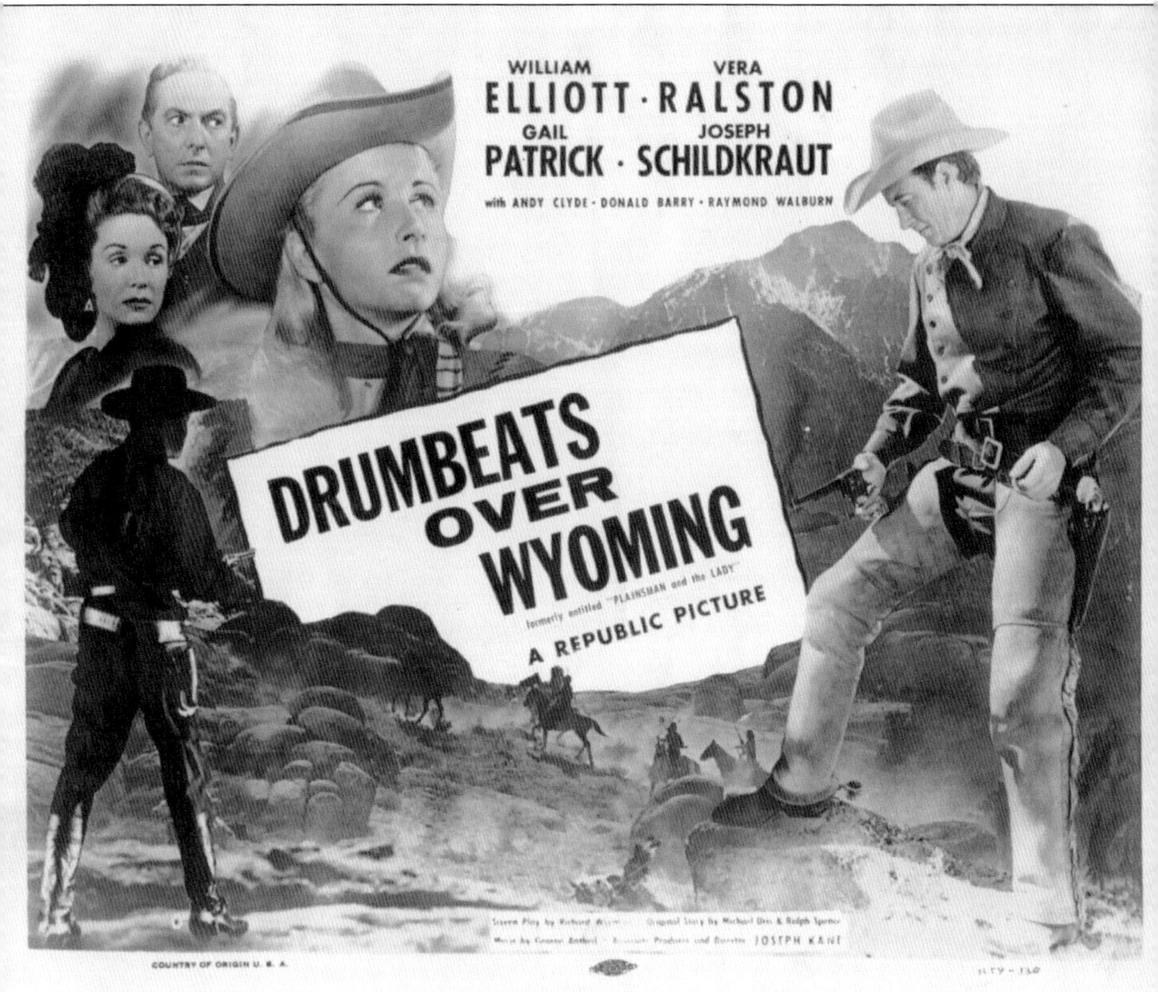


Above is the lobby card *Drumbeats Over Wyoming* (1946). The Western star Bill Elliott (far right) was famous for having his pistols inverted on his holster, as seen here. The lead role was turned down by John Wayne before being offered to Elliot, who was best known for starring in several episodes of the Red Ryder series, also filmed in the Alabama Hills.

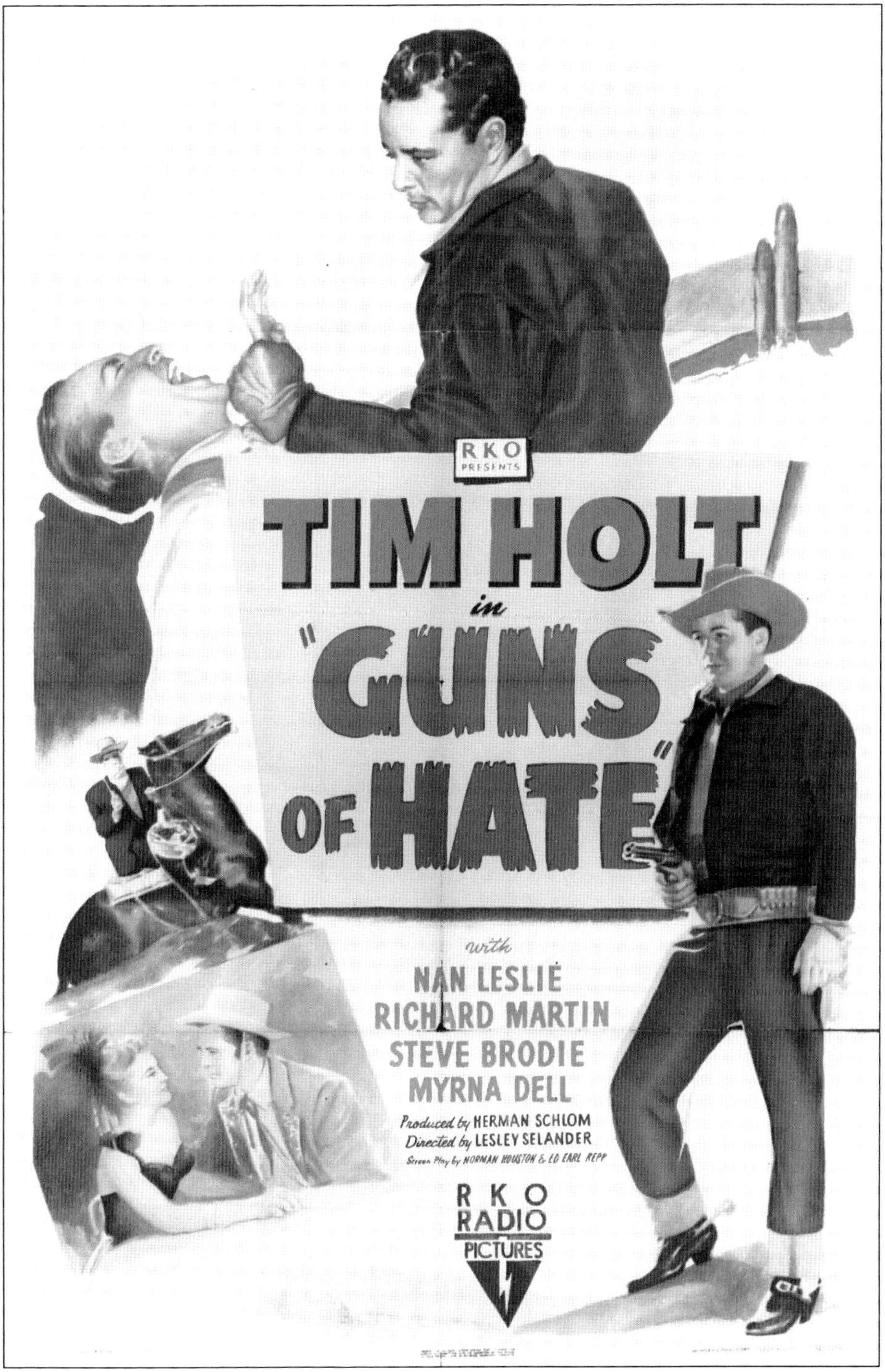


This is the lobby card for *Guns of Hate* (1948), which was filmed entirely in the Alabama Hills. Directed by Lesley Selander and starring Tim Holt, the film tells the story of two men falsely accused of murder who escape from jail and search for the real killers. Tim Holt's horse was named Duke.

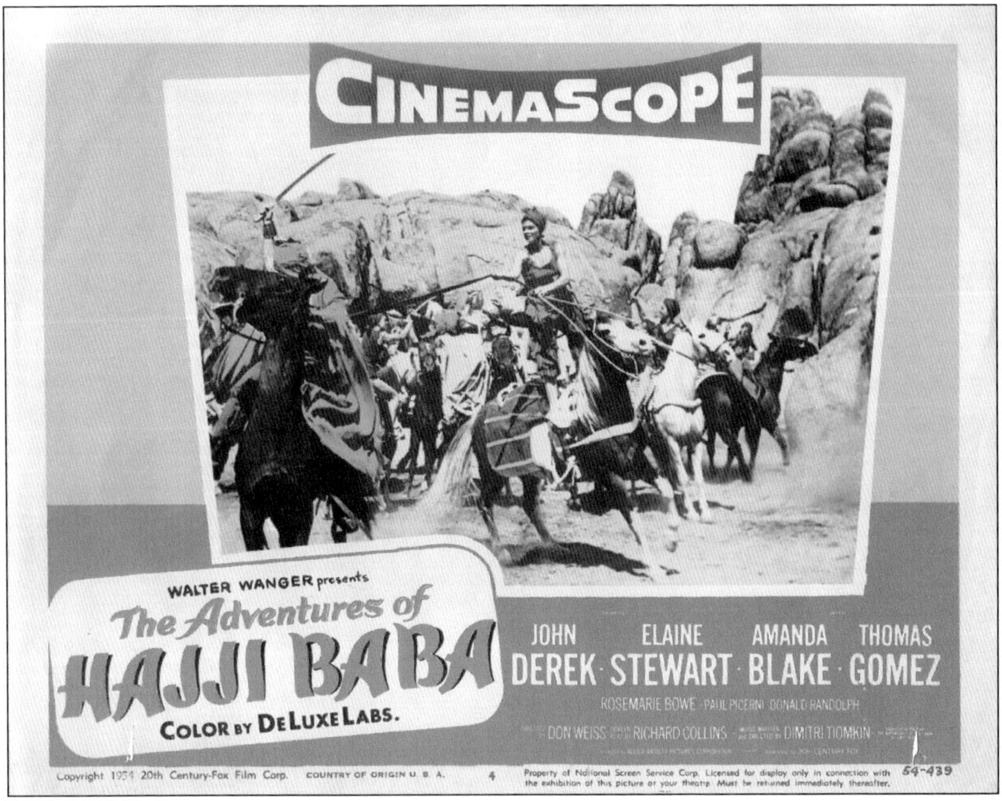


This lobby card is for *The Adventures of Hajji Baba* (1954). This film included many wonderful scenes showing locations in the Alabama Hills. Below is the lobby card for *The Violent Men* (1955). The film, starring Glenn Ford, centers around the Anchor Ranch, which is also the name of a real ranch located in Lone Pine. It also starred veteran actors Barbara Stanwyck and Edward G. Robinson. It became a magical place for Stanwyck, as her ashes were scattered in the winds of the Alabama Hills, her final resting place.

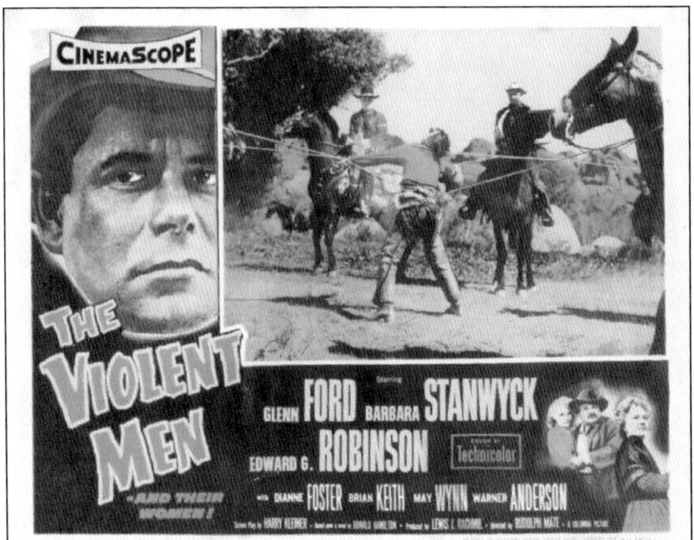

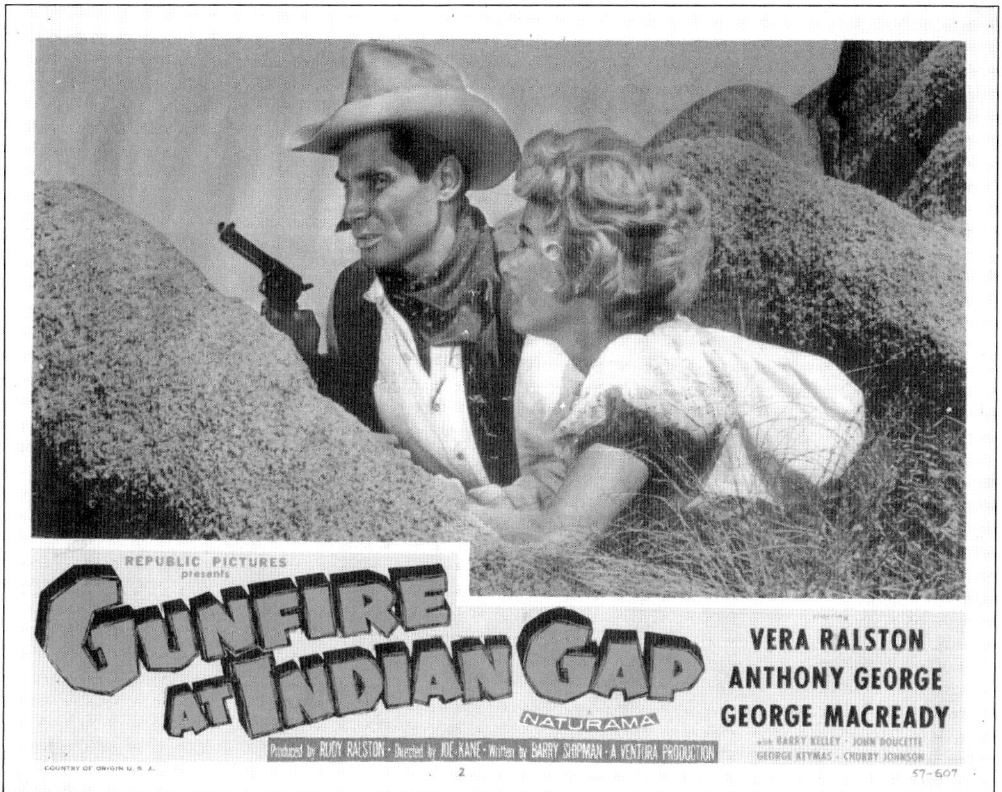


Pictured above is the lobby card for *Gunfire at Indian Gap* (1957), starring Vera Ralston in a classic Republic Western. Ralston was a Czech figure skater, actress, and wife of Republic Pictures founder and president Herbert J. Yates. Below is the lobby card for *From Hell to Texas* (1958). The film starred Don Murray (who costarred with Marilyn Monroe in 1956's Bus Stop), Dennis Hopper, and Chill Wills. The card shows the rocks of the Alabama Hills.

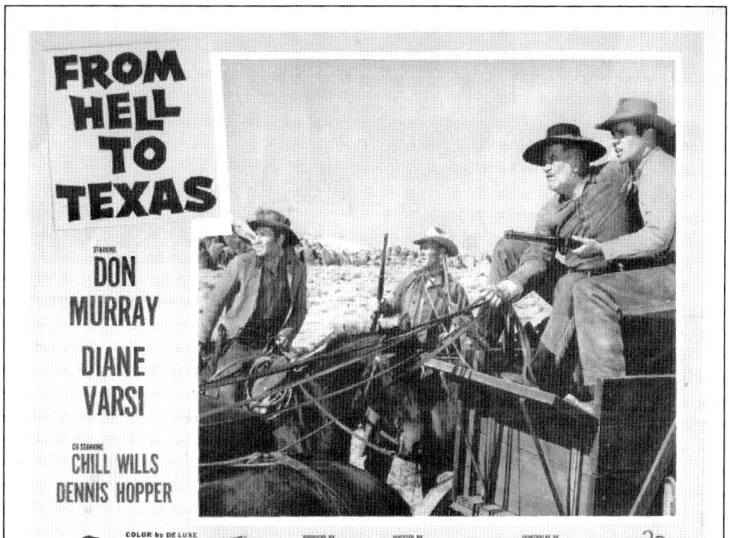

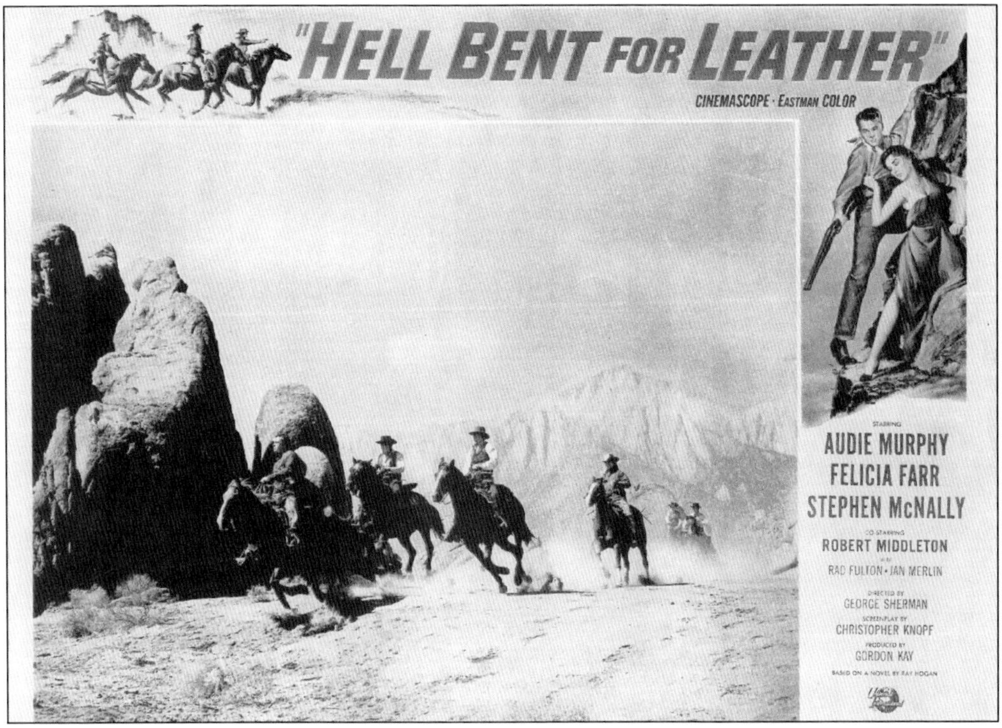


Above is the lobby card for *Hell Bent for Leather* (1960), starring Audie Murphy and Felicia Farr and featuring wonderful locations in the Alabama Hills. Below is a map is of the Ponderosa Ranch, from the television show *Bonanza*. The opening of each episode showed this map on fire as a catchy tune played the background. *Bonanza* episodes were filmed in the Alabama Hills. In the modern film *Django Unchained* (2012), also filmed partly in the Alabama Hills, actor Jamie Foxx is said to be wearing a vest and hat worn by Michael Landon in a *Bonanza* episode.

# *Three*

# Literary Fiction and Science Fiction

In the southern part of the Alabama Hills, one will venture along Horseshoe Meadow Road, along Whitney Portal Road, and past a private ranch on Lubkin Canyon Road and across a bridge, which both were significant to early Western literary fiction.

The Lubkin Ranch, which is private property, was the site of the original Bar 20 Ranch seen in film. The Bar 20 Ranch was the fictional home of the famous Hopalong Cassidy. In 1905, Clarence E. Mulford introduced Cassidy in a short story called "The Fight at Buckskin." Hopalong Cassidy, played by William Boyd, was the most marketed cowboy star, with merchandise including toys, and surpassed the fame of his predecessor, Tom Mix.

Also along Horseshoe Meadow Road, the explorer will find a monument to where the Gunga Din temple stood in the 1939 RKO classic. In the western part of the Alabama Hills, one will find sites called Whitney Portal Road, and Movie Road.

This area once saw a galloping Roman general, a giant killer worm, a mysterious temple, and a town called Red Dog. This location provided many camera angles and terrain that had a futuristic element to it. It was near here that Russell Crowe rode and camped in the film *Gladiator*. Another epic, Cecil B. Demille's *Samson and Delilah* was shot near here.

Due to their breathtaking combination of ancient geological formations, rolling hills, desert flatlands, boulder-strewn landscapes, and mountainous backdrops, the Alabama Hills are an ideal location for science fiction films.

Near here was where Robert Downey Jr., in *Iron Man*, shows off his successful experiment to the military and where Kevin Bacon evades a worm-like creature in the science fiction adventure *Tremors*.

Red Dog, a Western set built in the early days, was located along Whitney Portal Road near Horseshow Meadow Road; the intersection once stood where a wooden bridge now suspends the road. The town of Red Dog was complete with a saloon called the Red Dog saloon.

*Camel Spiders*, a 2011 film about killer spiders, was shot near Movie Road and the Anchor Ranch, which was once was invaded on film by a flying saucer. Speaking of camels, the 1953 film *Desert Legion* featured camels in a scene near the site of the Gunga Din temple monument site.

Science fiction and fantasy films have captivated the imagination and are a part of popular culture that fuels interest best when filmed at a place of wonder like the Alabama Hills.

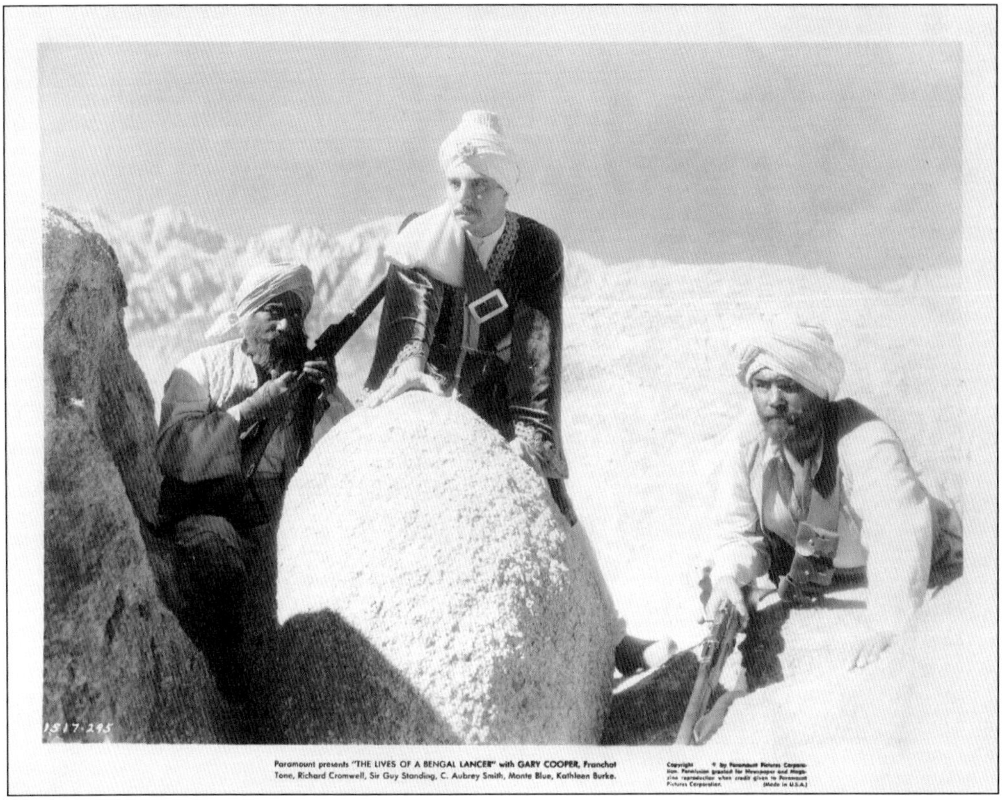


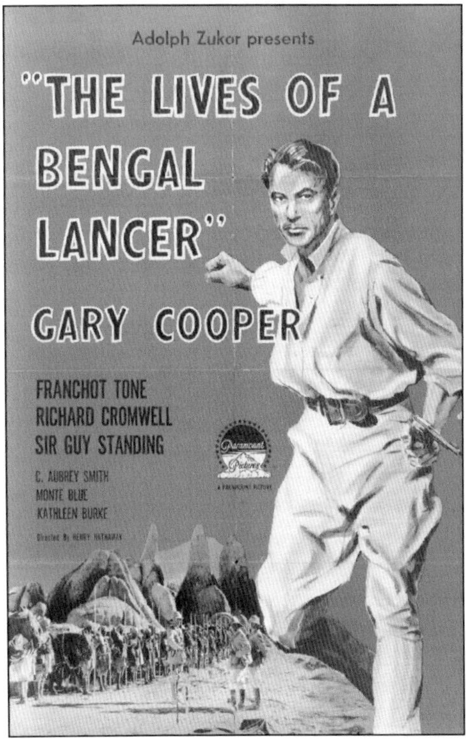


*The Lives of a Bengal Lancer* (1935) is an excellent example of an Eastern literary film. Starring Gary Cooper and Douglass Dumbrille, it was based on the 1930 novel of the same name by Francis Yeats-Brown and was shot in many locations in the Alabama Hills. The areas known as Background Rocks and Gene Autry Rock, as well as the burial site in *Rawhide* (1951), can all be seen in this film.

This is the lobby card for Paramount's *The Lives of a Bengal Lancer.*

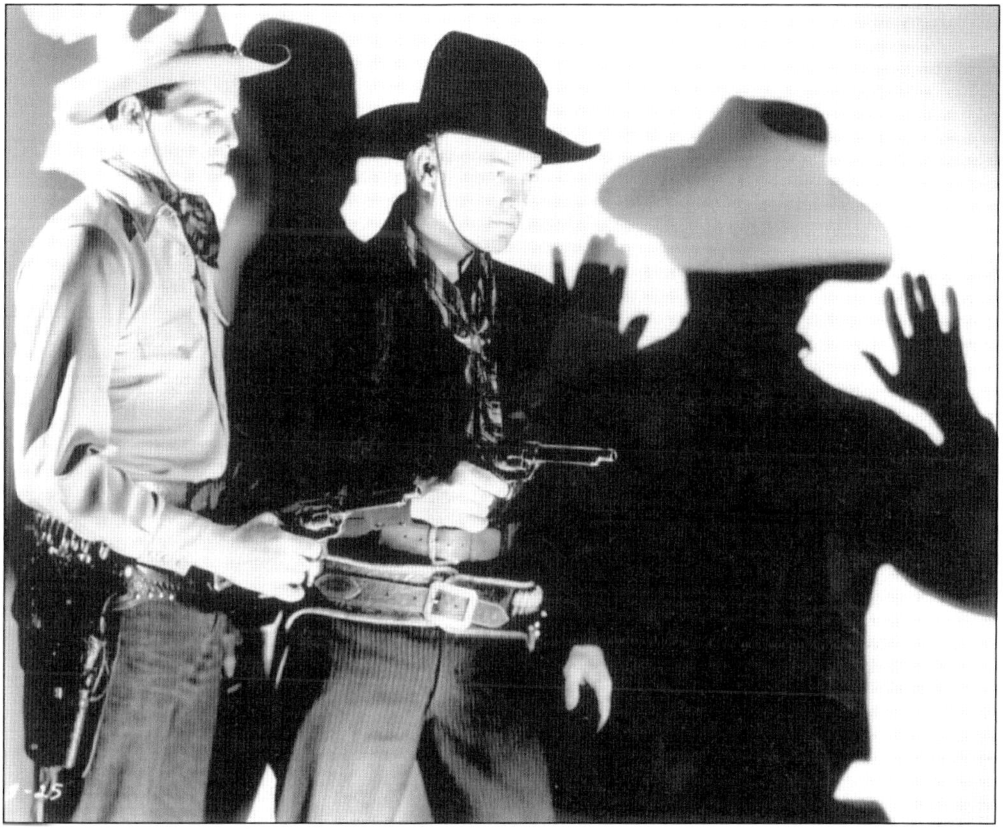

Clarence E. Mulford's character Hopalong Cassidy was portrayed by William Boyd, shown here in the black hat. Black hats in Westerns were symbolic of the villain, but not so for Hopalong Cassidy. Boyd loved bubble baths and would often sneak over to the Dow Hotel in nearby Lone Pine to soak after a hard day's work.

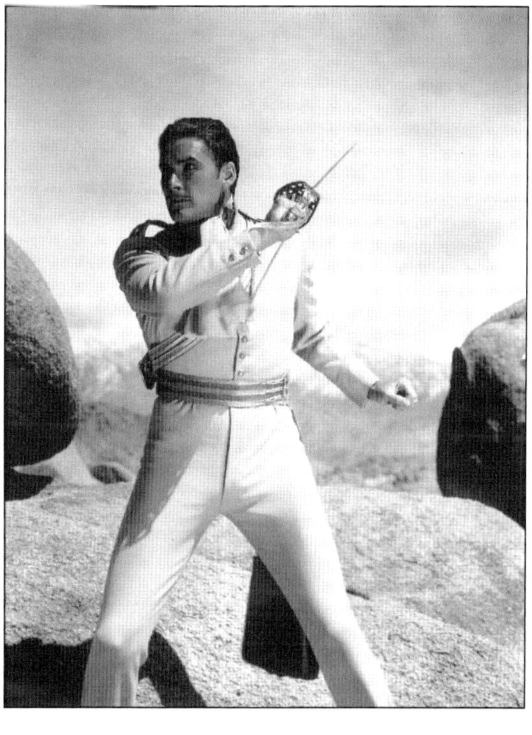

This wonderful publicity shot of Errol Flynn shows the Eastern Sierras in the background. Flynn made two films in the area: *Charge of the Light Brigade* (1936) and *Kim* (1950). Flynn disliked the wind and dust of the Alabama Hills and was prone to allergies. The sword in this photograph can be viewed at the Lone Pine Film History Museum, where it is on loan from the author.

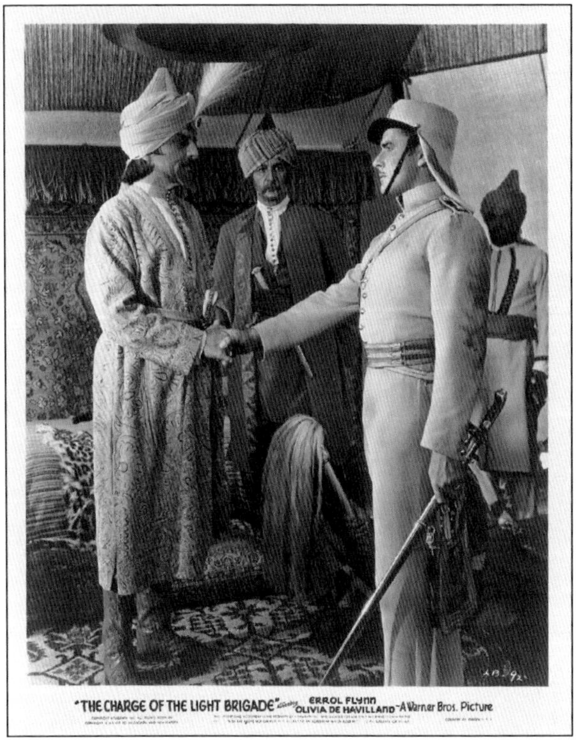


Errol Flynn is seen here in *The Charge of the Light Brigade* (1936), based on a poem by Alfred, Lord Tennyson. During filming, Flynn was almost deported for an expired visa, helped fight a hotel fire, and got into a brawl in which he defended a dog against mistreatment he had observed. Flynn now rests under a half-naked statue of a woman in peaceful Forest Lawn Cemetery in Glendale, California.

Tyrone Power (left) salutes in *King of the Khyber Rifles* (1953). Power would often pretend to blend in with the locals and play practical jokes, such as pretending to be a waiter or hotel clerk and seeing if people would notice him. He starred in *Brigham Young* (1940) and *Rawhide* (1951), both filmed in the Alabama Hills. He rests at Hollywood Forever Cemetery in Hollywood, California.

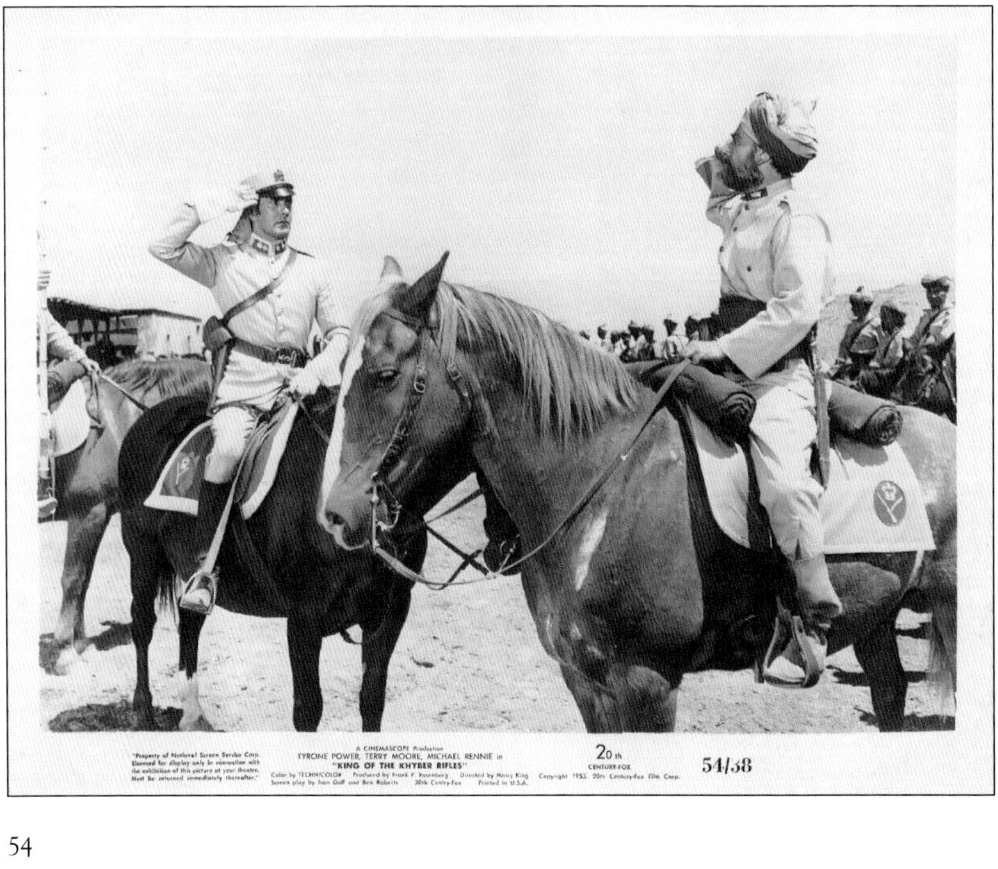

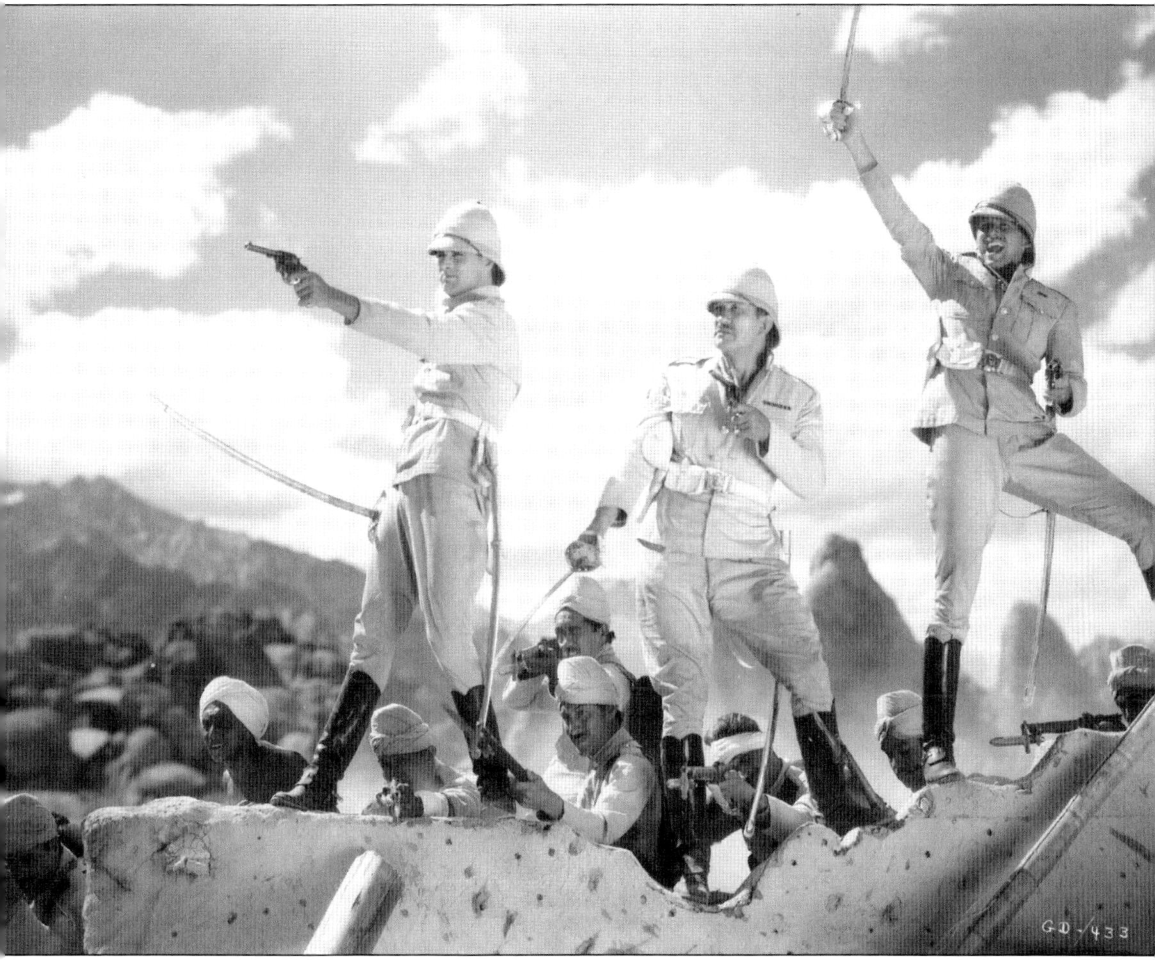


The critically acclaimed RKO Radio Pictures film *Gunga Din* (1939) is one of the most recognizable and noteworthy shot in the Alabama Hills. Adapted from an 1892 poem by Rudyard Kipling, this film was a large production and included elephants, a temple, a bridge, and hundreds of horses. Shown here are, from left to right, stars Cary Grant, Victor McLaglen, and Douglas Fairbanks Jr.

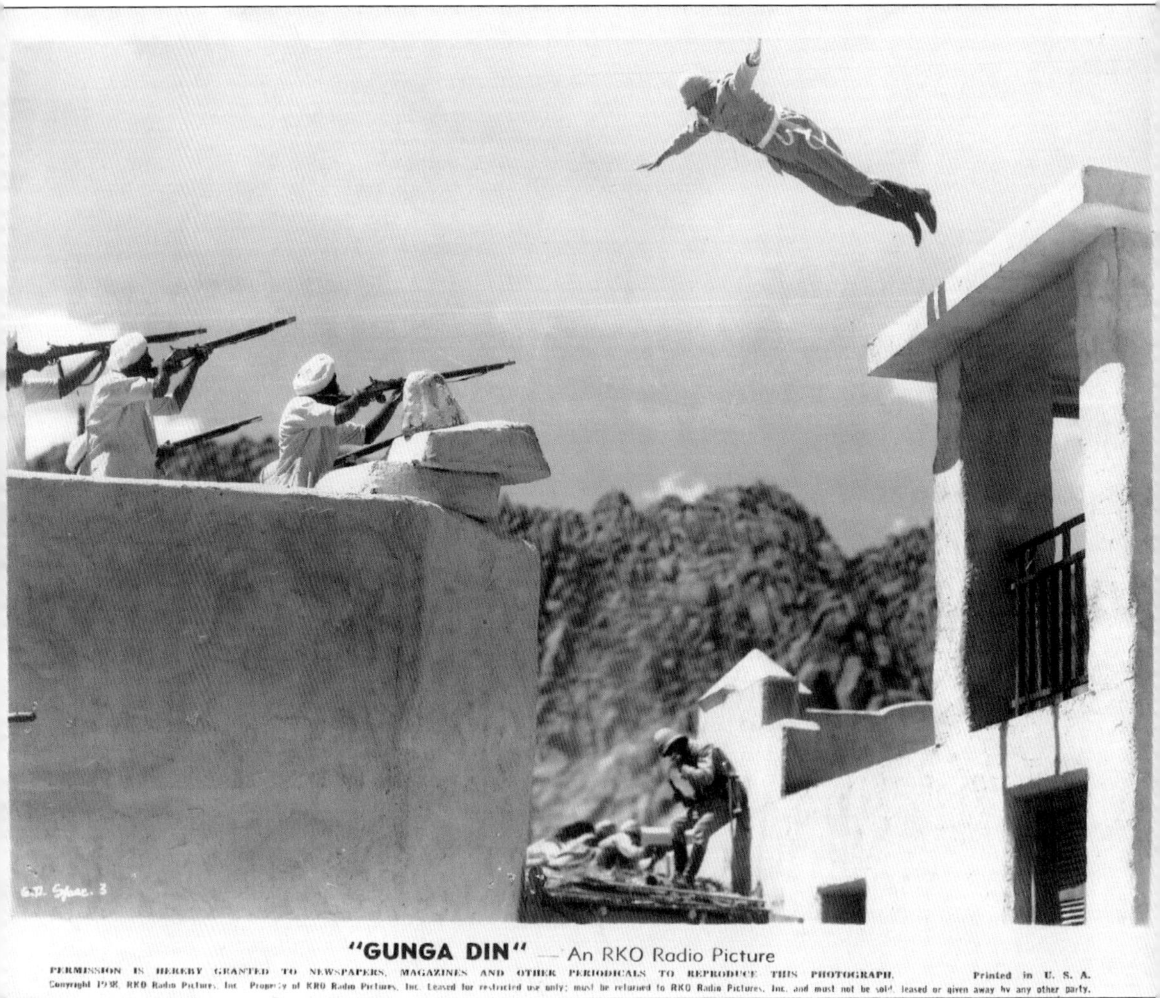


Victor McLaglen, a future founder of motorcycle clubs such as Victor McLaglen Motor Corps, is jumping off the wall of the set that was located in the northern section of the Alabama Hills. The movie crew and prop department of *Gunga Din* built Tantrapur in the Alabama Hills. The town no longer exists, but the location is easy to find northwest of Movie Road. When the set was torn down, parts of the material went to build the Anchor Ranch near Highway 395 in Lone Pine, California.

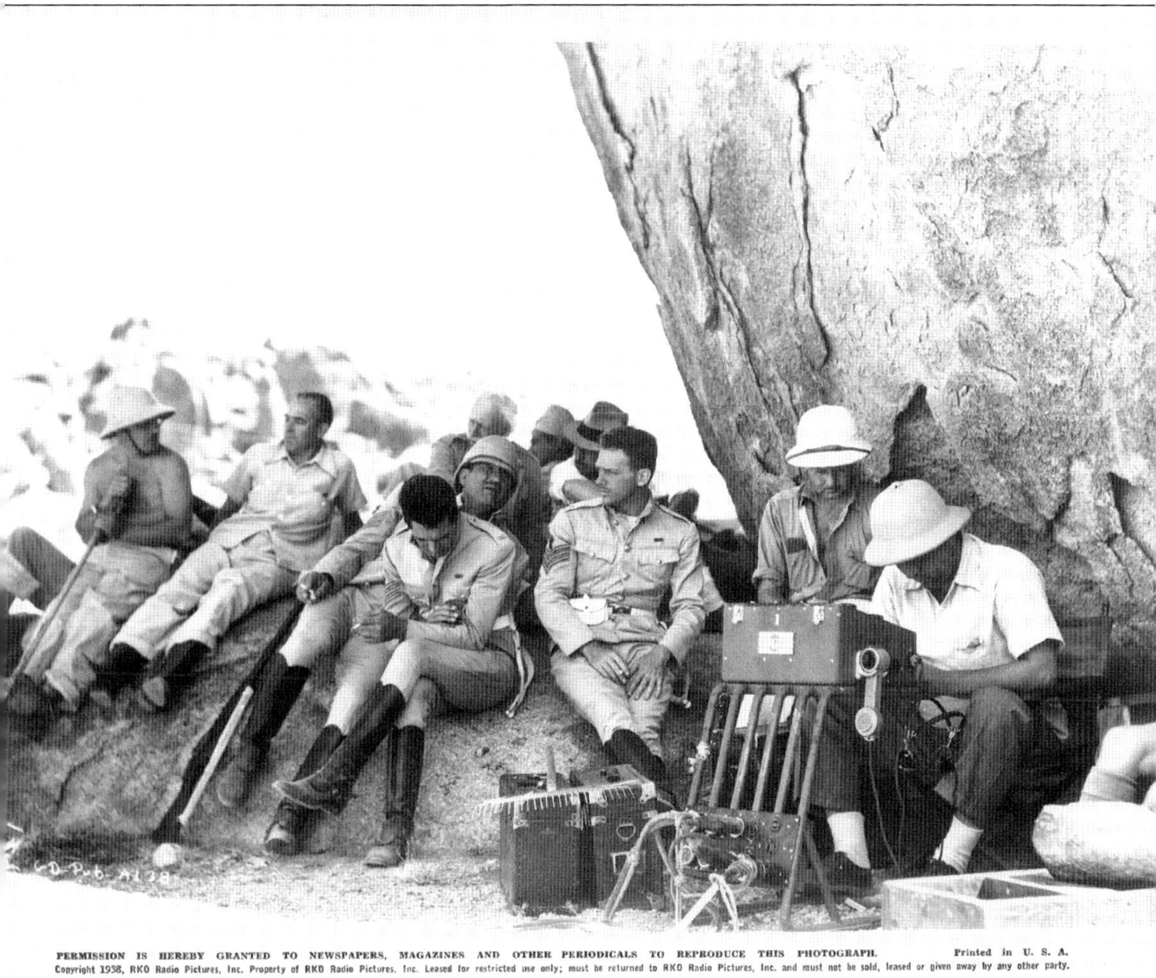


This very rare candid photograph shows the cast of *Gunga Din* seeking shelter under a huge boulder. The heat during filming was called "intense." The production took a toll on military veterans such as Victor McLaglen (third from left, behind Cary Grant) and Douglas Fairbanks (fifth from left). All three stars are smoking a cigarette, despite the heat. Douglas Fairbanks Jr. said in an interview that he suffered more injuries making movies like *Gunga Din* than during six years of military service (five of which were in combat).

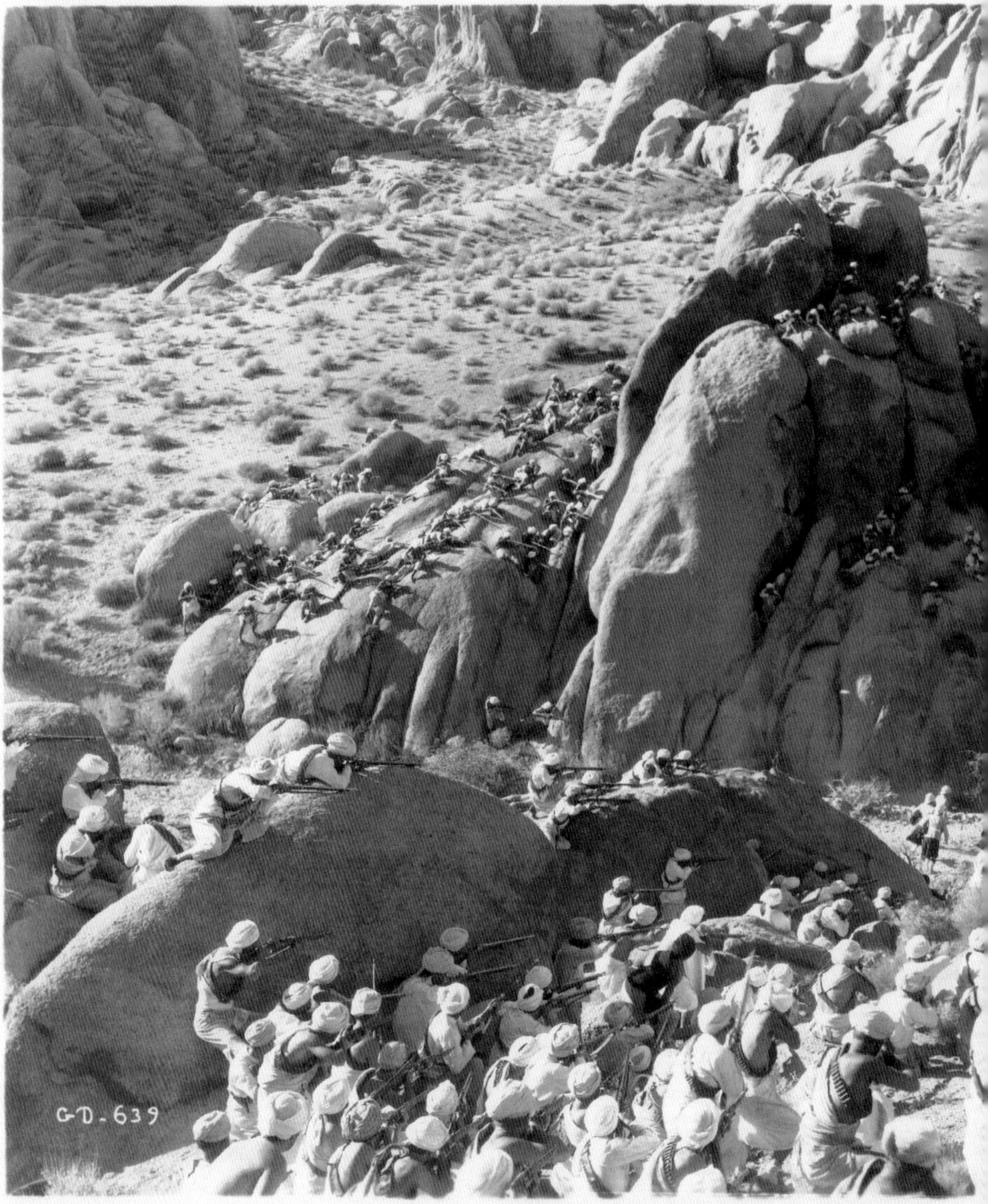


**"GUNGA DIN"** — An RKO Radio P

PERMISSION IS HEREBY GRANTED TO NEWSPAPERS, MAGAZINES AND OTHER PERIODICALS TO REPR

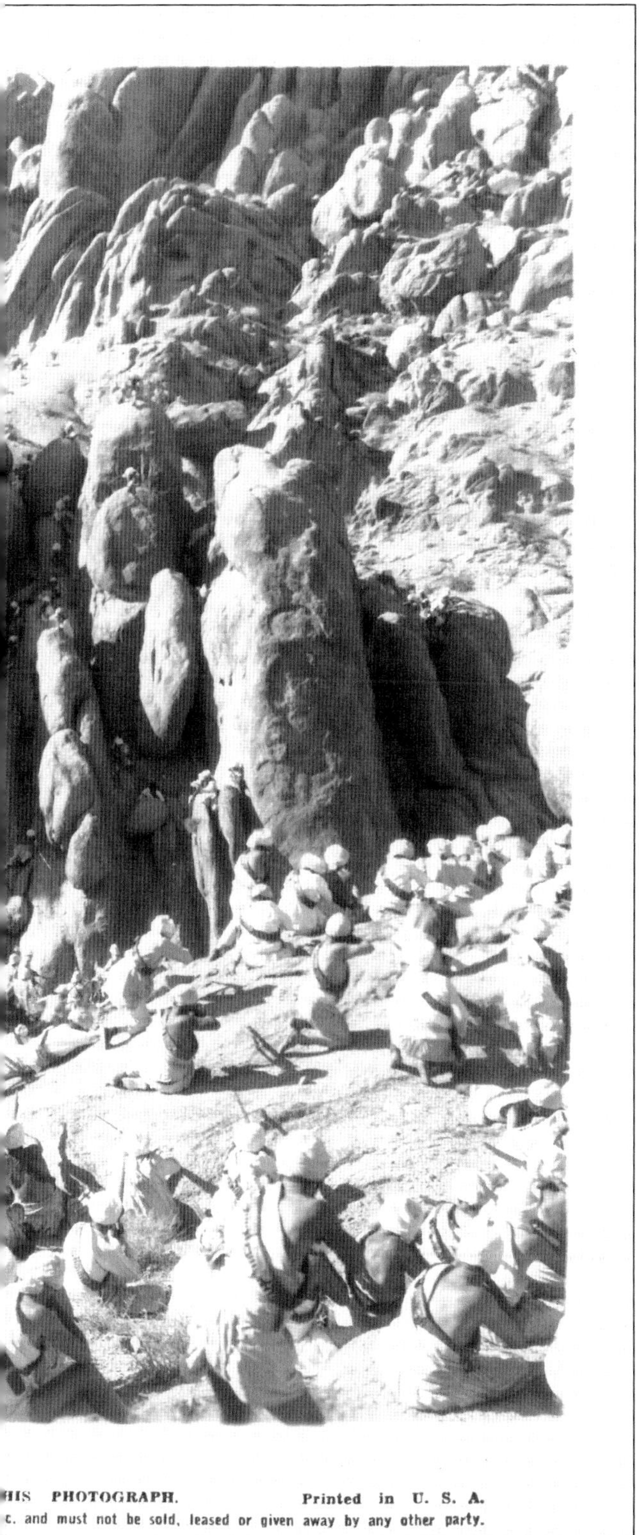


This view of the location for the climactic battle scene in *Gunga Din* (1939) shows the effort of thousands of extras and really gives the scope of how the Alabama Hills worked perfectly for a master epic. Note the soldiers scrambling among the rocks.

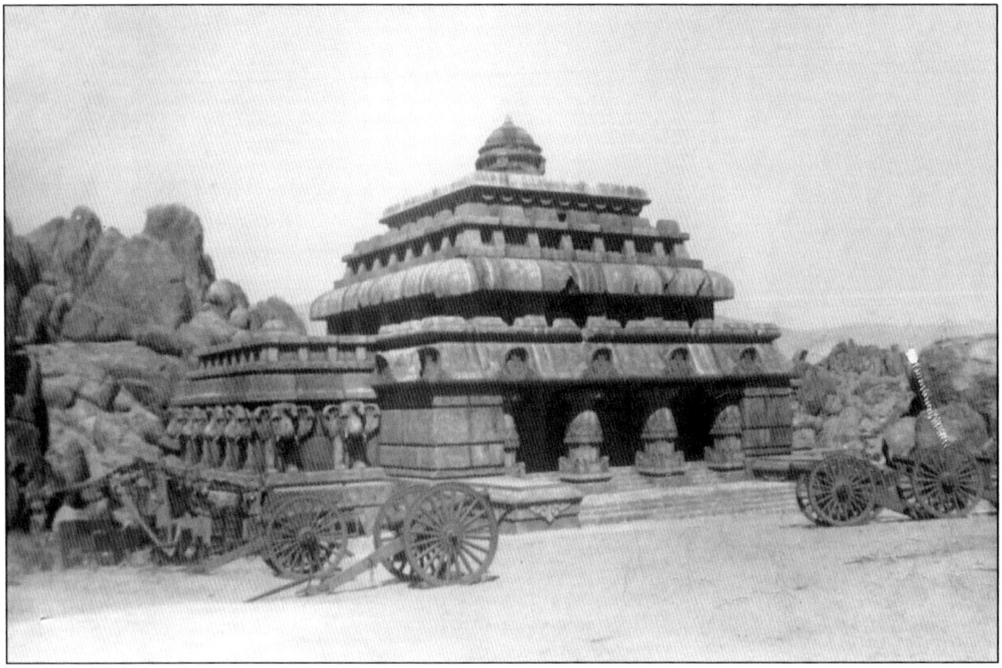

The image above is from a photograph that was glued onto a postcard and mailed during production. It shows the massive temple from *Gunga Din* (1939) that was located just off Horseshoe Meadow Road. There is now a marker designating the temple site. Below is the back of the postcard that was mailed on October 5, 1938, at 10:00 a.m. from Lone Pine, California.

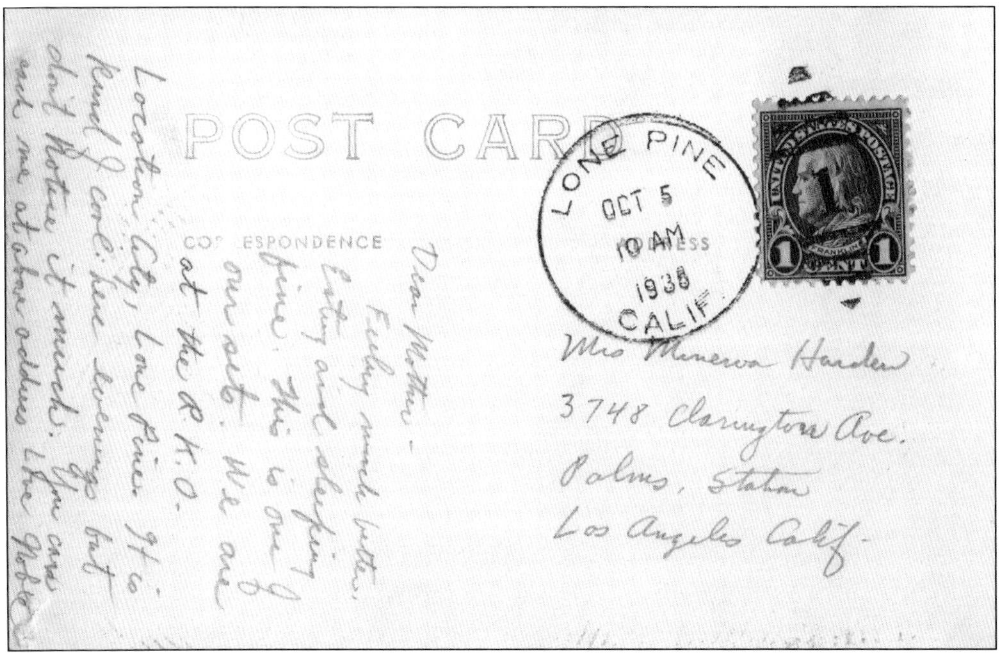

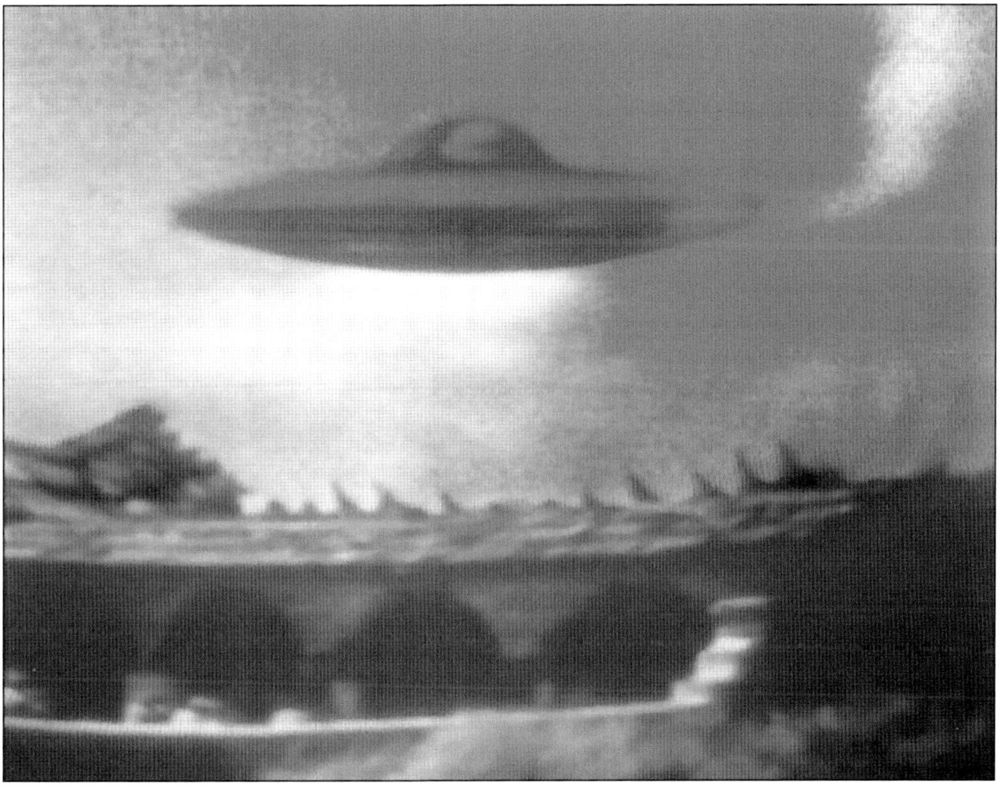

*Bamboo Saucer* (1968) is a great cult science fiction classic about a jet pilot who sees a UFO and follows a lead to find it in remote China. It is filled with great shots of a flying saucer and of men shooting Tommy guns in the Alabama Hills. This photograph shows a UFO flying over the Anchor Ranch located just off Highway 395, which was built from the old *Gunga Din* sets. Only a small outer wall remains of this once-massive structure.

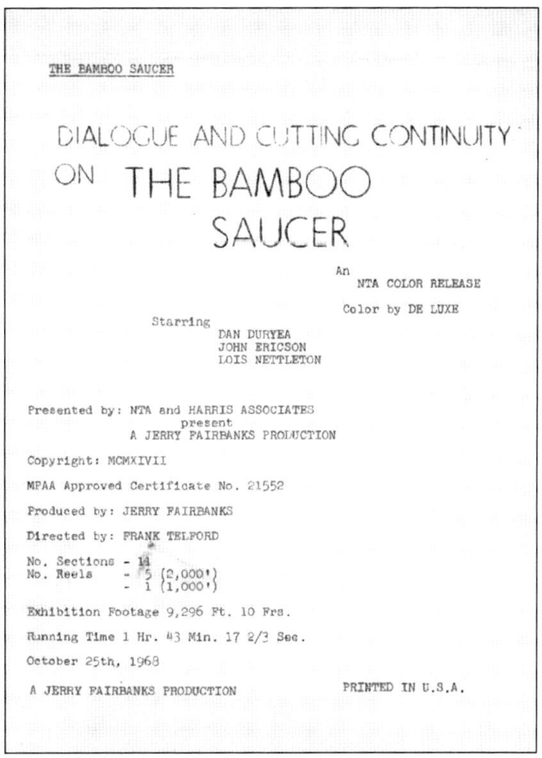

THE BAMBOO SAUCER

DIALOGUE AND CUTTING CONTINUITY
ON THE BAMBOO
SAUCER

An
NTA COLOR RELEASE

Color by DE LUXE

Starring
DAN DURYEA
JOHN ERICSON
LOIS NETTLETON

Presented by: NTA and HARRIS ASSOCIATES
present
A JERRY FAIRBANKS PRODUCTION

Copyright: MCMXIVII

MPAA Approved Certificate No. 21552

Produced by: JERRY FAIRBANKS

Directed by: FRANK TELFORD

No. Sections - 14
No. Reels - 5 (2,000')
- 1 (1,000')

Exhibition Footage 9,296 Ft. 10 Frs.

Running Time 1 Hr. 43 Min. 17 2/3 Sec.

October 25th, 1968

A JERRY FAIRBANKS PRODUCTION PRINTED IN U.S.A.

This is the front page of the script from *Bamboo Saucer.* The script is generally the first thing a director or actor reads before doing a film. This is an excellent example of how the movie-making process all starts.

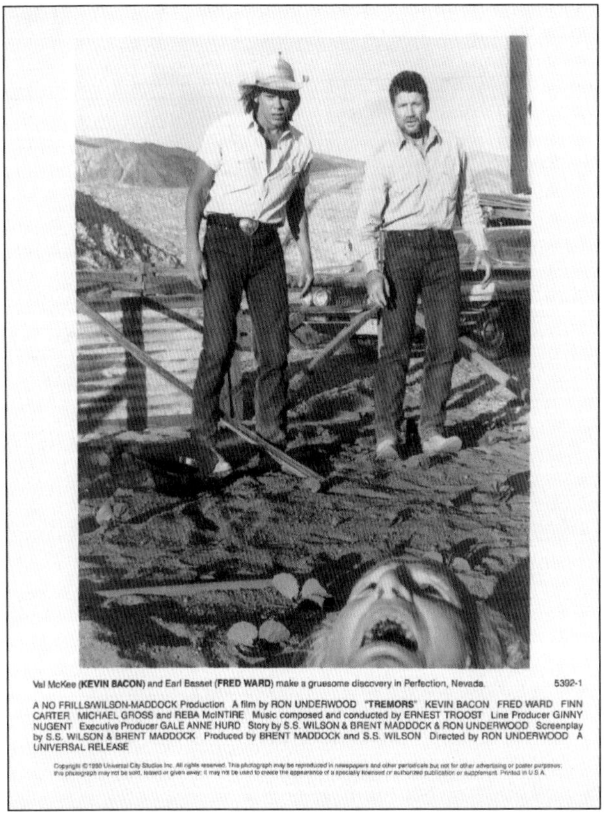


*Tremors* (1990), starring Kevin Bacon and Fred Ward, was filmed all over the Owen Valley, including the town of Keeler, "cactus flats," and in the Alabama Hills. It featured a killer worm creature that entertained audiences and still remains a classic science fiction film. Country-Western star Reba McEntire is seen in her first role.

*Iron Man* (2008) and *Chaplin* (1992), both starring Robert Downey Jr., were filmed in "the rocks." *Chaplin* was filmed along Movie Road, and *Iron Man* was filmed in the extreme northern area, known as the "bomb testing site." Other films in this area include *Transformers* (2007), *Tremors*, and *Man of Steel* (2013). Russell Crowe's character is seen camping in this area in *Gladiator* (2000), Demi Moore was filmed here in *G.I. Jane*, and Jamie Foxx is seen riding away at the end of *Django Unchained* (2012).

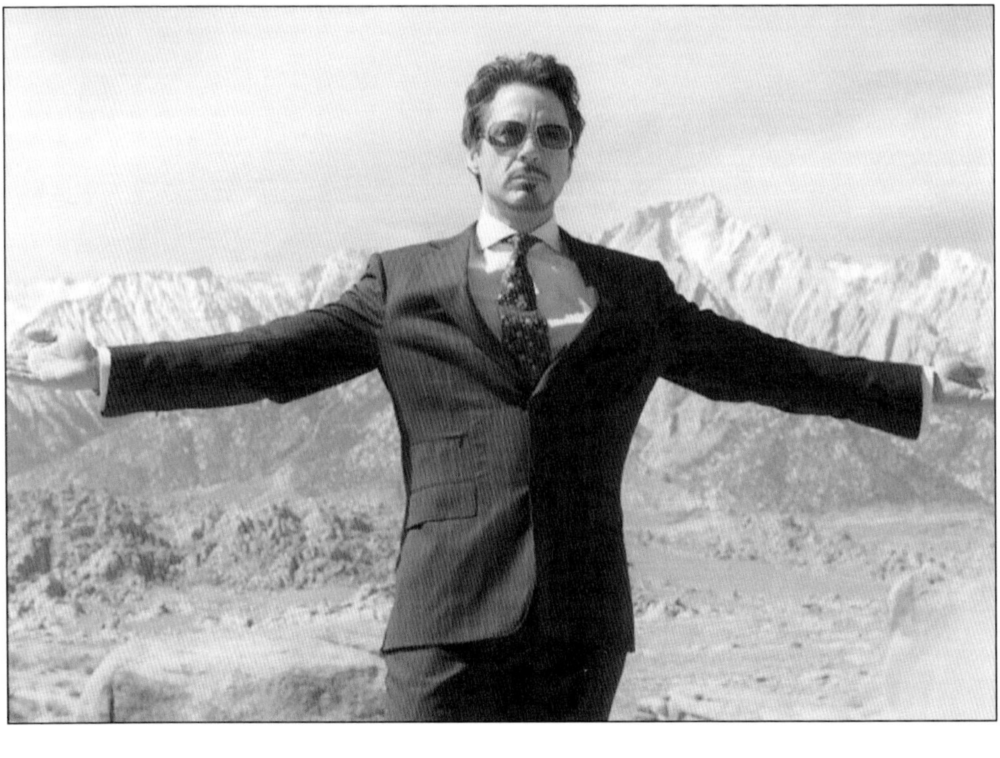

# *Four*

# Famous Directors and Filming Crews

The Alabama Hills have served as a diverse, convenient, and cost-effective filming destination for nearly 100 years. Location managers quickly discovered that in a mere three-hour drive from Hollywood, directors could utilize terrain that included desert landscapes, mountain backdrops, rolling hills, and spectacular geological rock formations. Thus, the Alabama Hills have featured in productions ranging from B Westerns and historical films to contemporary dramas and science fiction blockbusters.

Directors and filming crews have worked in numerous iconic areas in and around the Alabama Hills, including, but not limited to, Skull Rock (where Leo Powell's portrayal of The Lone Ranger serial began filming), Anchor Ranch (the location of several Hopalong Cassidy and Tim Holt films) and Ruiz Hills (as seen in early Tom Mix, Fred Humes, and Jack Hoxie features).

Examples of directors who filmed throughout the Alabama Hills area include the late Clarence Badger, William Witney, William Wellman, Cecil B. DeMille, Henry Hathaway, Raoul Walsh, Lesley Selander, and contemporary directors Ridley Scott and Quentin Tarantino. Clint Eastwood (1972's *Joe Kidd*) and Mel Gibson (1994's *Maverick*) starred in films shot throughout the Alabama Hills area and later became Academy Award winning directors (Eastwood for 1992's *Unforgiven* and 2004's *Million Dollar Baby*, and Gibson for 1995's *Braveheart*, his first film following *Maverick*).

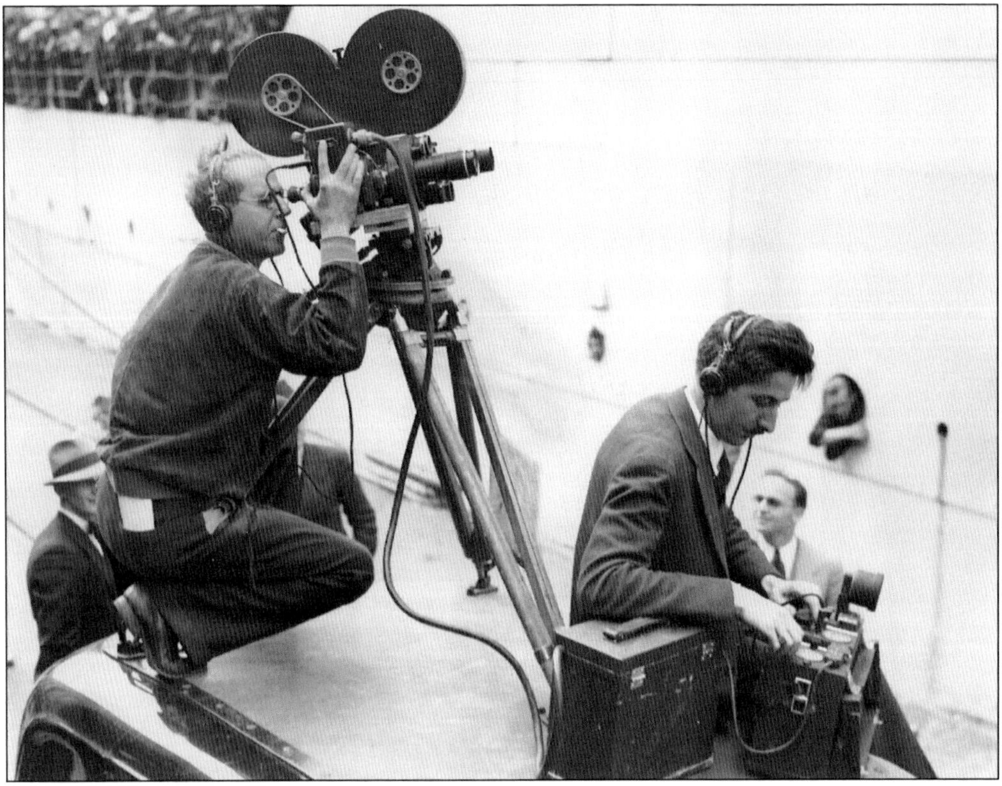

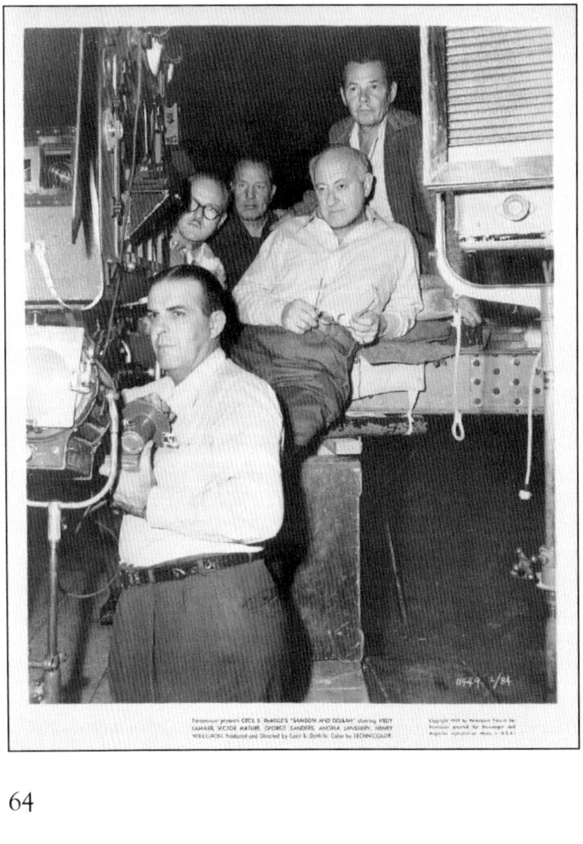


The Eastern Sierras and Alabama Hills has witnessed tragic plane crashes. On May 28, 1935, Allyn Alexander (left) and Lewis Tappan (right) from Movietone News lost their lives when their plane crashed near Mount Whitney.

Cecil B. DeMille (center), who directed the first movie in Hollywood, travelled up near the Alabama Hills to film *Chimmie Fadden Out West* (1915). He then returned to shoot scenes from one of his epics among the boulders. The Paramount movie was called *Samson and Delilah* (1949) and starred Hedy Lamarr, Victor Mature, and Angela Lansbury.

HS
D1952

HARRY SHERMAN PRODUCTIONS
5255 CLINTON STREET • HOLLYWOOD, CALIF.
TELEPHONE HOLLYWOOD, 1101

May 6, 1942

r. Harry Wilkinson
ollywood Amuseum
2 Darling
arblehead, Mass.

ear Mr. Wilkinson:

t must be a difficult job to review motion pictures, plays, tcetera, and to advise others as to their merits, but it's ven more difficult to produce pictures that will merit the upport of the public in all respects. As a producer of any years standing I can assure you that my whole organiza- ion has but one thought and that is to make good pictures, ictures that will please and entertain and contribute onstructively to the industry of which we are proud to be part.

hat I'm writing to you about is the prevailing custom of eferring to western pictures as "horse operas." Many great rtists in the various branches of writing, acting and pro- uction pour their talents into making these highly enter- aining films and to pass them off so slightly is to discount he intelligence of the vast audiences they entertain.

et me pass on a few interesting bits of information:

he fact that western pictures have been from the beginning f the industry, and still are, for a majority of the theatres n the United States the so-called bread and butter pictures nd the profit pictures. Many community theatres make no rofit at all on society dramas and "artistic" pictures, but epend upon the family trade which comes to see westerns to ay their rent of the theatre and make the living expenses f the exhibitor.

The Great Train Robbery" was a terrific success at the box ffice; "The Covered Wagon" established road show prices in owns that never before knew what road show prices were. ou can't call "Billy the Kid" anything but a picture depict- ng early American life, and you certainly wouldn't call it "horse opera," and do justice to the hundreds of people who y their joint efforts brought this picture to the screen. he same thing is true of "Jesse James," "Stagecoach," "They ied With Their Boots On," "Union Pacific," "The Plainsman," nd dozens of other great financially successful pictures eleased in past years.

-2-

The three highest paid actors the industry has ever known were William Farnum, Tom Mix and William S. Hart. They were western stars. They brought thousands upon thousands of new fans to moving pictures, starting with the youngsters who were four and five years of age.

Westerns took a decided spurt in popularity in 1935 when Bill Boyd, star of many big specials, mounted a white horse and rode into the hearts of the movie fans everywhere as "Hopalong Cassidy."

There are thousands of other nice things that can be truth- fully said about western pictures, but I don't want to bore you with a lengthy letter. In my humble opinion it is unfair for anyone to refer to pictures that bring America to Americans and the rest of the world as "horse operas." Such reference infers that these pictures are unworthy of appreciation by motion picture audiences when all the facts prove conclusively that they are the backbone of the industry. It is both unfair and unrealistic to refer to western pictures as a class in a derogatory way.

Would it be asking too much to solicit your personal interest in this problem and to ask that as much credit be given western pictures as is given any other kind of photoplay? The thousands of people engaged in producing, distributing and exhibiting western pictures will be grateful to you for your support, not overlooking the millions of western fans who genuinely like their entertainment in this form.

With all good wishes, I am

Cordially yours,

Harry Sherman

Harry Sherman

Harry Sherman, the producer who bought the rights to Hopalong Cassidy, was one of the first to understand the importance of movie rights. Sherman first held the rights to the *Birth of a Nation* (1915), and with the money from the rights to that film, he formed Harry Sherman Productions in 1935. His production company was made famous by the Hopalong Cassidy serial. After producing 54 films, Sherman turned the company over to star William Boyd so that he could produce bigger films, such as *Ramrod*. Harry Sherman still very much cared about the Westerns and knew the importance of these films. He sent this letter to Harry Wilkinson, a movie critic from Massachusetts, defending the Westerns and making sure they would not be referred to as "horse operas." In the late 1940s, Western films were actually considered to be a dying genre. However, the Western still clearly survives today.

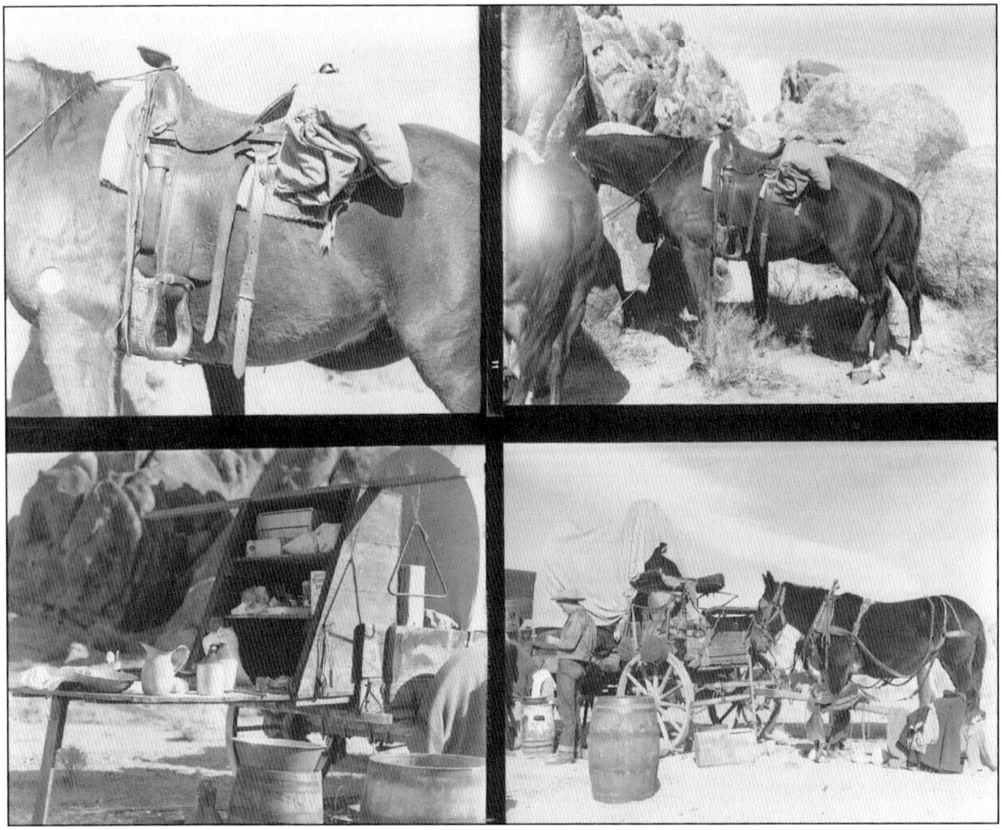

These four shots demonstrate the prop department's great attention to detail and commitment to help a picture look authentic. These images are from the Hal Roach Studios' 1943 film *Dudes Are Pretty People*.

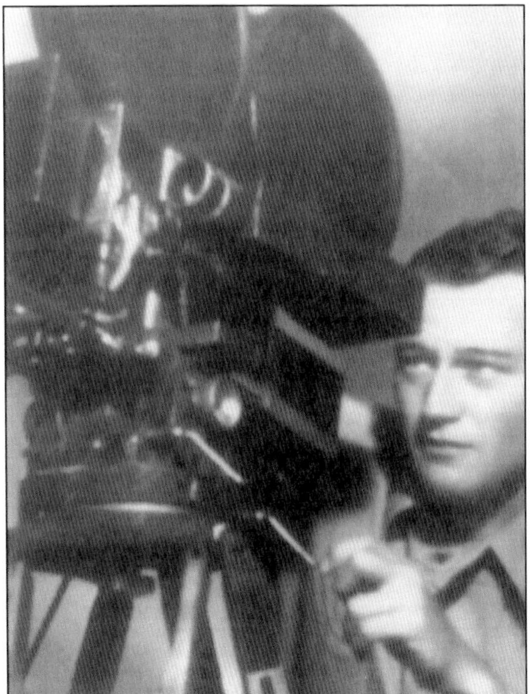

This is a publicity still for a film that John Wayne was in called *I Cover the War* (1937). Wayne went on to direct many films himself; one of his favorite—and biggest—projects was *The Alamo* (1960), which he produced, directed, and starred in. It was filmed in another familiar movie location, Brackettville, Texas. John Wayne made his first movie with Republic Pictures, *Westward Ho* (1935), in the Alabama Hills and stayed with Republic until he left to shoot *The Alamo*.

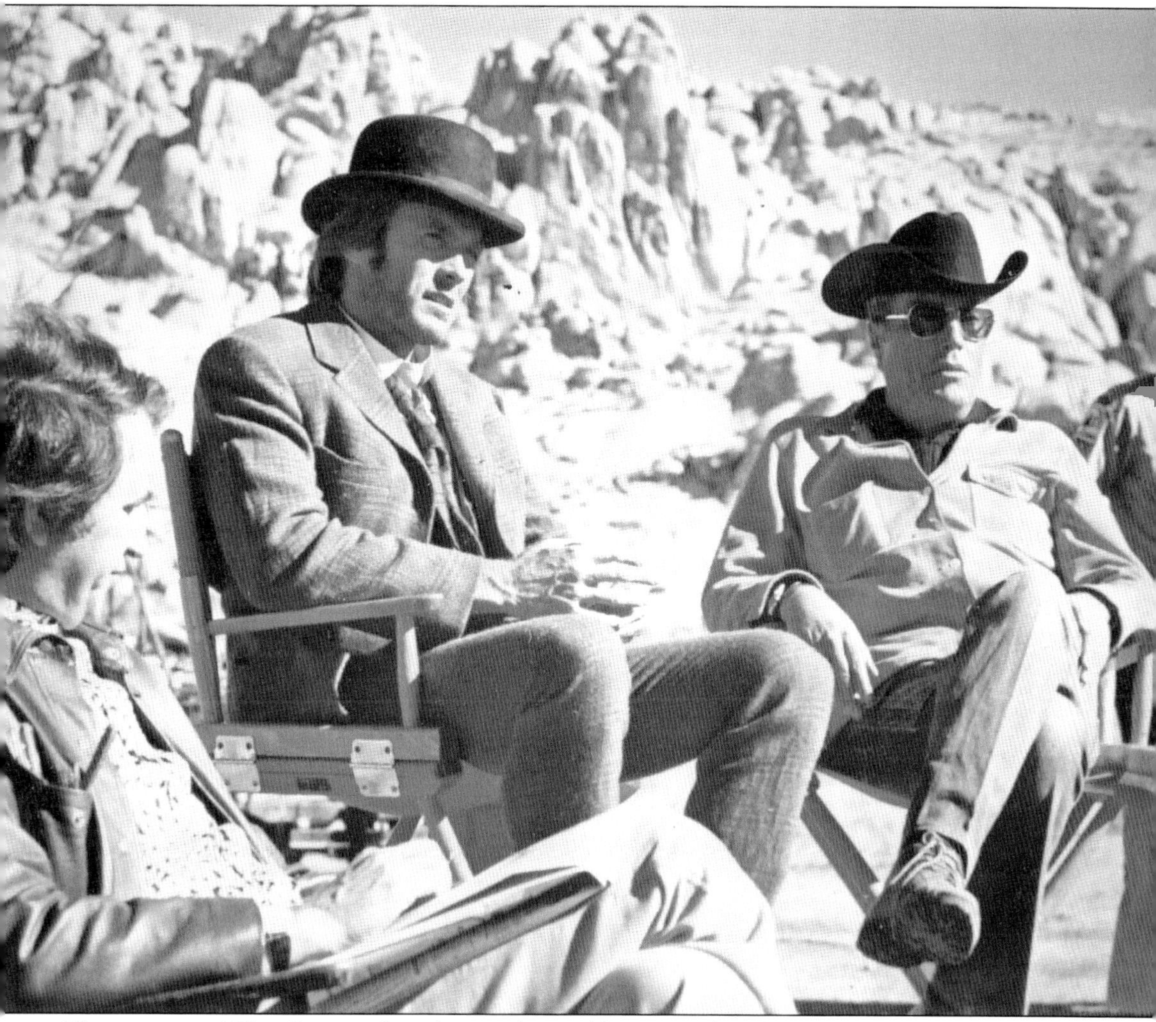

This image is of Clint Eastwood on the set of *Joe Kidd*. Eastwood worked on films in the area a few times, most notably appearing in *Joe Kidd* and 1973's *High Plains Drifter* (also filmed near Bishop, California). It was rumored that he once drove a pickup all the way up from Los Angeles with the flu but learned upon arriving to one of these locations that he had been named *Time* magazine's sexiest man alive. He quickly felt a lot better, and the next day arrived on set ready to work.

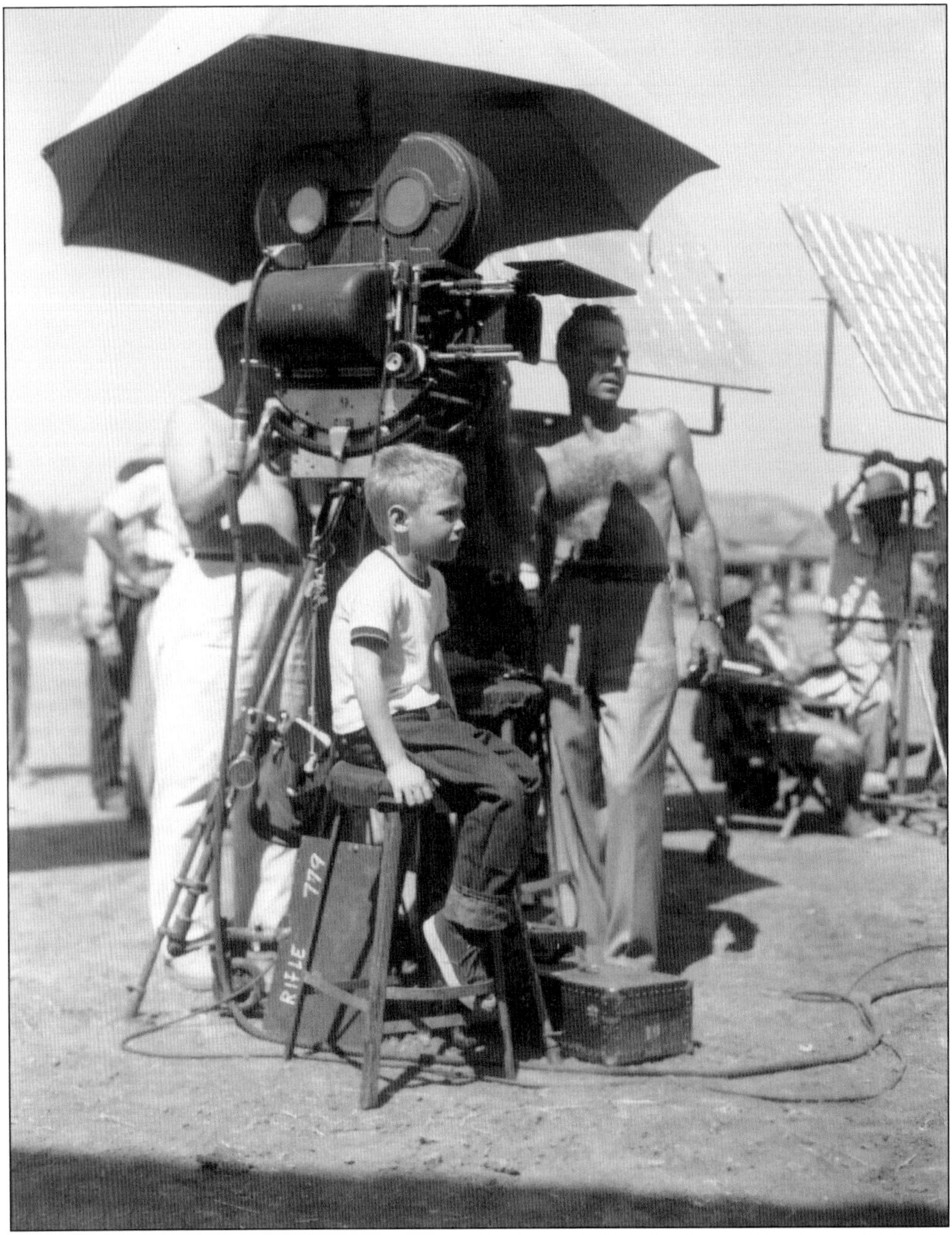


This shot here is of the wonderful Gary Cooper film *Springfield Rifle*, directed by André De Toth. This image shows the reflectors that the different gentlemen are holding to direct light onto the various actors to get more radiance on the performer. What is great about this shot is that it shows that the Alabama Hills has a very interesting climate; it can be extremely hot, windy, or bitterly cold.

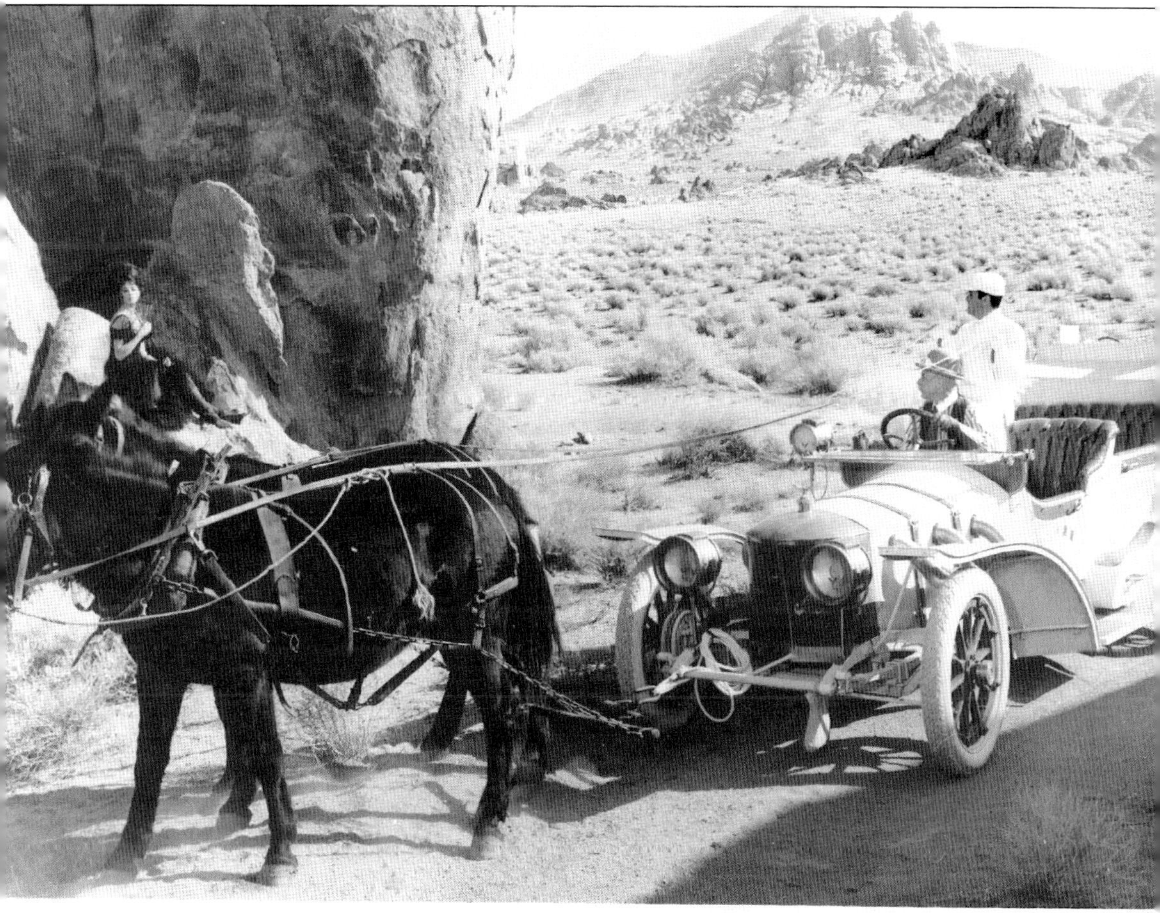

Story-in-Pictures THE GREAT RACE Photo 4

the Western desert, Maggie's Stanley Steamer breaks down but she is rescued by Leslie, whose car is porarily forced to use non-mechanical horsepower. Printed in U.S

This image of the *Great Race* (1965) depicts the scene when the Stanley Steamer breaks down but is rescued by Leslie, who is forced to use mechanical power. In this shot are Leslie (played by Tony Curtis) and Natalie Wood. The location was easily accessible along the road. The film's director, Blake Edwards, was most notable for his Pink Panther movies starring Peter Sellers.

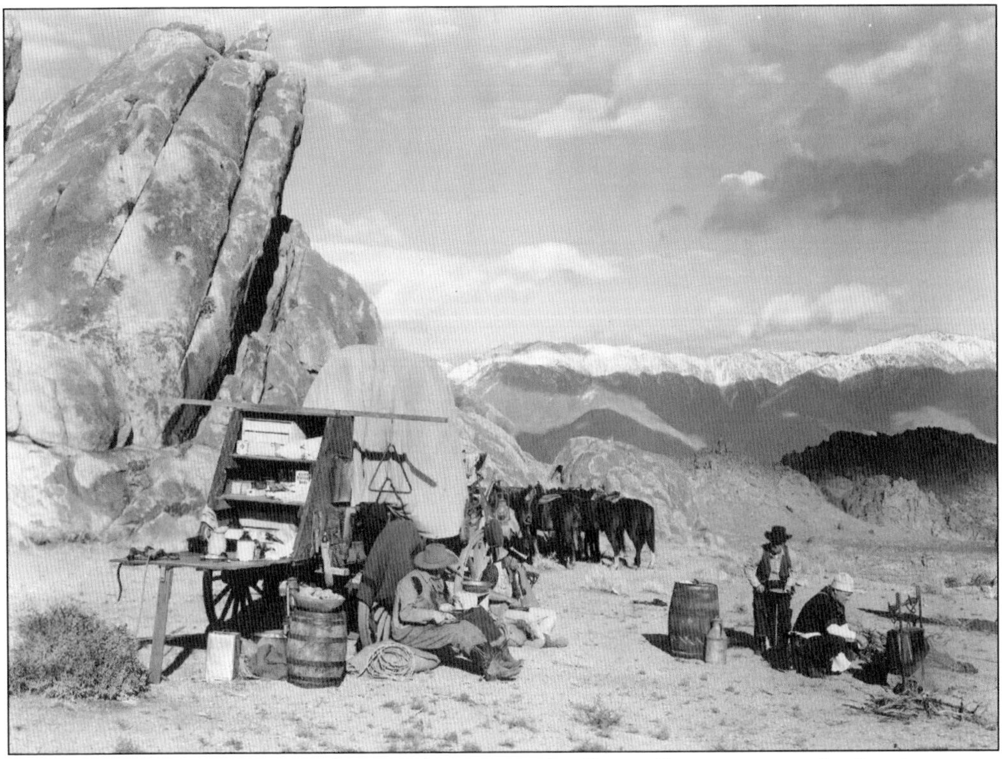

The image above shows a site that is right next to the *Gunga Din* suspension bridge that was a very popular filming location in the Alabama Hills. An interesting note about shooting in the Alabama Hills is that when directors film a scene from multiple angles, the background terrain significantly changes. Therefore, directors are rewarded by having the option to select the best background for one particular shot or can even film various scenes at the same location. These pictures show a scene from *Dudes Are Pretty People* (1943). Note the markers that are used to signify where the actors are to stand. These views show strategic placement of sagebrush and various other props to keep the actor within the shot as the director desired. Below is a close-up view of the same site. It actually shows a different gentleman than the previous image; this was an often-used tactic for directors to perfect the shot. Note that in the first shot there is a man sitting on a blanket next to the front wheel, whereas the next image shows just a gentleman sitting on the right of the wheel. Directors can be very intense individuals that pay close attention to detail, and it often requires more than one or two takes to get it right.

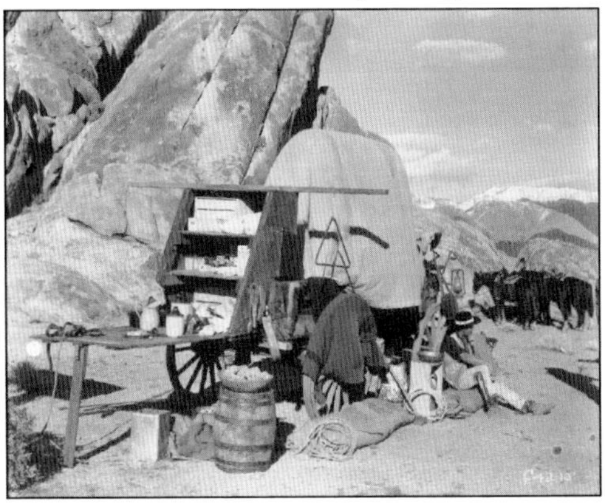

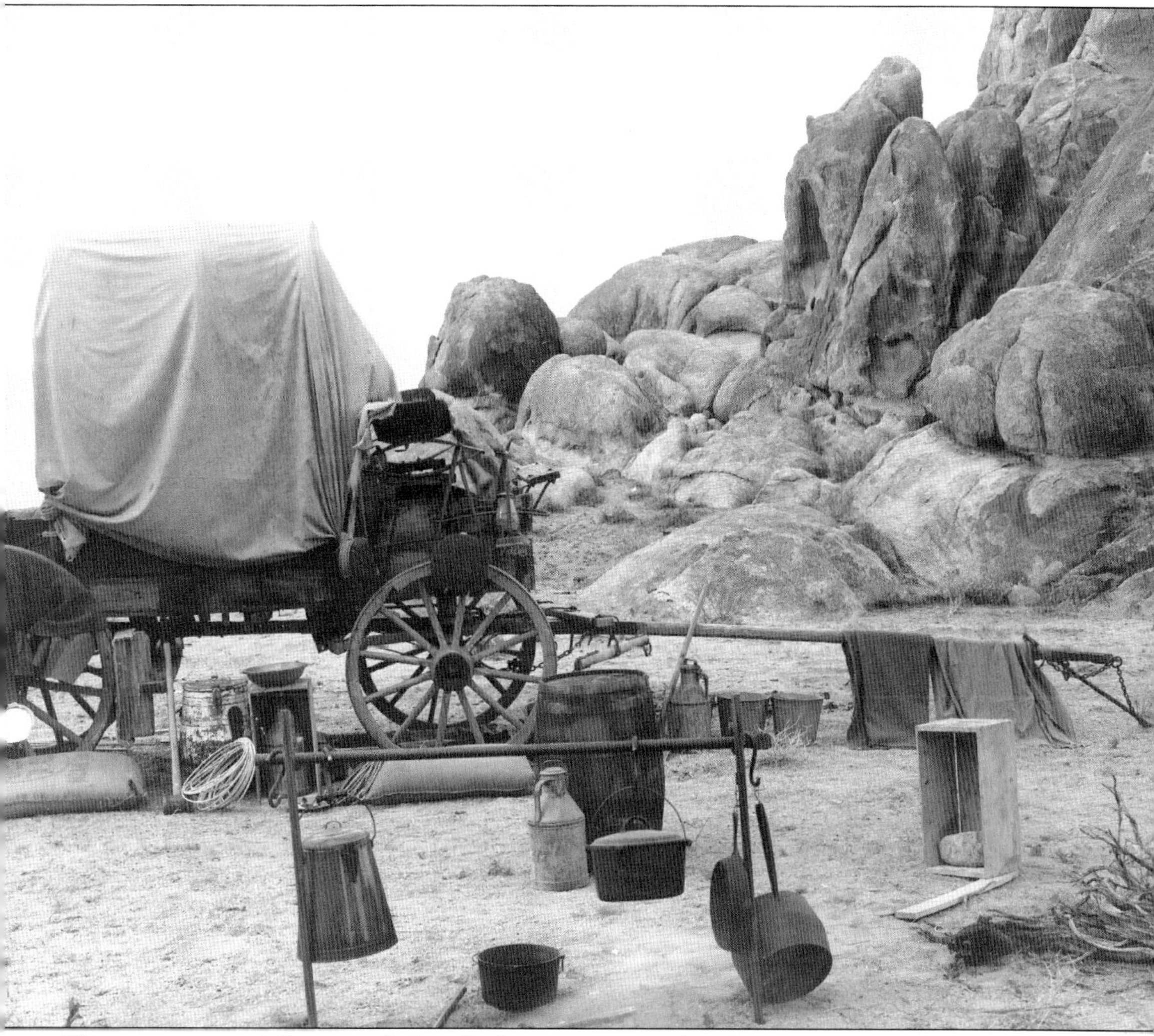

This next view is a different angle from *Dudes Are Pretty People*. Changing the shot alters the scene considerably. This technique of shooting the same scene from different angles is still used. Such changes create more visual depth and substance for the scene while simultaneously enhancing the acting performances.

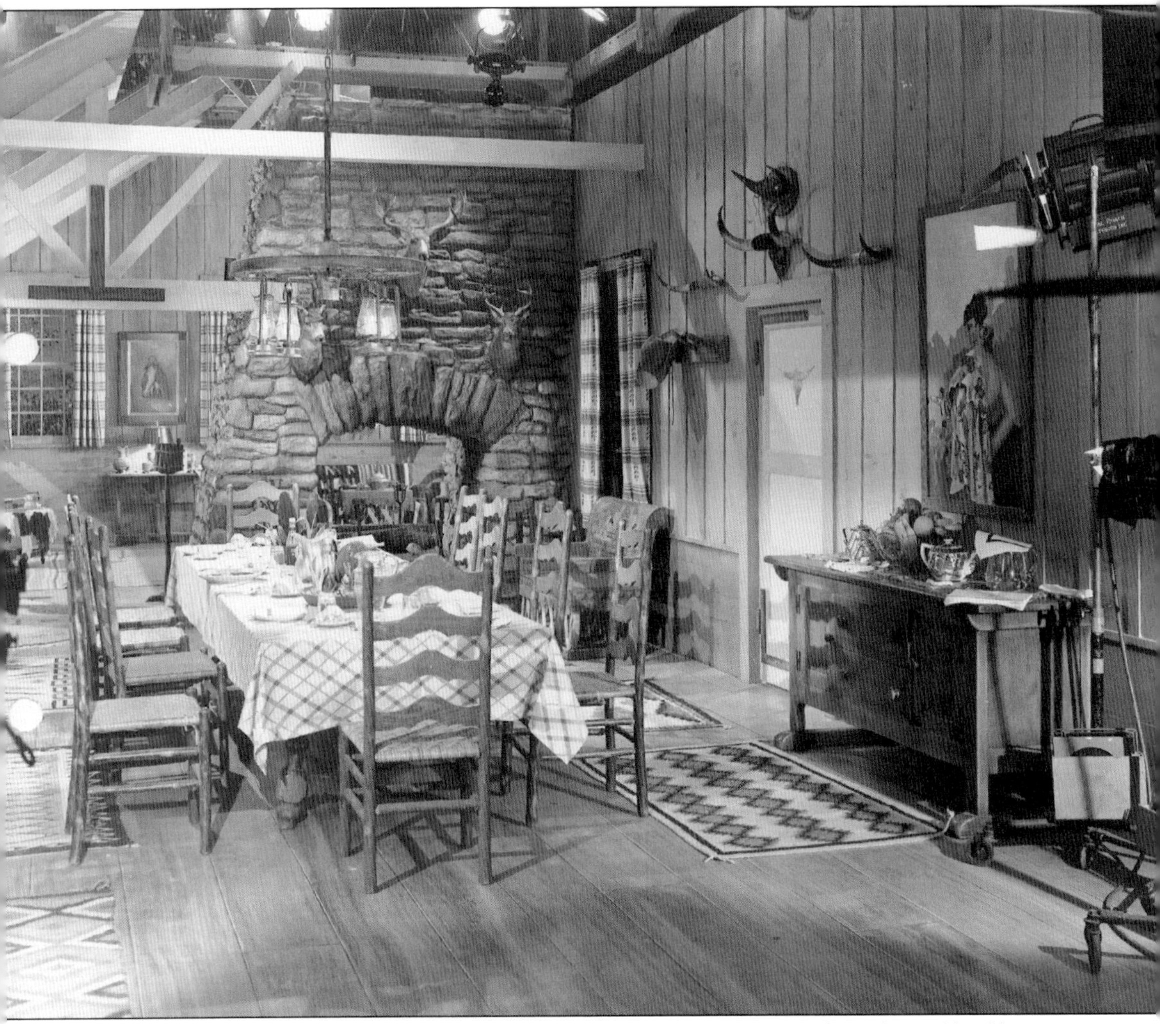

This wonderful interior shot of a studio exemplifies the meticulous work performed by film crews. Note the lighting above, reinforced bars, and T-angled supports, which represent the attention to detail required when filming Western scenes. Also note the lack of roof, which is typical of a soundstage. The Alabama Hills have served as a filming location for many productions when a soundstage could not be used. Western films commonly shot interior scenes on a soundstage and then traveled to the Alabama Hills to add scope, scale, and grandeur to the production. Reducing costs was another reason to film in the Alabama Hills, as large studio sets usually did not have to be built. The upper right-hand corner of this picture designates this as Hal Roach Studios film. Hal Roach was also famous for creating *Our Gang*, which is better known as *The Little Rascals*.

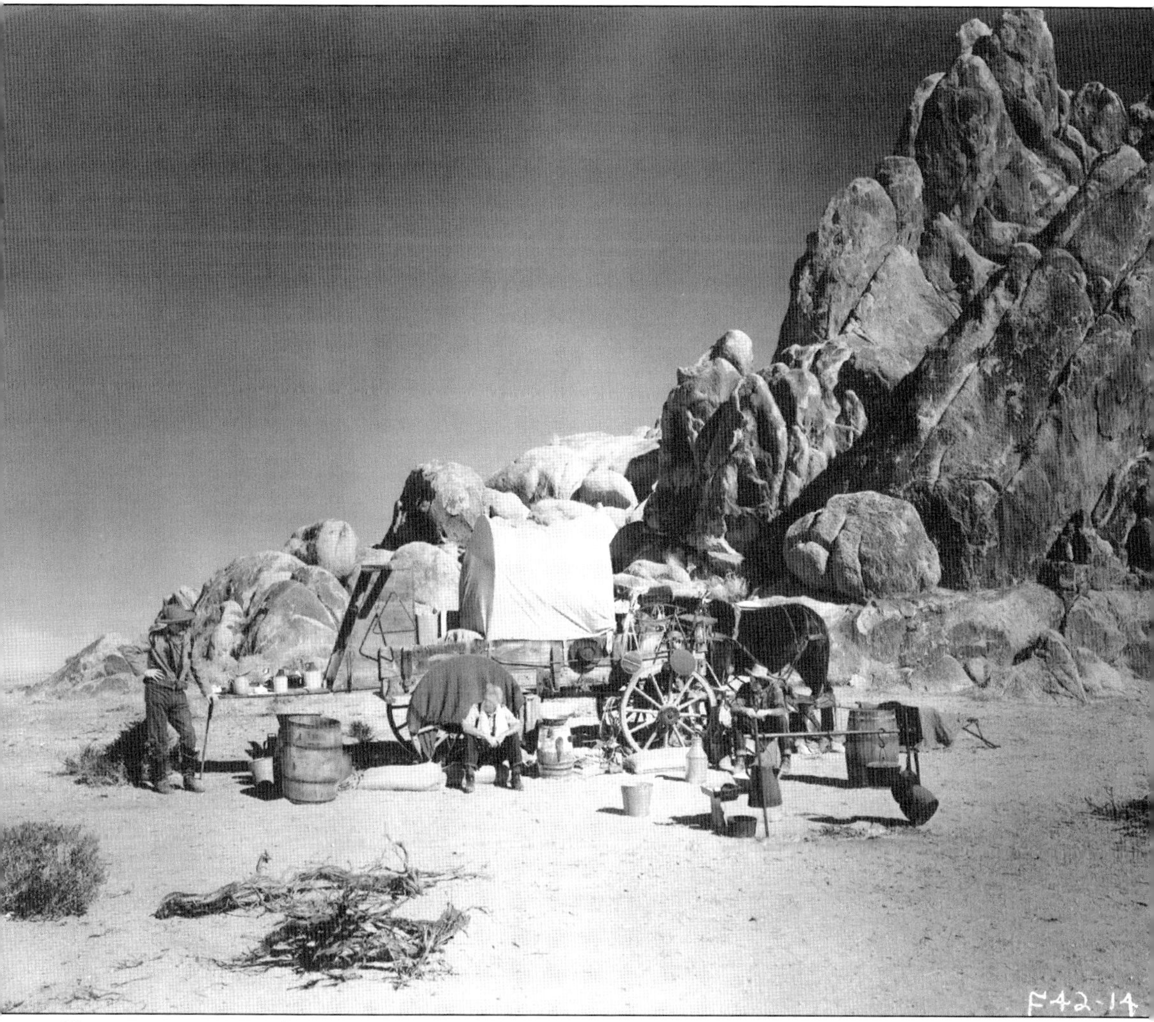


Visitors can come to this common filming location to stand where the stars once stood. Directors or location managers frequently select certain filming areas for reasons that include lighting, weather, shade, or access to other resources. In the distance to the left is a primary filming location for RKO's classic *Gunga Din* and the suspension bridge where Cary Grant and an elephant once stood. Four years later and a few yards away, the same location serves as a Western setting in *Dudes Are Pretty People* (1943).

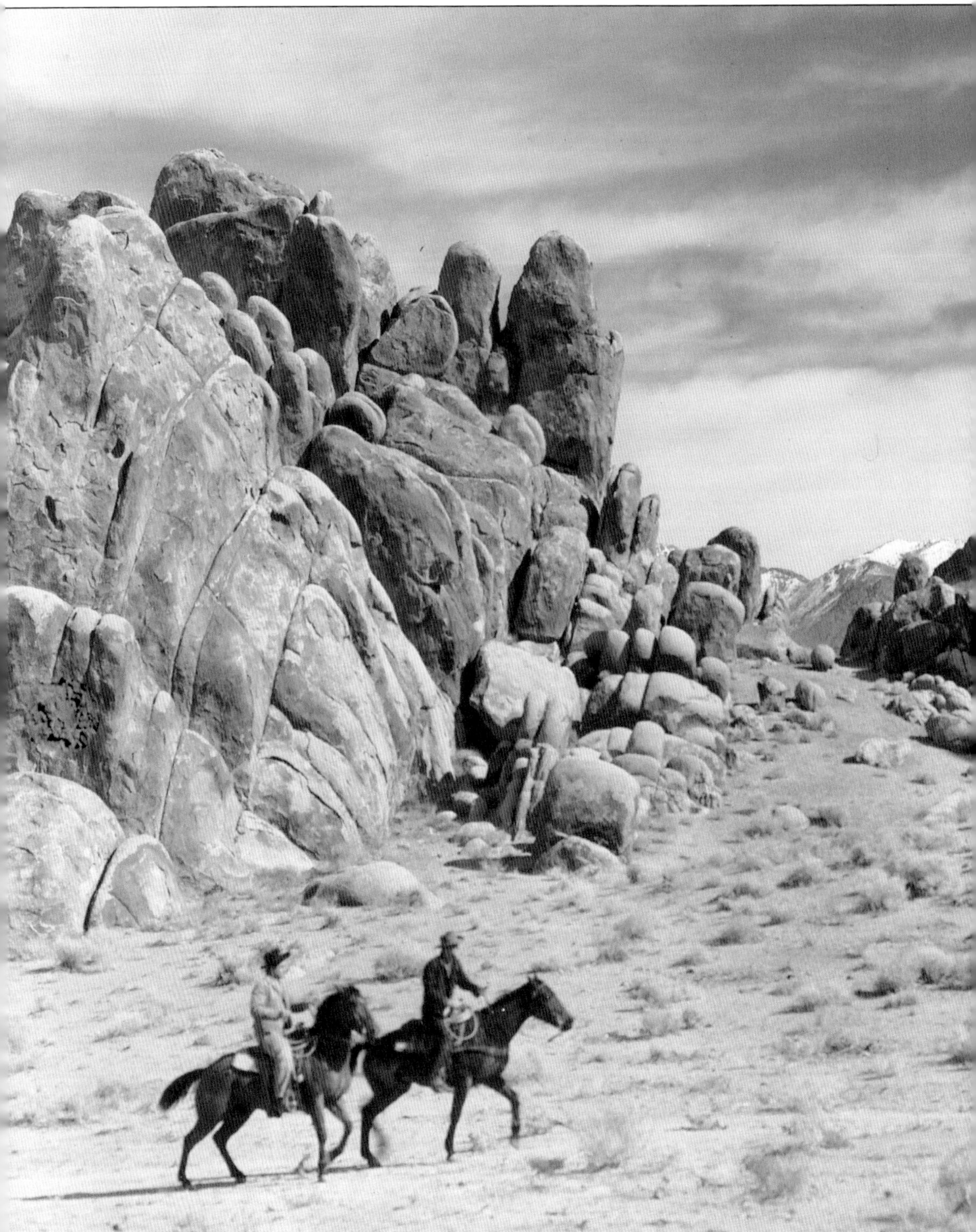

This shot illustrates how great directors combine multiple elements of an image, such as background, foreground, and action, to achieve a beautiful scene. The resulting scene articulates a piece of the

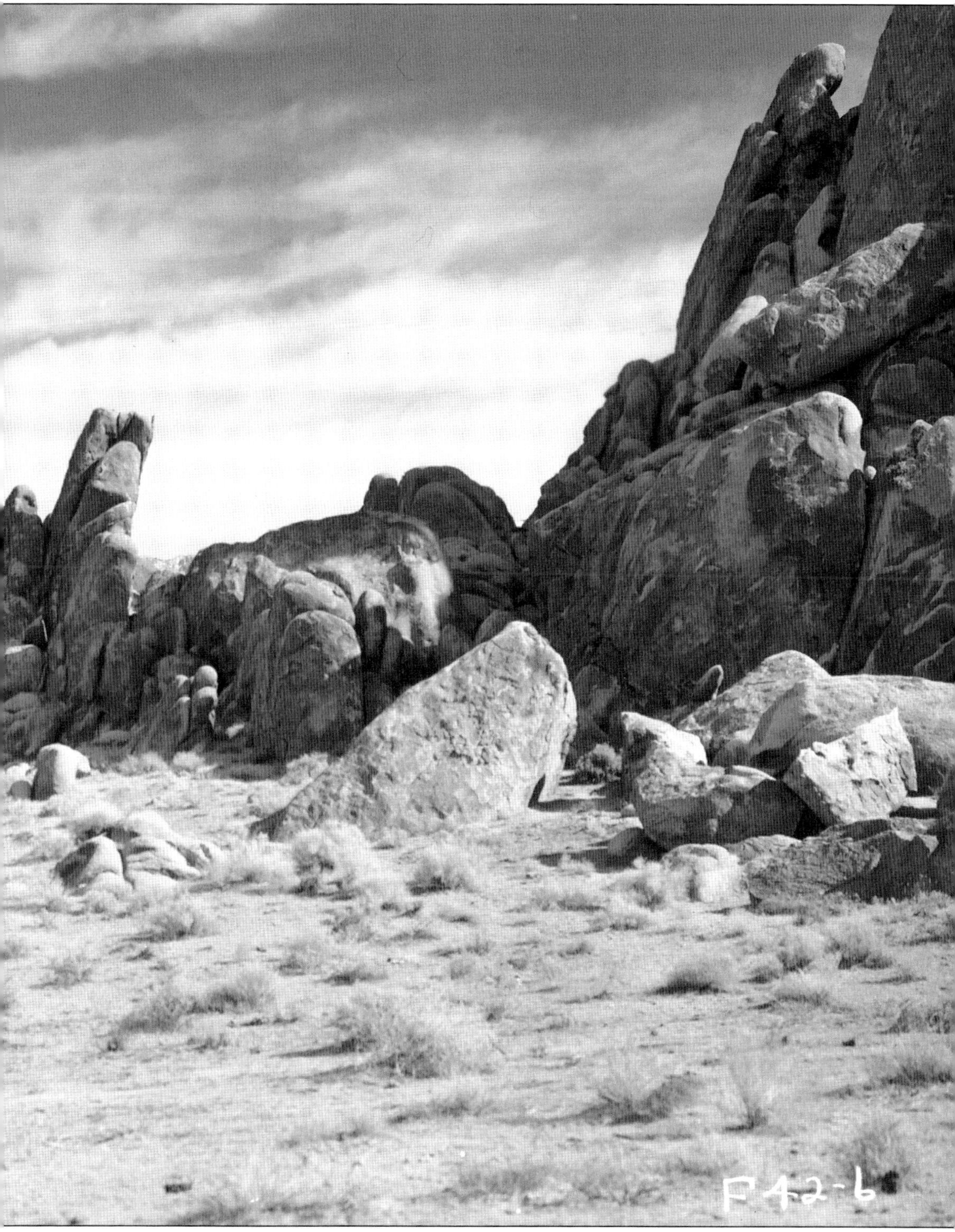


story that, when combined with others, culminates in a lasting piece of history and film.

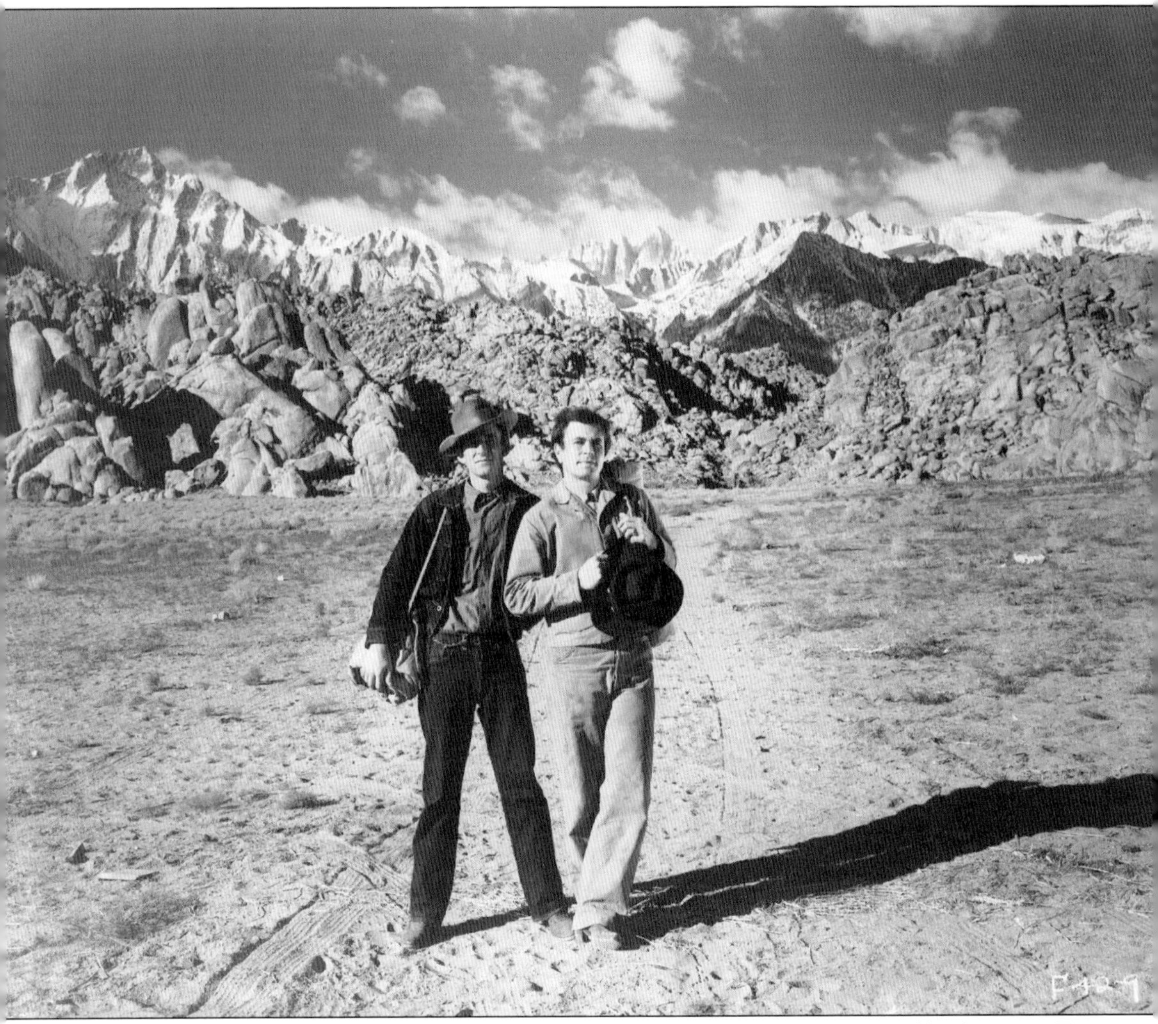

The Alabama Hills feature a variety of landscapes and terrains that are coveted by directors. For example, a director may crop the above image to make it appear that the two men are standing in a dusty, desert-like environment. The director could then alter the image to show the dirt and rock formations slightly above them, or, further yet, focus solely on the upper half of the image to highlight the towering mountains that might double as peaks in such distant places as Tibet, India, or Afghanistan. Such diversity of landscape is a fundamental reason why so many movies and commercials have been shot in the Alabama Hills.

Ida Lupino came up to shoot *High Sierra* (1941) with Humphrey Bogart. Lupino was very much into film noir and suspense, and having starred in *High Sierra* and revering the movie locations of the Alabama Hills, she returned to direct a very interesting and suspenseful film called *The Hitch-Hiker* (1953). In *The Hitch-Hiker*, the Alabama Hills are used to represent Mexico.

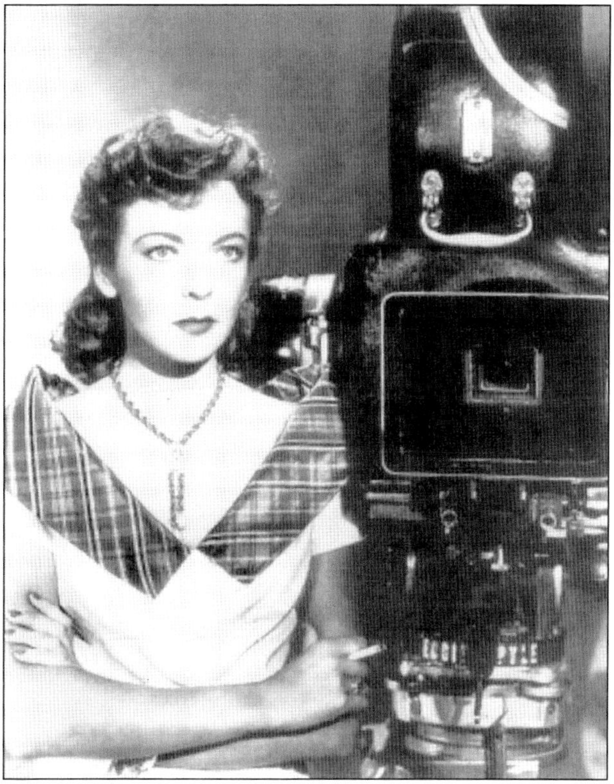

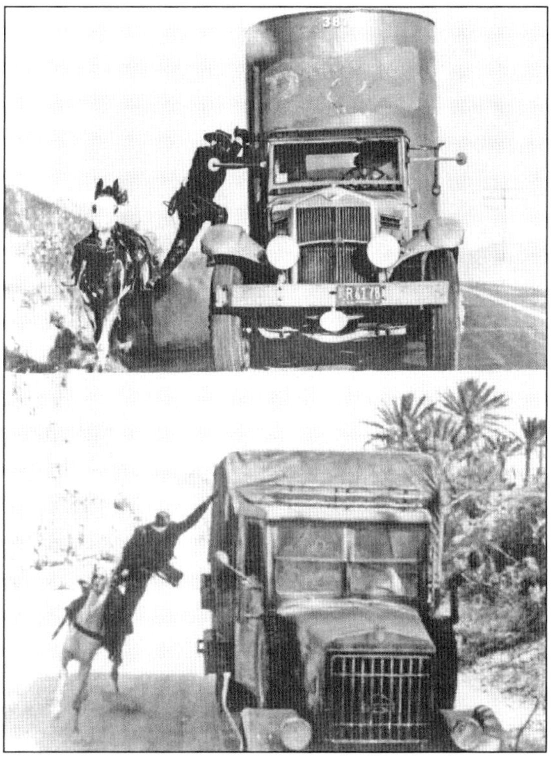

Some stunts are repeated. Yakima Canutt, a famous stuntman, climbed back up from under a moving stagecoach during a Lone Ranger serial in 1938. Similar scenes were captured in *Zorro Rides Again* (1959), again with Canutt (top), and with stuntman Terry Leonard in 1981's *Raiders of the Lost Ark* (bottom). In both scenes, the stagecoach has been replaced by a moving truck.

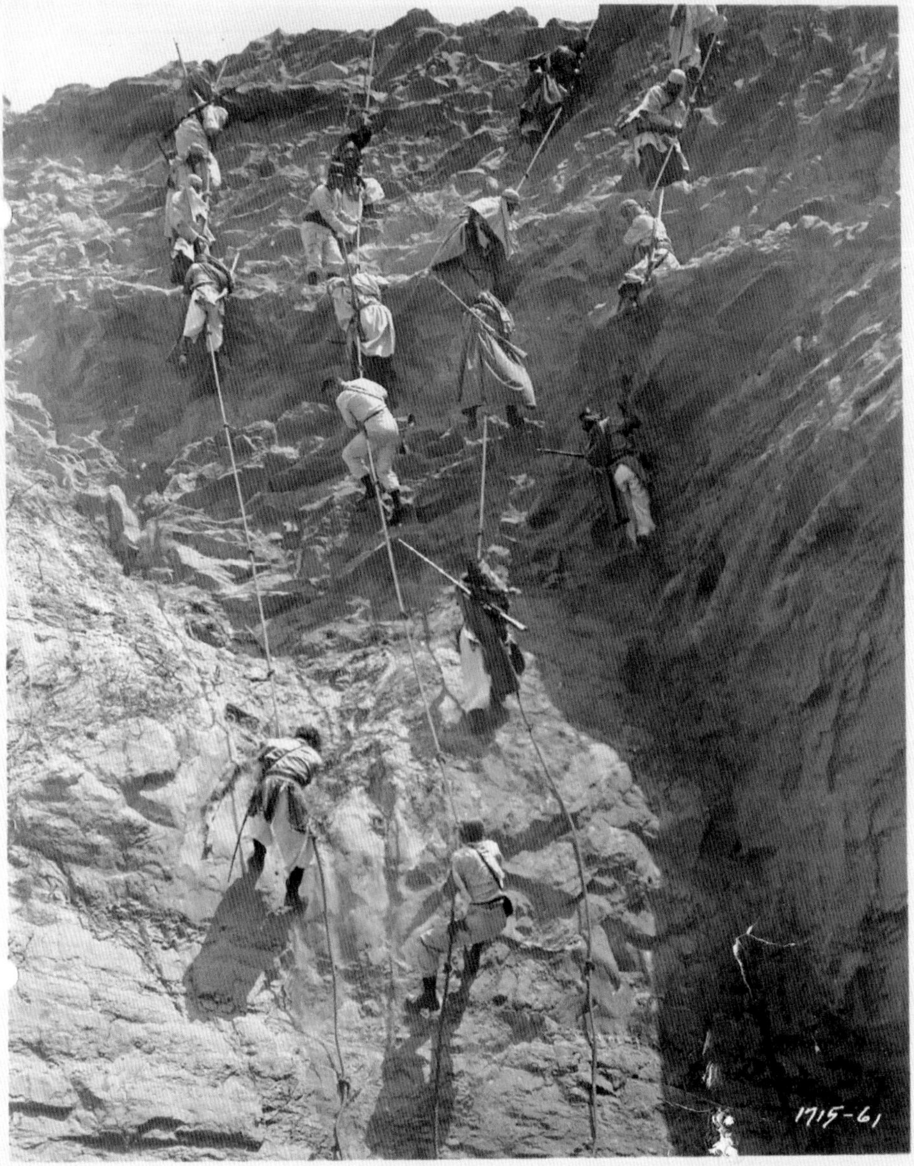


"Copyright 1953 Universal Pictures Company, Inc. Permission granted for newspaper and Magazine reproduction. Any other use, including television, Prohibited." Printed in U.S.A.

This interesting shot from *Desert Legion* (1953), starring Alan Ladd and Richard Conte, shows a challenging stunt and the great care that has gone into ensuring safety. Safety is important, and emergency personnel are always present. Sometimes, a film requires special training—for example, repelling in this scene—months before the production.

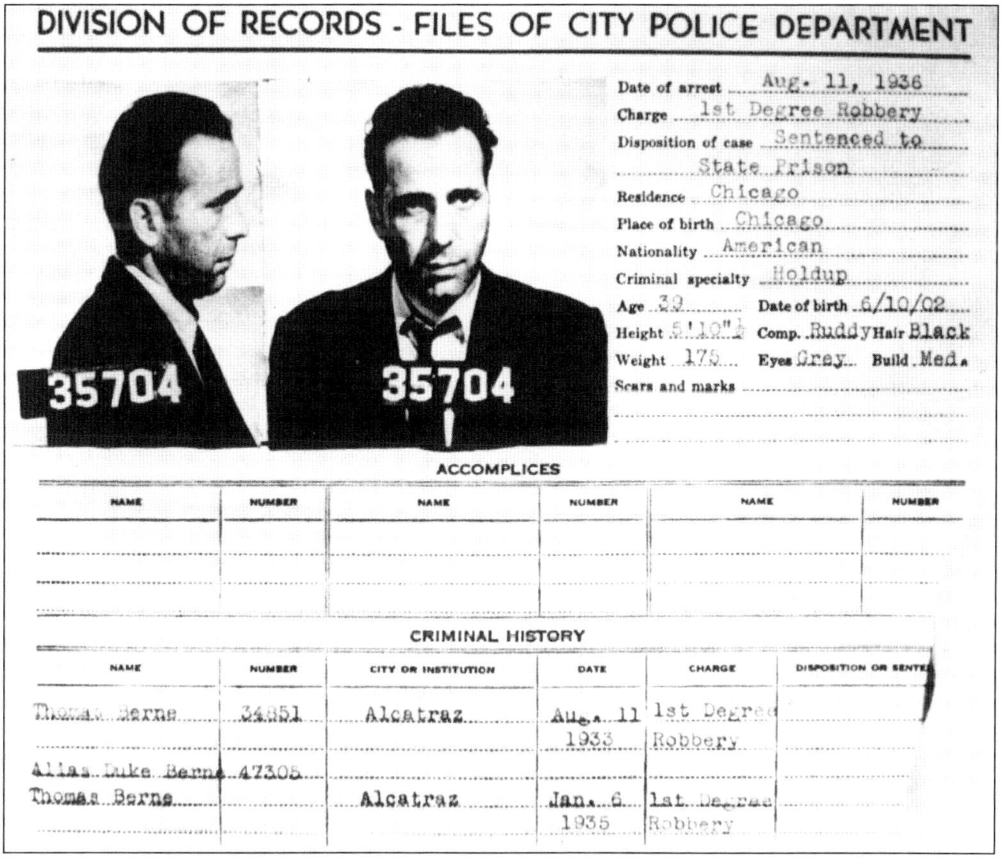

DIVISION OF RECORDS - FILES OF CITY POLICE DEPARTMENT

35704

Date of arrest Aug. 11, 1936
Charge 1st Degree Robbery
Disposition of case Sentenced to State Prison
Residence Chicago
Place of birth Chicago
Nationality American
Criminal specialty Holdup
Age 39 Date of birth 6/10/02
Height 5'10"½ Comp. Ruddy Hair Black
Weight 175 Eyes Grey Build Med.
Scars and marks

ACCOMPLICES

| NAME | NUMBER | NAME | NUMBER | NAME | NUMBER |
|---|---|---|---|---|---|
| | | | | | |

CRIMINAL HISTORY

| NAME | NUMBER | CITY OR INSTITUTION | DATE | CHARGE | DISPOSITION OR SENTENCE |
|---|---|---|---|---|---|
| Thomas Berne | 34851 | Alcatraz | Aug. 11 1933 | 1st Degree Robbery | |
| Alias Duke Berne | 47305 | | | | |
| Thomas Berne | | Alcatraz | Jan. 6 1935 | 1st Degree Robbery | |

This next image is a prop used in the noir film *High Sierra* (1941). Great detail is put into very small items that may only be shown on screen for one or two seconds.

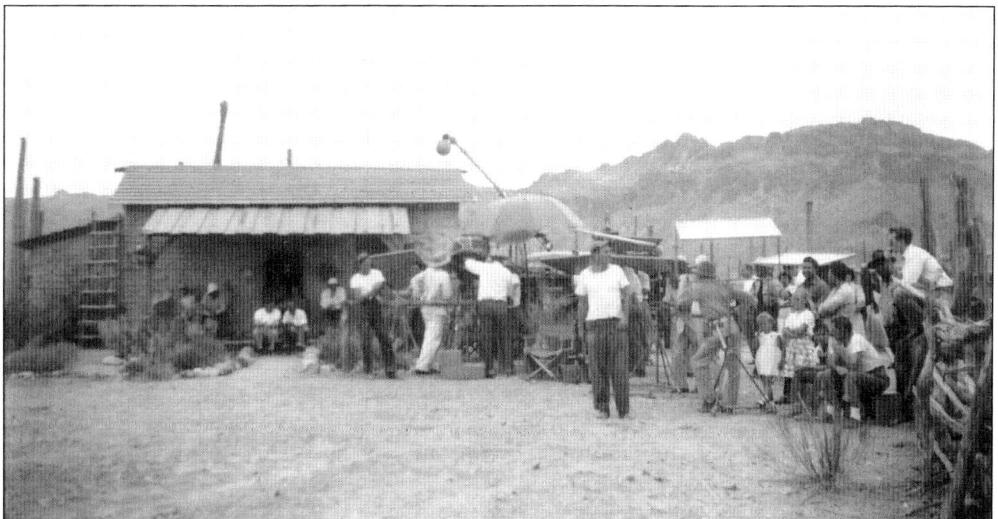

This photograph shows a typical film crew from a Gene Autry Western. Note the sound recorder. Recording sound and mixing is essential to a film. In 1981, Ben Burtt recorded sounds in the Alabama Hills to serve as echoing gunshots in *Raiders of the Lost Ark*.

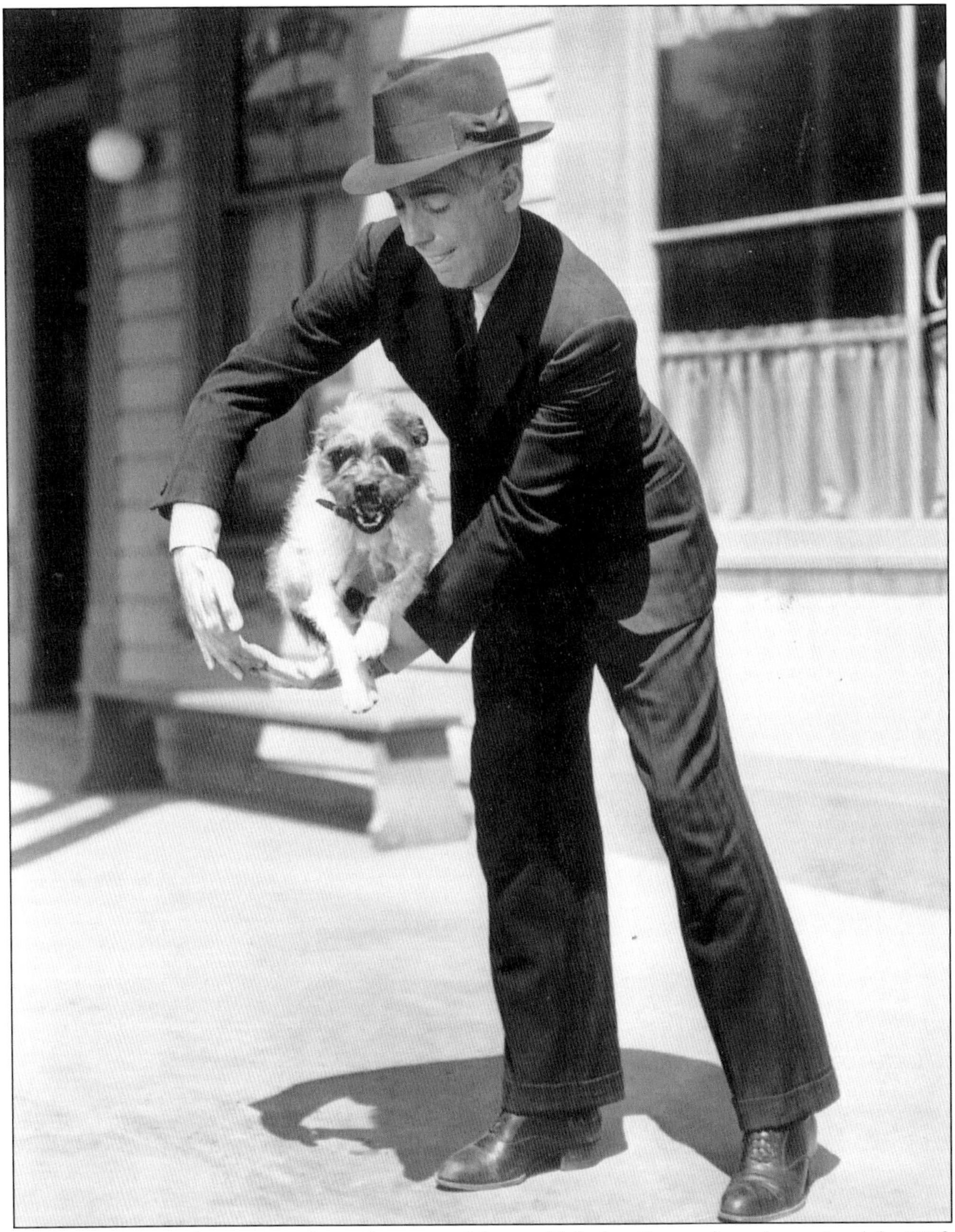

This photograph shows Humphrey Bogart and his real-life dog Zero, whom he trained for *High Sierra*. Filming crews sometimes include animal actors. Other famous animals actors to be shown in various movies filmed throughout the Alabama Hills include notables such as Trigger and Gene Autry's horse Champion, who also starred in his own series.

# *Five*

# Celebrity Heroes and Film Noir

In the western part of the Alabama Hills, one will find the locations known as Whitney Portal Road, Background Rocks, and Movie Road. It was here that famous favorite celebrities who served in the armed forces made films that will never be forgotten.

Humphrey Bogart was in the US Navy and can be seen in the 1941 classic *High Sierra*, filmed along Whitney Portal Road and Lone Pine. Desi Arnaz, who was a World War II veteran, can be seen in the 1953 film *The Long, Long Trailer* with Lucille Ball, also shot along Whitney Portal Road. Tyrone Power was a decorated US Marine Corps pilot who flew over Iwo Jima and starred in front of Background Rocks in the 1940 film *Bringham Young* and 1953's *King of the Khyber Rifles*, also filmed along Whitney Portal Road.

Robert Ryan and Lee Marvin were in the Marines and starred alongside US Navy veteran Ernest Borgnine in the 1955 film *Bad Day at Black Rock*, which is a film location in this area near Movie Road. Kirk Douglas starred in the 1951 film *Along the Great Divide* and served in the US Navy as well. David Niven was at D-Day and is seen in the 1936 film *Charge of the Light Brigade*. Douglas Fairbanks Jr. was a commando in World War II who starred in *Gunga Din*, released in 1939. The RKO classic *Gunga Din* was filmed almost entirely in all areas of the Alabama Hills.

Edward G. Robinson served in World War I and starred alongside Glenn Ford, who served in World War II, Korea, and Vietnam. Both served in the US Navy and can be seen in the 1955 film *The Violent Men* with Barbara Stanwyck.

And Audie Murphy, the Medal of Honor recipient and soldier/cowboy in World War II, starred in the 1963 film *Showdown* and others that were filmed along Movie Road and elsewhere in the Alabama Hills.

Film noir is a genre of films that captures the imaginations of viewers by featuring men wearing fedora hats, cigarette-smoking femme fatales, dimly lit alleys, cliffs with winding roads, staircases, gumshoe detectives, gangsters, and plenty of locations filled with crime and suspense. Several film noir productions were filmed in the Alabama Hills, including *The Hitch-Hiker* (1953) and *Bad Day at Black Rock* (1955).

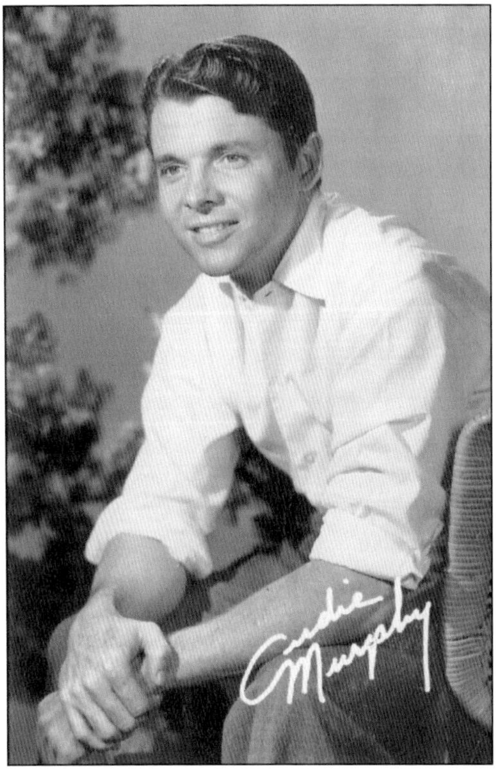


The highest-decorated soldier of World War II was Medal of Honor recipient Audie Murphy. Murphy starred most notably in *Showdown* (1963). In it, he can be seen galloping along Movie Road just as the Roman hero Russell Crowe does in *Gladiator* (2000). His personal pistol is on display at the film museum in Lone Pine, California, from the collection of Jim Phillips, who is a distant relative of Roscoe "Fatty" Arbuckle.

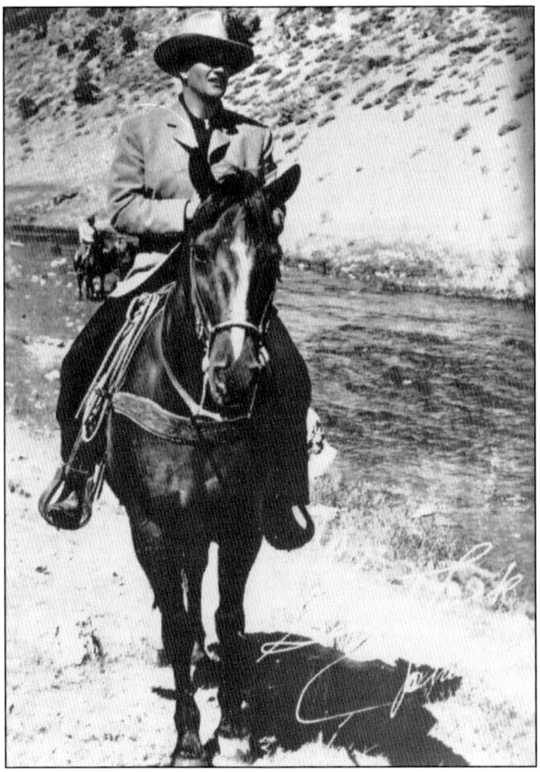

John Wayne, born Marion Morrison, filmed his last scene on Movie Road in late August 1978. It was a commercial for Great Western Savings Bank. His last movie was *The Shootist* (1976), filmed in Nevada. In it, he gives his horse Dollar to a young Ron Howard. Dollar was the real name of the last horse John Wayne owned. His first horse was named Bo Bo. After filming in the Alabama Hills, Wayne, like many actors, would return to the Hollywood studios. Near one of these studios, he would frequent a train car that had been converted into a restaurant called the Formosa Café, which still operates today. One evening after having dinner, he fell asleep in one of the booths. The staff did not want to wake him up, so they locked him in. The next morning when the staff returned, John Wayne had cooked breakfast as a thank-you. "The Duke," as Wayne was known, is buried in Newport Beach, California. He lived there and owned an old World War II minesweeper converted to a pleasure boat named the *Wild Goose*.

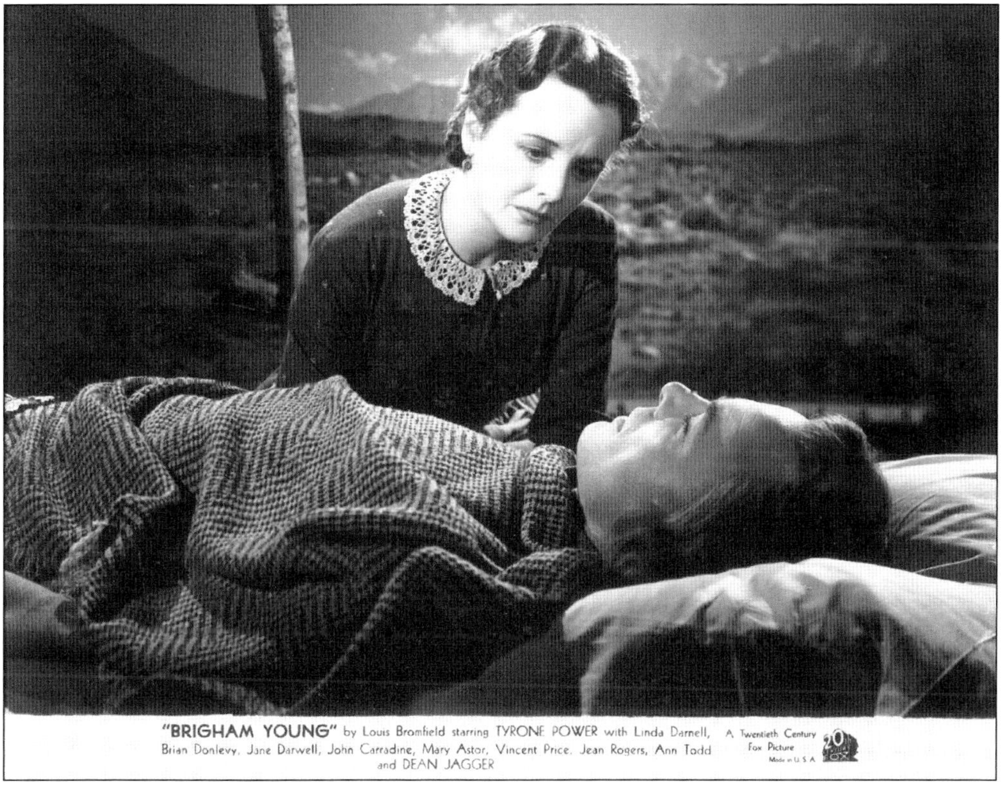


*Brigham Young* (1940) had an all-star cast that included Brian Donlevy, who was a World War I veteran, and John Carradine, father of famed Kung Fu master and actor David Carradine. Mary Astor from *The Maltese Falcon* and Vincent Price from *House of Wax* also starred alongside each other. Other stars included in this film were Linda Darnell, who later tragically died in a house fire while watching *Star Dust*, another movie she starred in that year, and Tyrone Power, who became a decorated US Marine Corps pilot during World War II and was involved at Iwo Jima. Tyrone Power and his wife, Annabella, rented and stayed at a house on Brewery Street in the town of Lone Pine during the filming. This film location is out on Movie Flats; the Sierras are seen in background.

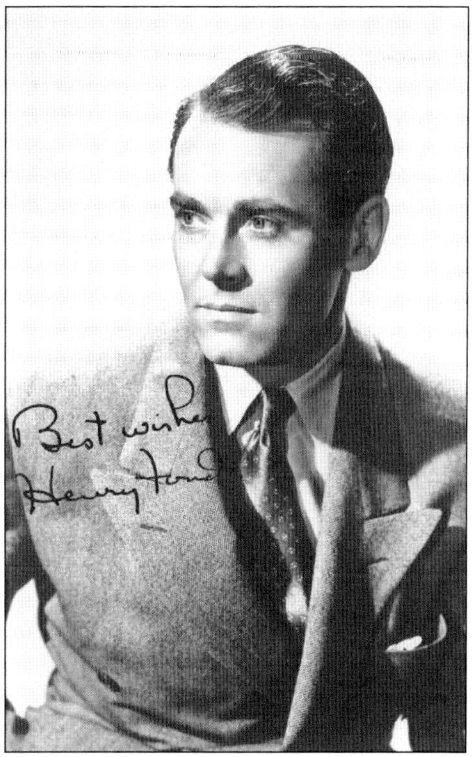


Here is a nice photograph of Henry Fonda, who starred in *How the West Was Won*. Fonda served in the US Navy and won a Bronze Star. He represented many celebrities who volunteered for World War II and contributed to many organizations for veterans.

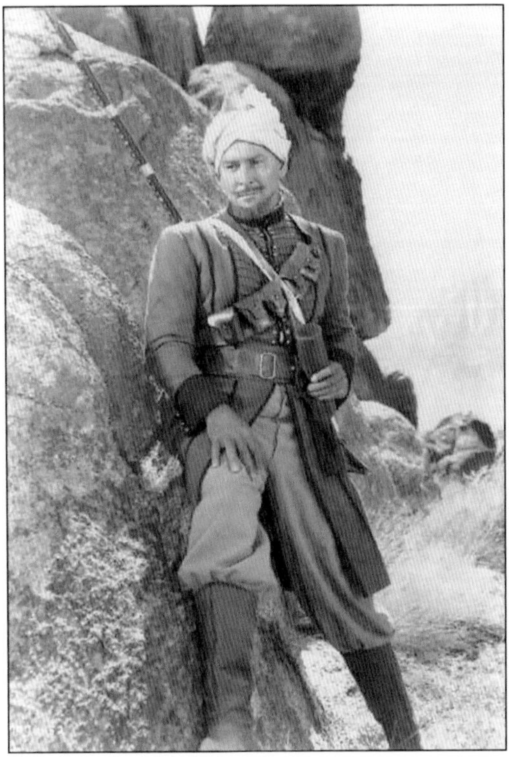

Errol Flynn was born on June 20, 1909, in Australia. He is seen here starring in *Kim* (1950), which was filmed partly in the Alabama Hills due to its resemblance to the Khyber Pass in Afghanistan. Flynn once ate camel dung on the set, according to Dean Stockwell. Having become a naturalized US citizen in 1942, he tried joining the Army Air Corps, the Army, and the Navy during World War II but was rejected because he had had tuberculosis and malaria as a child. Flynn also suffered congestive heart disease, which caused Warner Bros. much difficulty in insuring him for many of his films. Flynn also loved animals, including dogs and horses, and was an early animal activist.

This image shows a scene from an early film noir, *Woman Trap* (1936). It is about jewels thieves, bandits, and hot pursuits and shows great locations around Lone Pine and the Alabama Hills.

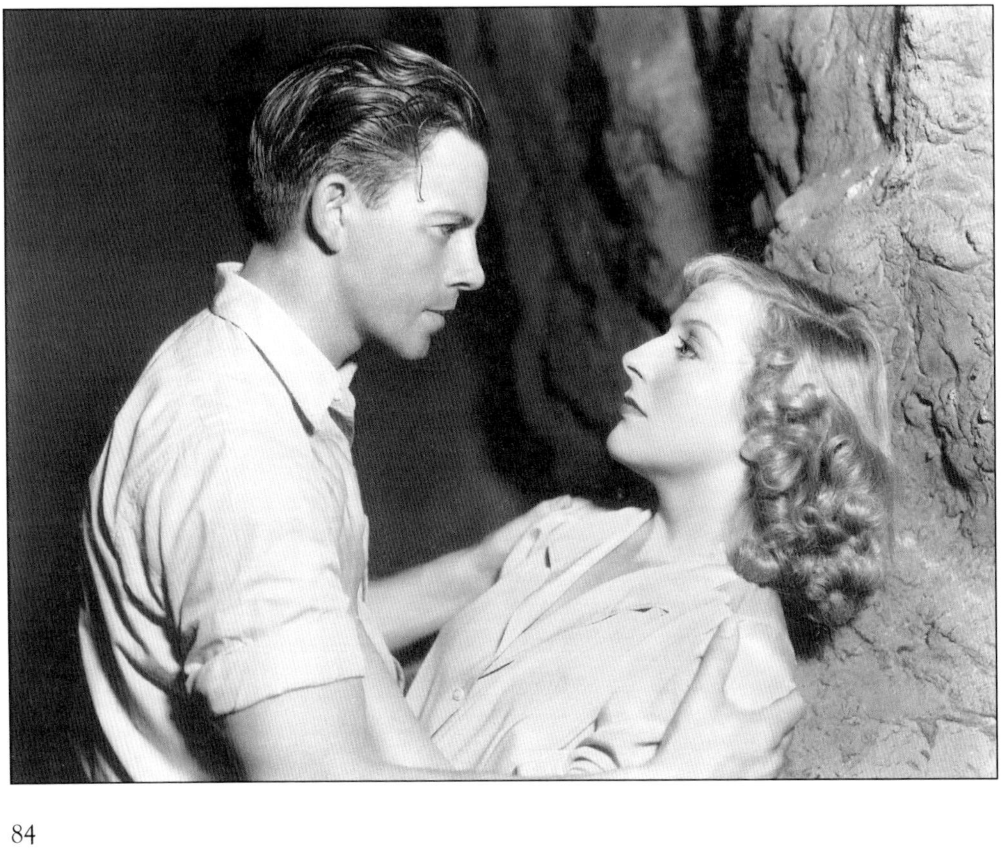

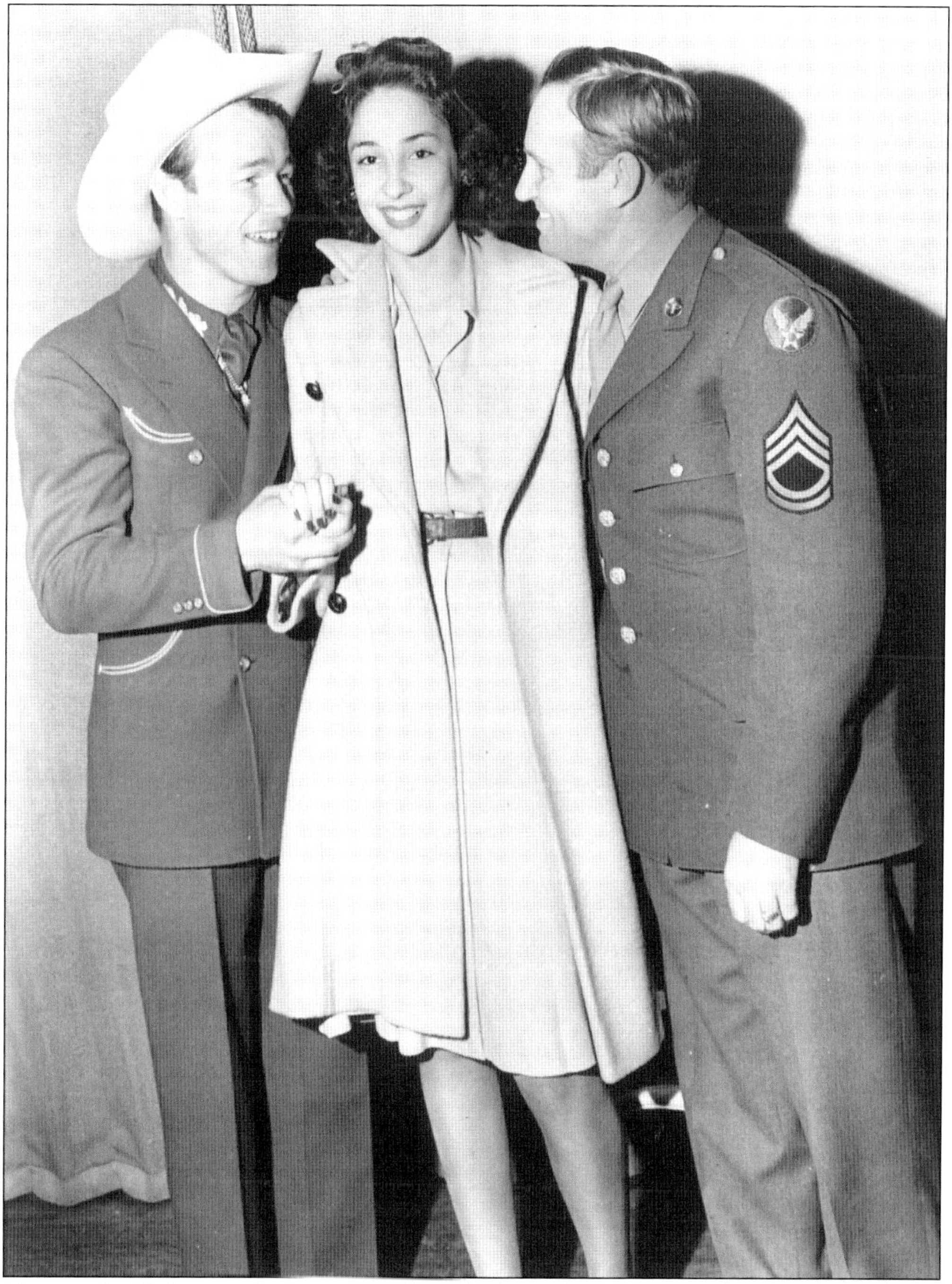

This wonderful photograph shows Gene Autry (right) and Roy Rogers entertaining a nice young woman during the war years. Autry served in the Air Transport Command and went on to own the baseball team now called the Los Angeles Angels of Anaheim. He built Anaheim Stadium in 1964. There is a statue of him as a cowboy at the stadium in Anaheim, California. Roy Rogers dedicated the monument on Movie Road at the first film festival commemorating film production in the Alabama Hills.

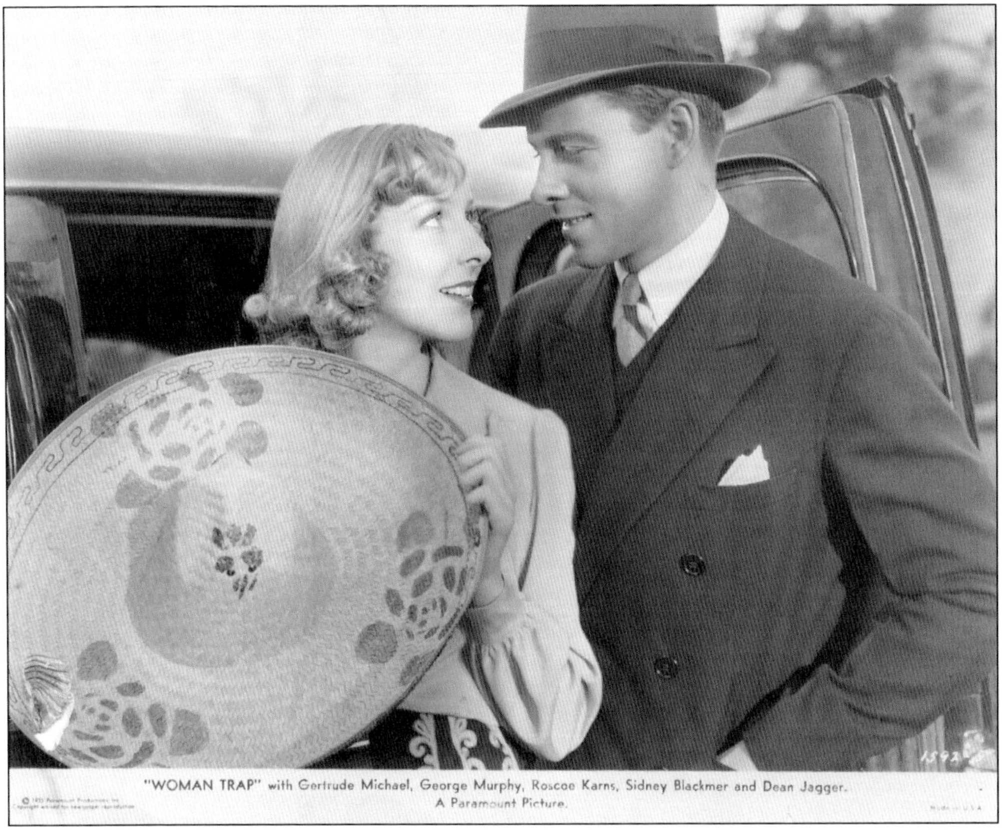


Here is another scene from *Woman Trap* (1936), starring Gertrude Michael and George Murphy. The hideout and Mexican town in the film are actually the old Anchor Ranch, and at the end of the film, local California Highway Patrol officers are shown.

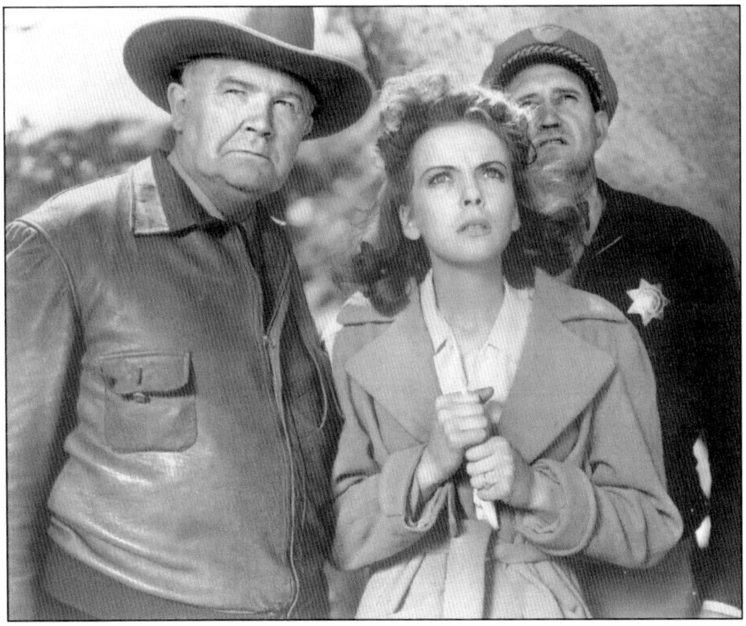

*High Sierra* (1941) was another film noir that remains a favorite of movie history. This scene shows Ida Lupino looking with anticipation to see what Bogart's fate will be in the film. Ida Lupino enjoyed the location and returned to Lone Pine to shoot *The Hitch-Hiker* (1953).

This publicity shot shows Bogart atop Whitney Portal Road. Raoul Walsh directed *High Sierra*, as well as many other films. The screenplay of *High Sierra* was written by W.R. Burnett and John Huston, who went on to direct *Treasure of Sierra Madre* (1948).

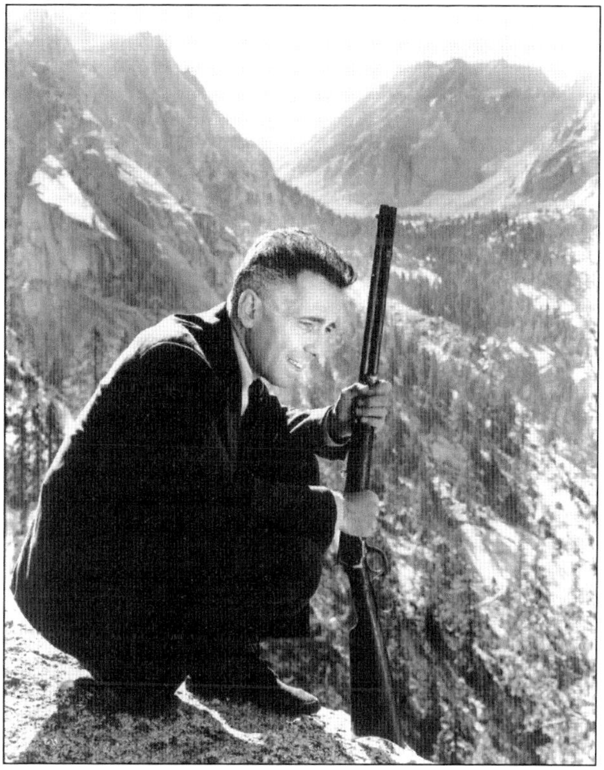

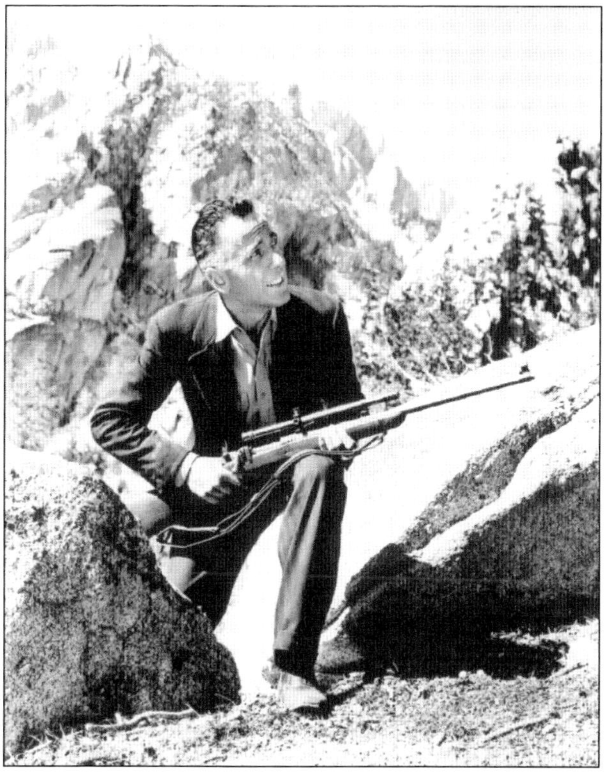

This rare photograph shows Bogart awaiting his fate after fleeing from the Alabama Hills up Whitney Portal Road. The getaway car (a 1937 Plymouth Coupe) that Humphrey Bogart drives in *High Sierra* can be found at the Lone Pine Museum. Edward G. Robinson, Paul Muni, George Raft, and James Cagney all turned down Bogart's part. During filming, Bogart was under suspicion for being a Communist. *Colorado Territory* (1949) was a Western remake of this film with Virginia Mayo but was not shot in the Alabama Hills. *I Died a Thousand Times* (1955) with Jack Palance is another remake of the film.

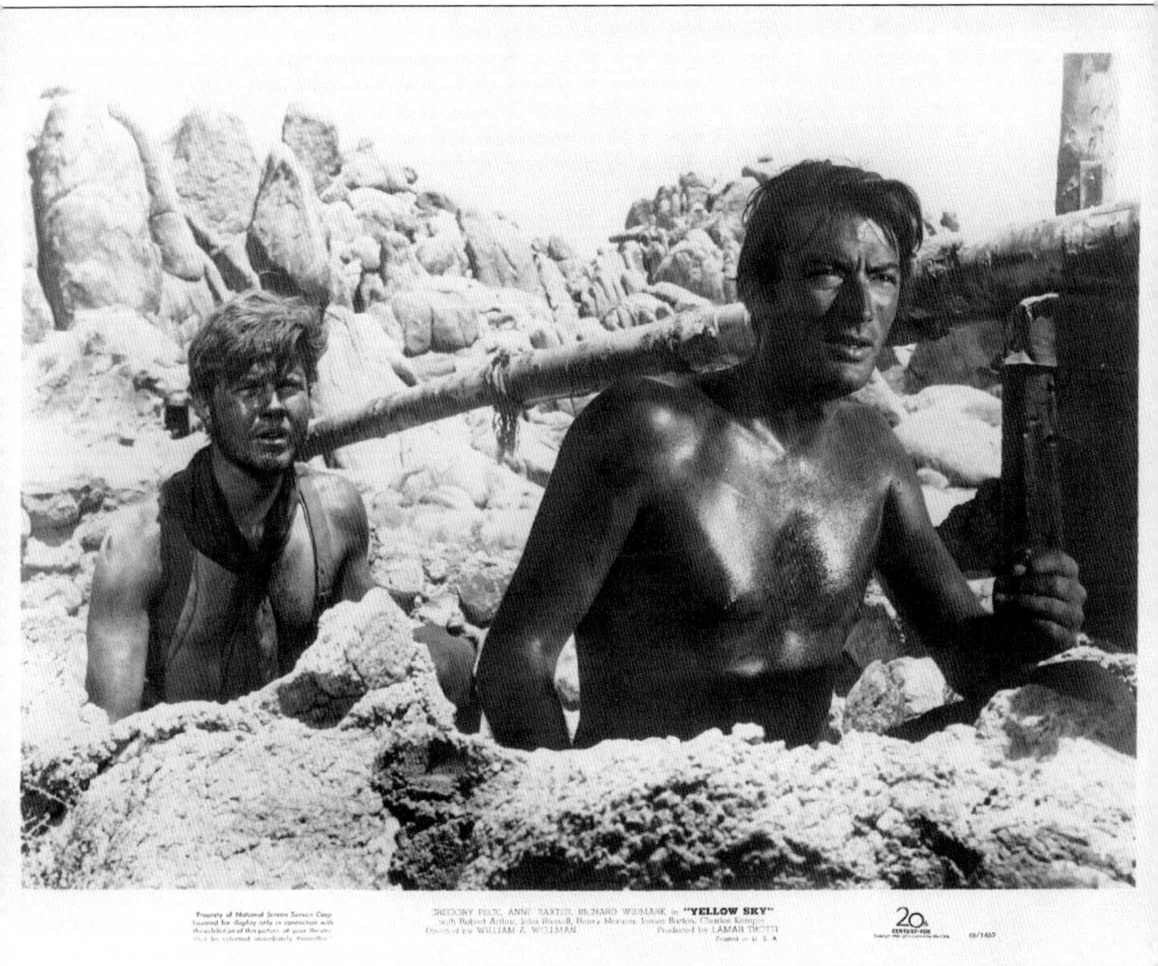


Gregory Peck (right) is shown here in *Yellow Sky* (1948), taking cover behind aristae that can still be seen between Movie Road and the Ruiz Hills area of the Alabama Hills, offering the best evidence of early filmmaking. According to Dave Holland, a local was paid to dismantle the set but for whatever reason left this piece of movie history.

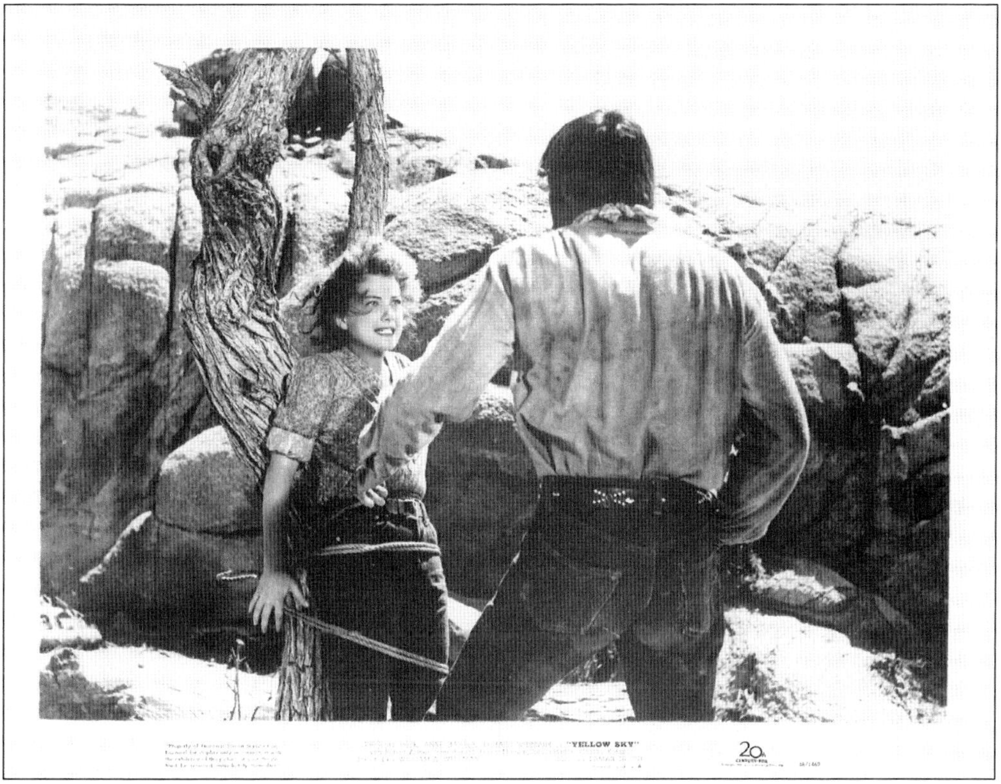

This action scene from *Yellow Sky* (1948) shows Anne Baxter and Gregory Peck. Gregory Peck's role in this film goes from bad guy to good guy, and the movie is considered one of the better Westerns ever filmed in the Alabama Hills. In one scene, Gregory Peck goes in a saloon, and the bartender is Victor Killian. Killian was found murdered at the Lido Apartments after visiting the Chinese Theatre in Hollywood; some say the theater is haunted by his spirit.

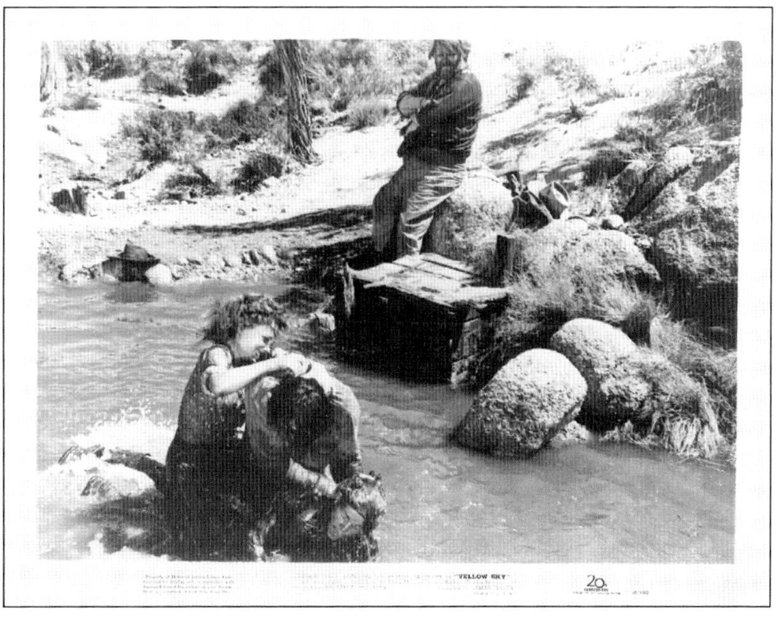

This action scene from *Yellow Sky* (1948) shows a tough Anne Baxter, whose character defends her grandfather's fortune and her home. This location was a dry depression that was filled with water to create a small creek bed.

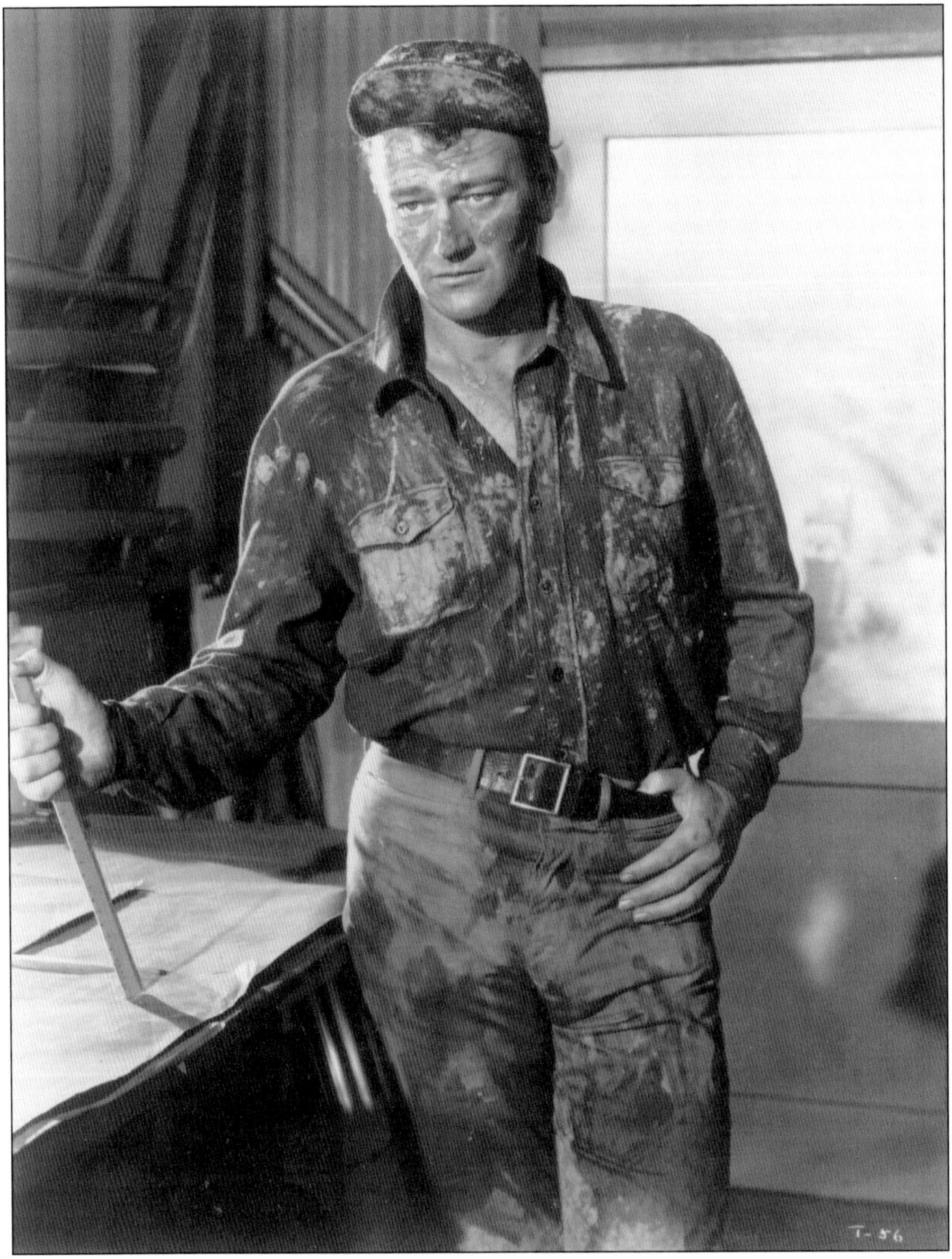


John Wayne is seen working hard on the set of *Tycoon* (1947). It was filmed in the Ruiz Hills area of the Alabama Hills, and where the mine was in the film, traces of the set can still be seen.

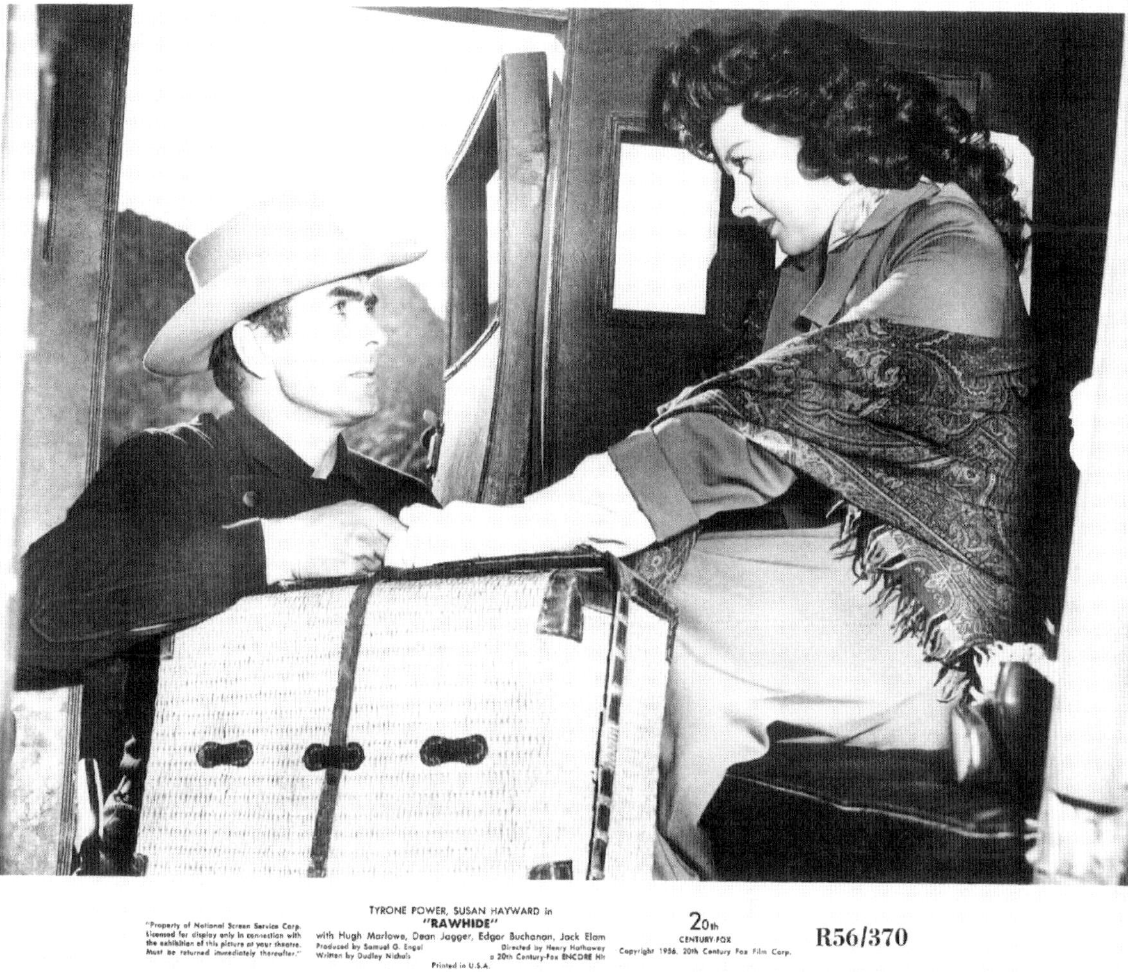


*Rawhide* (1951) starred Tyrone Power and Susan Hayward. Director Henry Hathaway filmed a burial scene similar to *Lives of a Bengal Lancer* (1936). The burial scene in *Rawhide* is along Movie Road, and the road looks the same as it did when it was filmed. Twin children were used during filming; one would cry for some scenes as needed, and the other would not cry. Power often pretended to be a local in town, posing as a hotel clerk as a practical joke to see if he would be noticed. Hayward was rumored not to wear undergarments while relaxing in town.

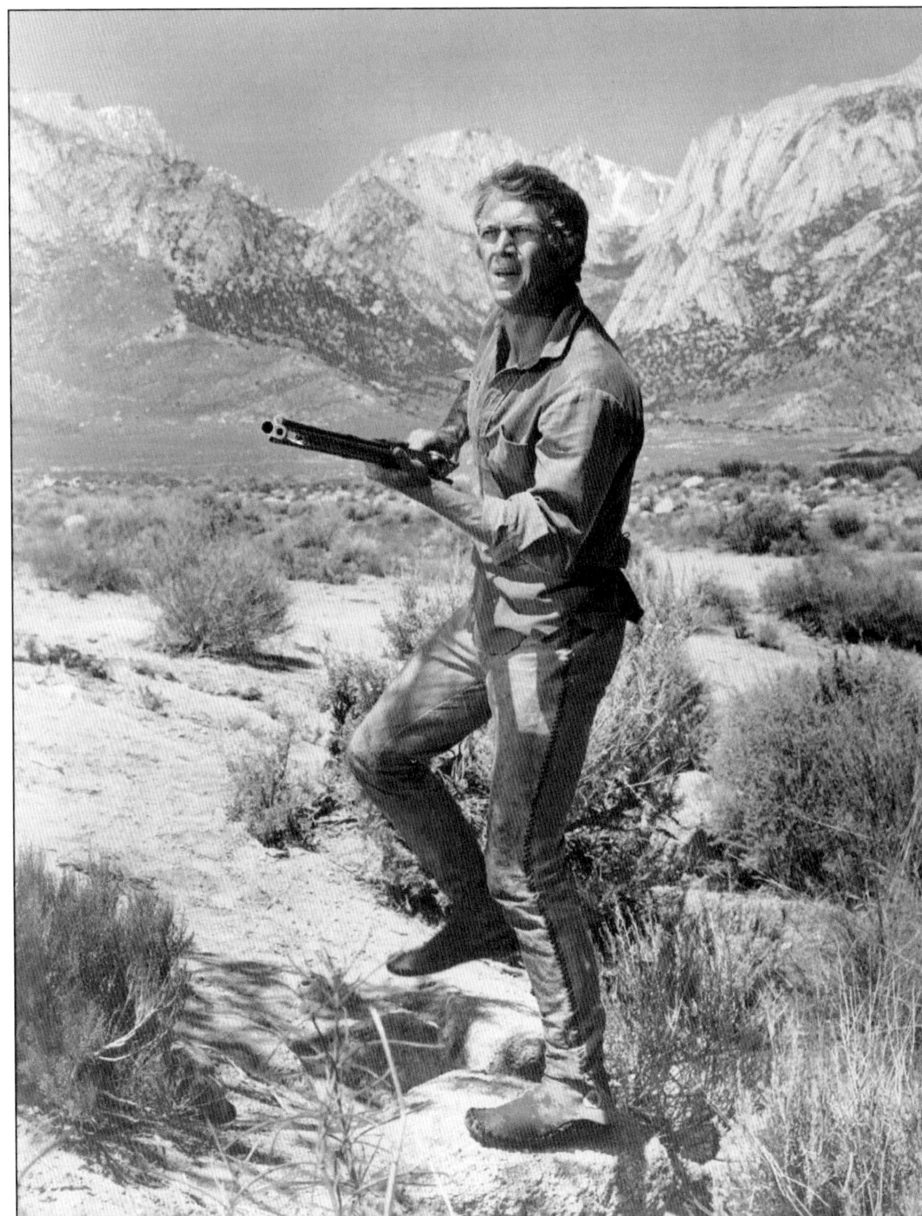


Steve McQueen was in the US Marine Corps and starred in the 1966 film *Nevada Smith*.

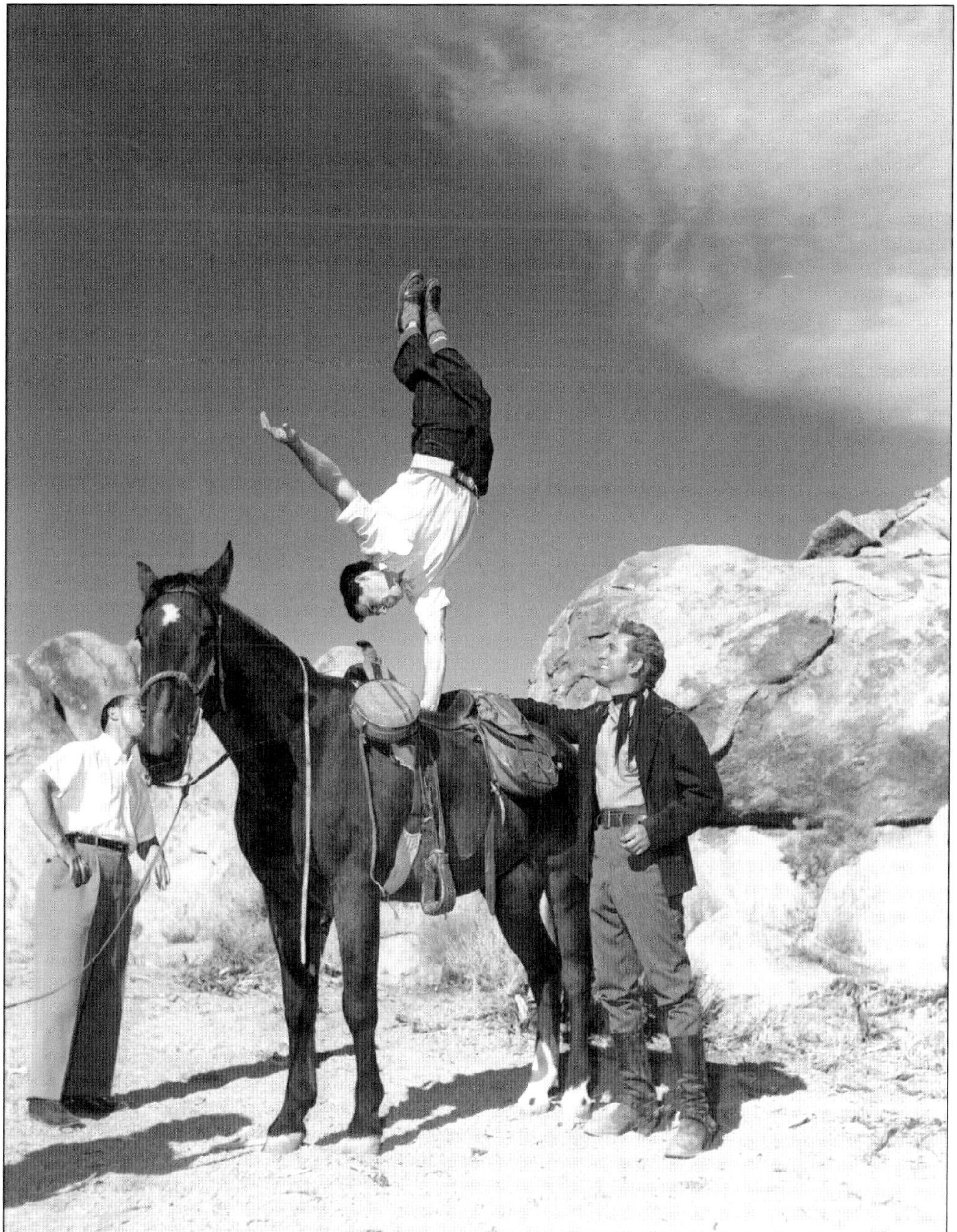

*Along the Great Divide* (1951) starred Kirk Douglas, a US Navy veteran, in his first Western, and Virginia Mayo. This location can be found near Lone Ranger Canyon. Robert Mitchum, another great actor, starred in the 1944 Western *Nevada* (which is the only film to mention a "lone pine" in reference to the town of Lone Pine), also filmed in the Alabama Hills. Mitchum was previously seen in the movie *Riders of the Deadline* (1943).

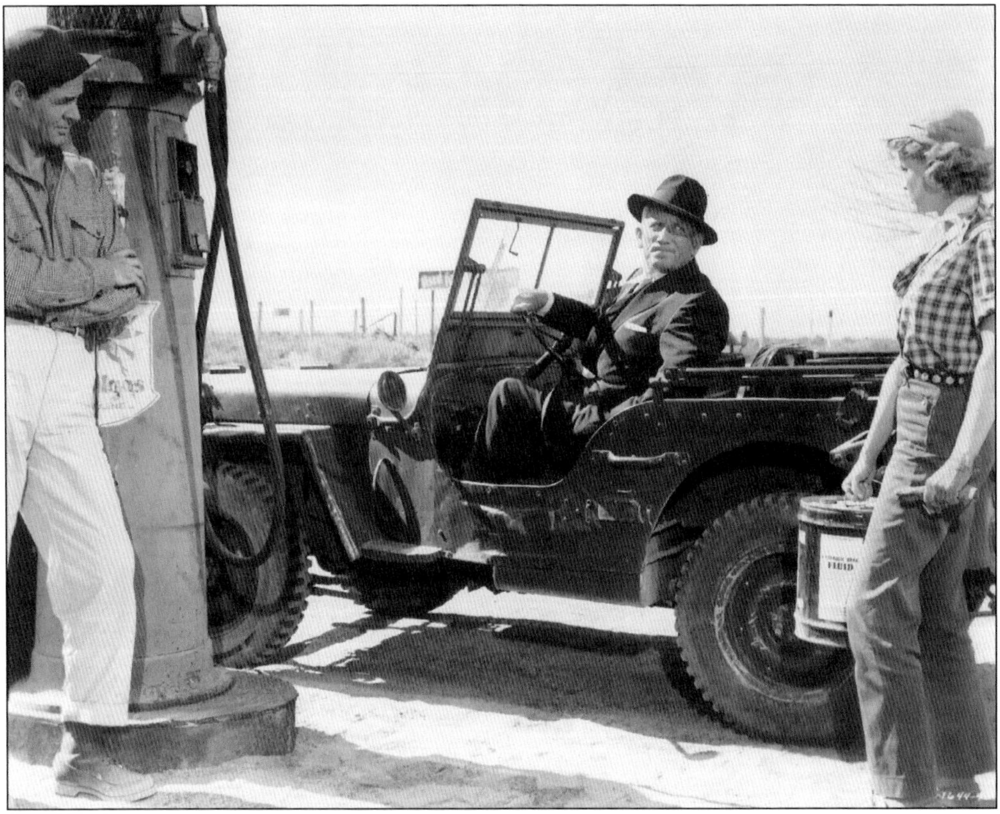

*Bad Day at Black Rock* (1955) was filmed east of Lone Pine and in the Alabama Hills. One of the scenes featured a Plymouth sedan driven by Ernest Borgnine, chasing a Willys jeep driven by Spencer Tracy. Robert Ryan and Lee Marvin were in the US Marine Corps and starred alongside US Navy veteran Ernest Borgnine in the colorized suspenseful film noir.

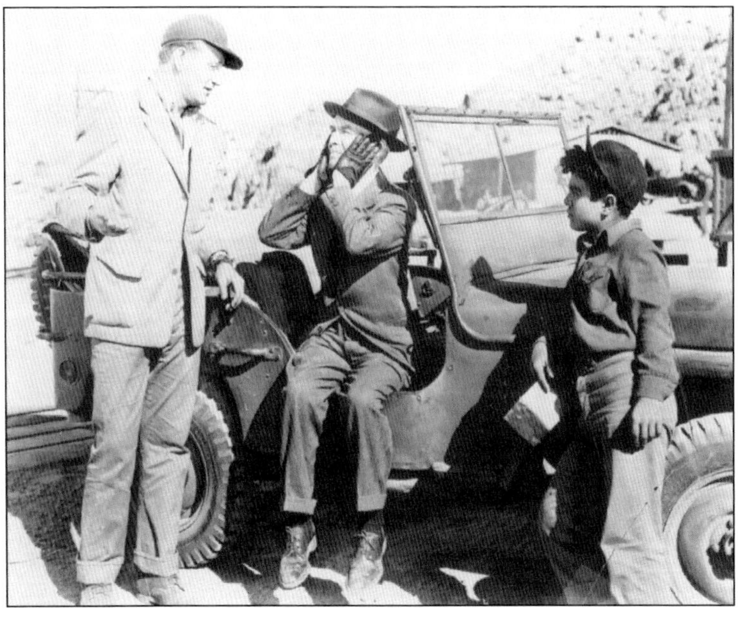

This image is from *Tycoon* showing a Willys jeep like the one in *Bad Day at Black Rock* in 1955. The Willys jeep was reliable in wartime as well as in movies filmed in the Alabama Hills. This location is in the Ruiz Hills area.

# *Six*

# Filming Near the Alabama Hills

In addition to the spectacular locations of the Alabama Hills, many production companies also filmed in the Eastern Sierras and along Highway 395. Starting from the dry lake at Victorville, California, visitors will pass a location for *Stagecoach* (1939). Continuing on Highway 395 are very small towns near Red Mountain where *Hidalgo* (2004) was filmed. A Star Trek location can be found at the Trona Pinnacles, located near the turnoff to Trona. The town of Randsburg follows, where Johnny Depp starred in *The Brave* (1997) and Kirstie Alley appeared in *Nevada* (1997).

When directors filmed in the Alabama Hills, they often chose to add a shot or "pick up" scene to contribute to the final touches of a production. For example, places like Corraganville, Malibu Creek State Park, Melody Ranch, Paramount Ranch, Bronson Canyon, Universal, or the Warner Bros. back lot were used as locations to add to films shot in the Alabama Hills.

Moreover, most of the riding sequences in the introduction to the Lone Ranger were filmed in the Alabama Hills. However, the latter part of the introduction (where the Lone Ranger rears up his horse, Silver) was shot at Iverson Ranch near Chatsworth, over 200 miles away.

Vasquez Rocks and Red Rock Canyon were a favorite filming location for science fiction productions, such as Star Trek, and Western singing cowboy movies starring Roy Rogers and Gene Autry. In the 2013 *Lone Ranger*, starring Johnny Depp, an added shot was filmed on the Owens Valley Dry Lake, even though most of the filming took place in Monument Valley, Utah. Owens Valley Dry Lake was also the filming location for numerous car commercials and *Star Trek V: The Final Frontier* (1989).

In addition to movies, Gatorade commercials, music videos, and a Twilight Zone episode were shot in and near the Alabama Hills. Death Valley is featured in scenes from *Star Wars Episode IV: A New Hope* (1977) and *Star Wars Episode VI: Return of the Jedi* (1983). Rock Creek Lake was an early 1920s movie location, and several scenes from *Indiana Jones and the Temple of Doom* (1984) were filmed in and around the ski resort town of Mammoth. Diaz Lake, another recreational area, is where the *Charge of the Light Brigade* (1936) and many Westerns were filmed.

In the Inyo County towns of Lone Pine, Independence, Big Pine, and Darwin, numerous filming locations exist. Outside of Lone Pine, along Lone Pine Narrow Gauge Road, a bustling train station once stood and served as a filming location for a Gene Autry production. An area near Big Pine was inspiration for the film *Man of a Thousand Faces* (1957), starring James Cagney, and the town of Darwin, with a population of 43 as of the 2010 US Census, was featured in *Kalifornia* (1993), starring Brad Pitt and David Duchovny.

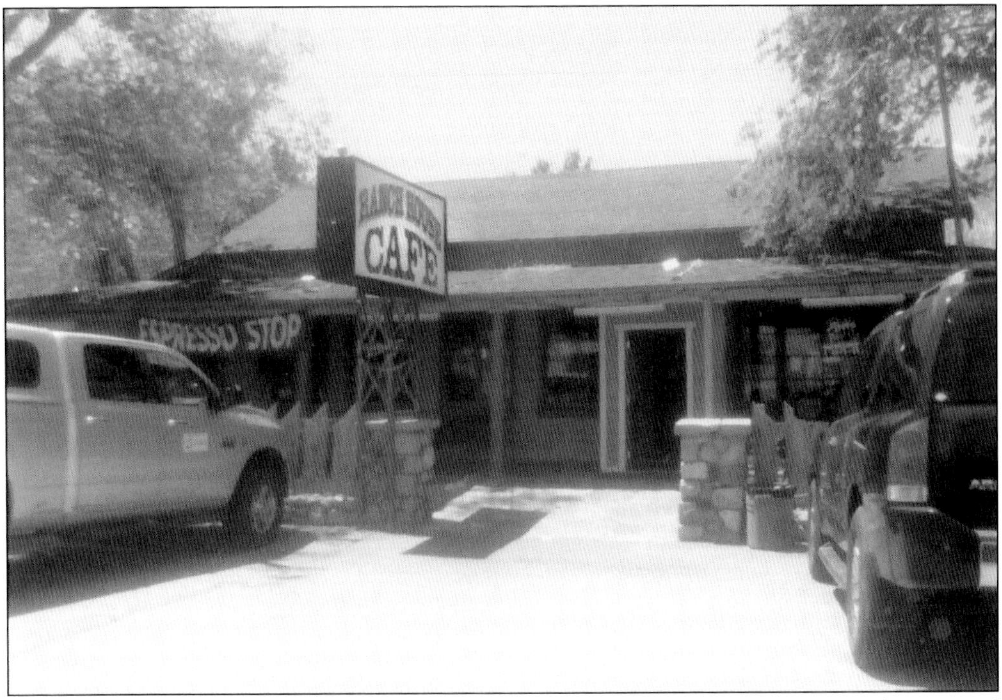


This image shows the Ranch House Café, a great breakfast place on Highway 395 where *Camel Spiders* was filmed. The movie, which featured giant spiders taking over a small town, is science fiction cult classic that was also filmed in the Alabama Hills.

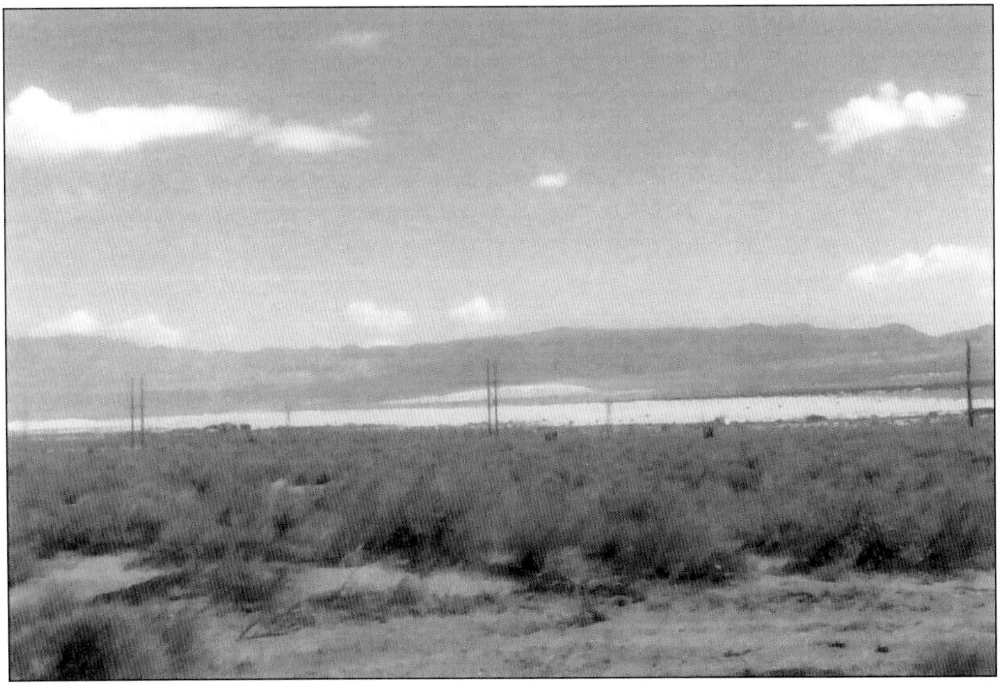

The sand dunes of Olancha served as a location for another science fiction film, *Crossworlds* (1998), as well as many other productions, like *Bagdad* (1949) and *Iron Man* (2008).

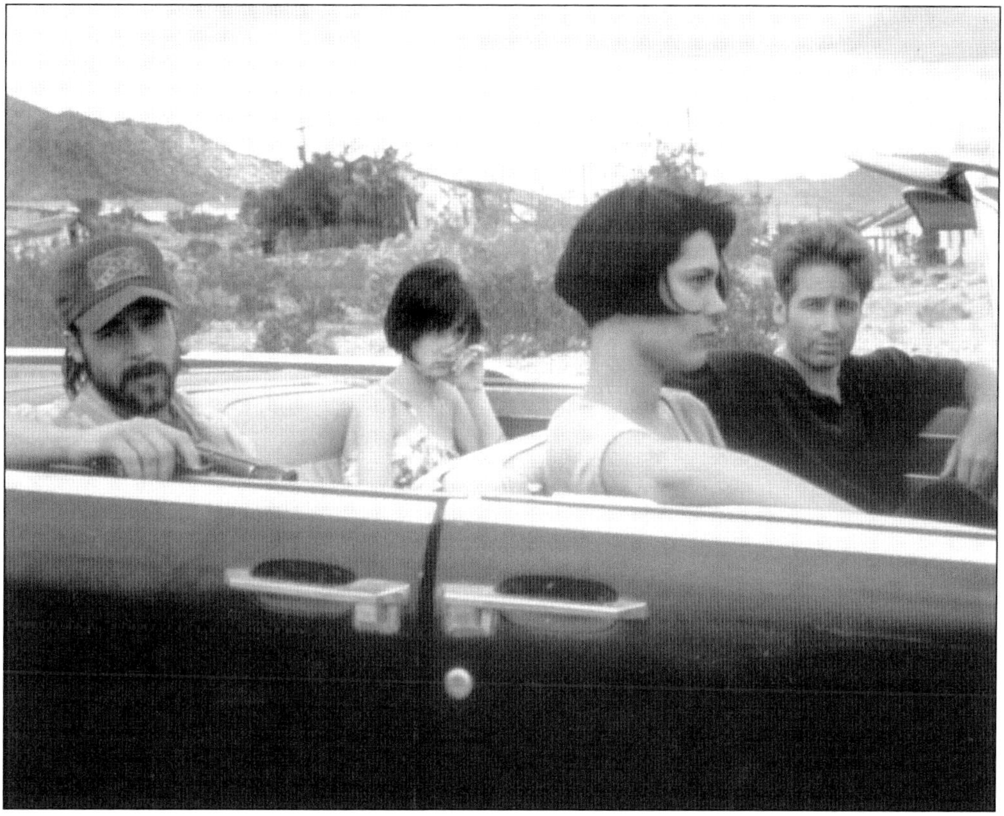

The town of Darwin, near Lone Pine, California, was the location of *Tremors* (1990) and *Kalifornia*, starring, from left to right, Brad Pitt, Juliette Lewis, Michelle Forbes, and David Duchovny.

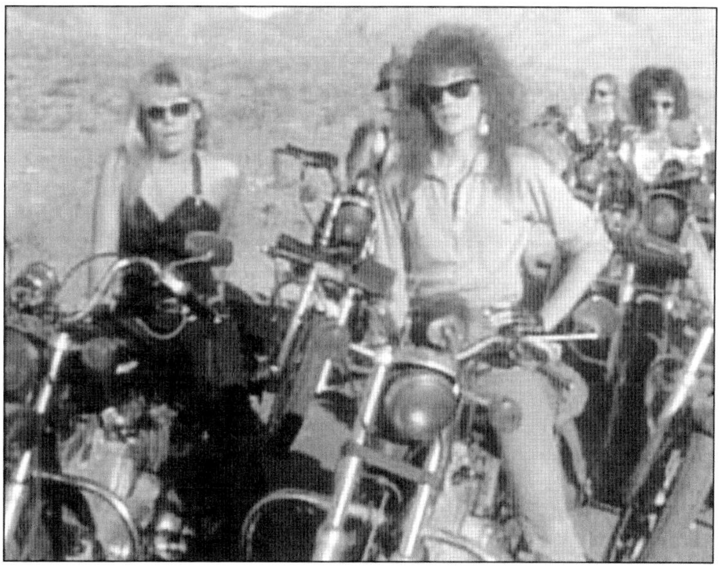

Shown here is *Chopper Chicks in Zombie Town*, one of Billy Bob Thornton's first films, made in Randsburg, California, which doubled for the fictional town of Zariah, population 127.

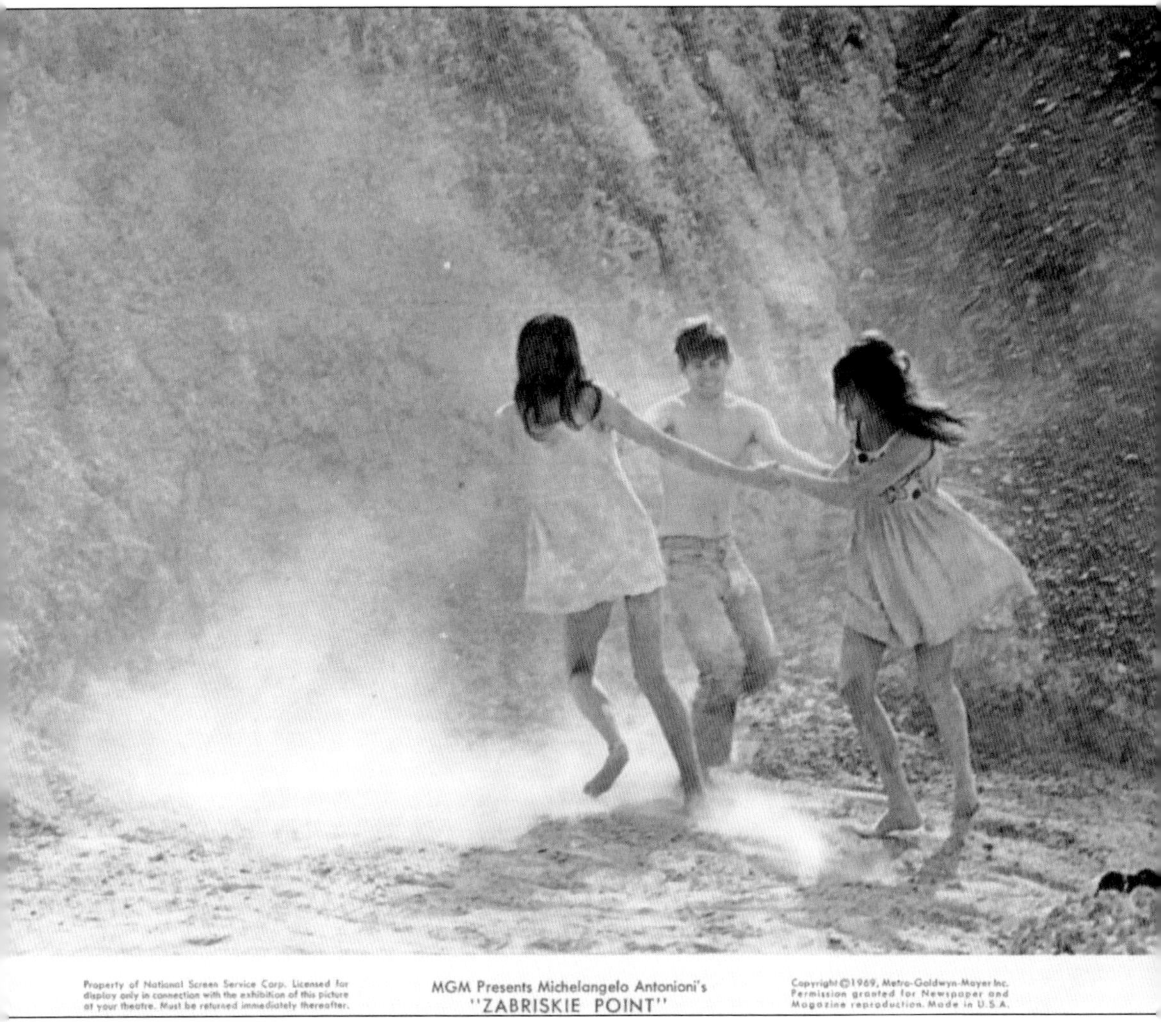


Death Valley can be reached from Lone Pine, California, and is shown in this still from *Zabriskie Point* (1969). Death Valley was used for many filming locations, including *Star Wars*. Not far from this location is where Barker Ranch once stood and where the infamous Charles Manson was captured in 1969.

Pictured here is a Lone Pine High School patch from Lone Pine, California, where the town itself served as locations for movies. Jamie Foxx from *Django Unchained* (2012) donated to the sports teams in exchange for use of the high school gym.

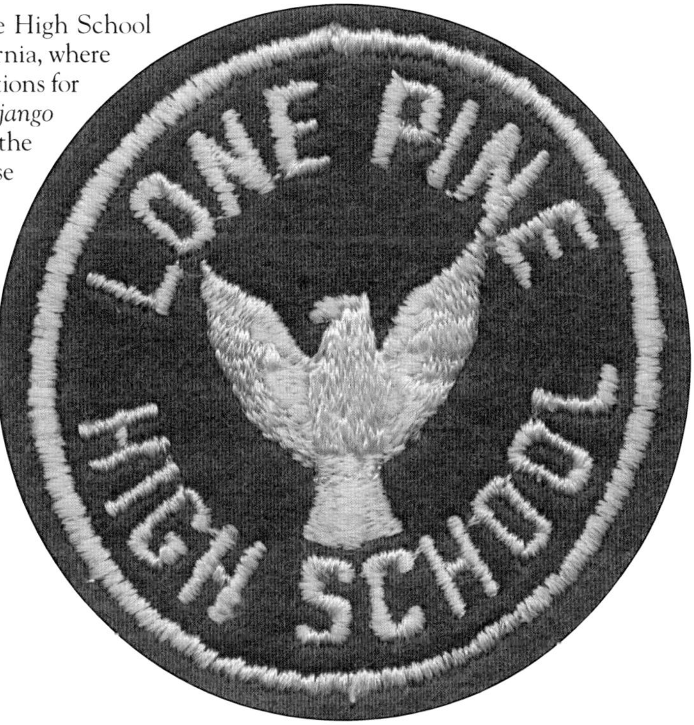


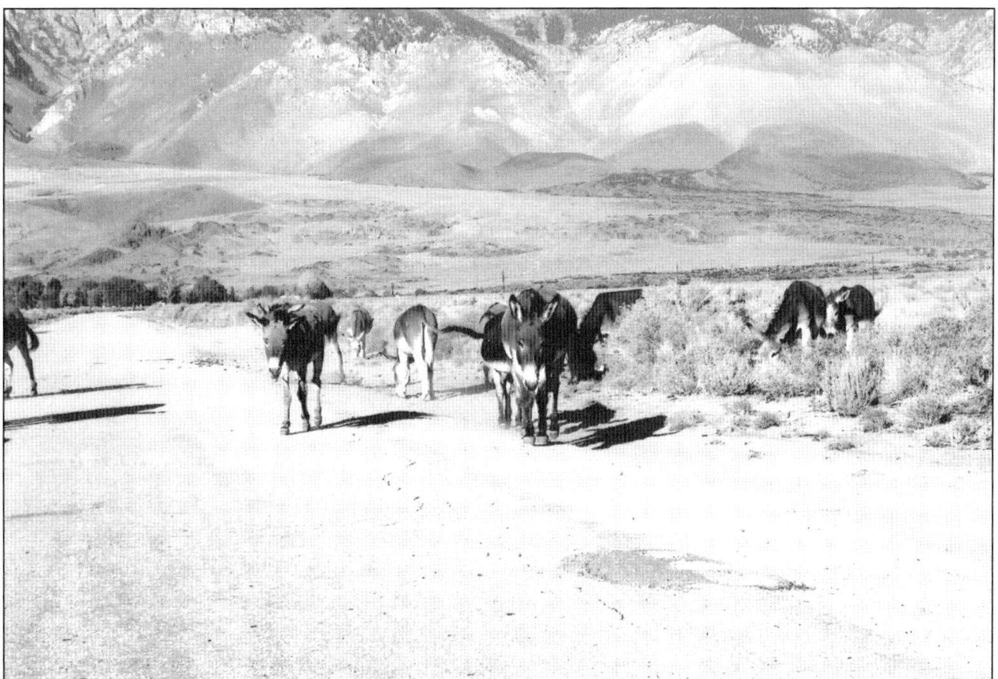

Aberdeen is a filming location of *Camel Spiders*. It has a nice restaurant that used to be on old Highway 395, and in the area are wild burros, as pictured here.

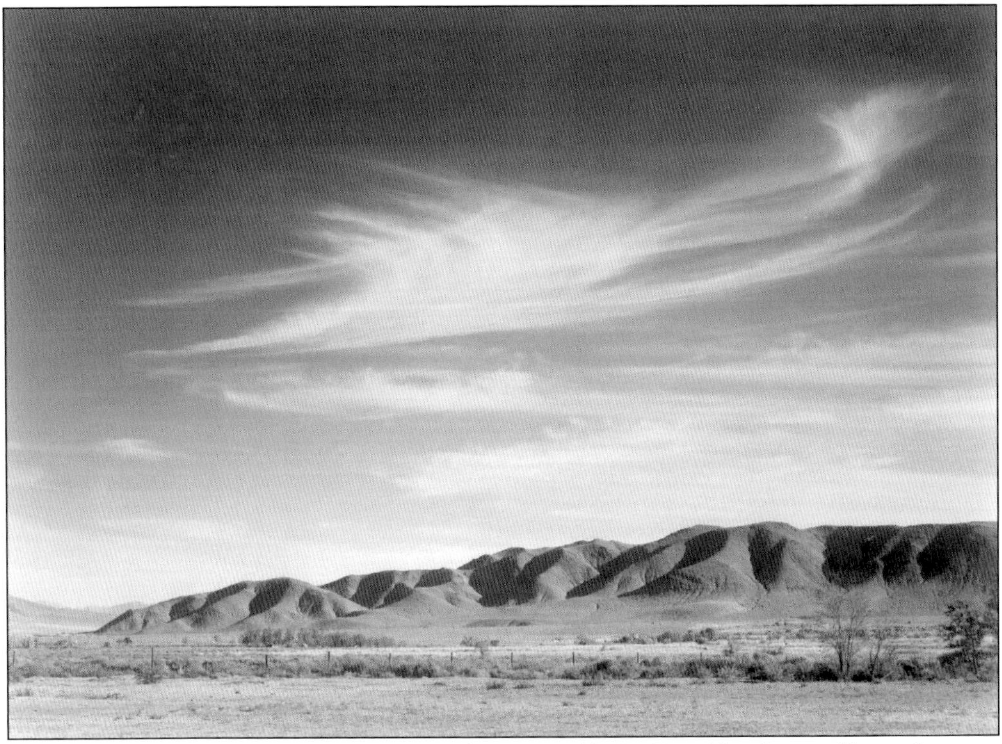

Manzanar was a Japanese internment camp during World War II and has been a filming location as well. The view above, looking south from Manzanar to Alabama Hills, was taken by famous photographer Ansel Adams in 1943. Below are the author and his dog at the abandoned Manzanar gatehouse. (Above, courtesy of Library of Congress.)

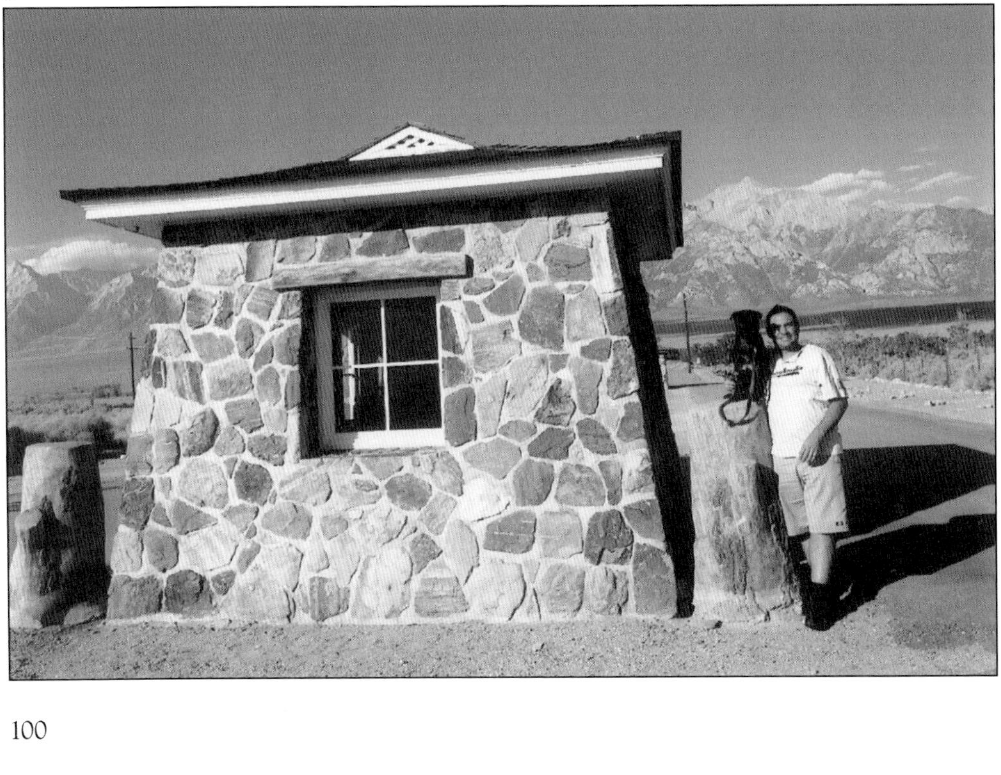

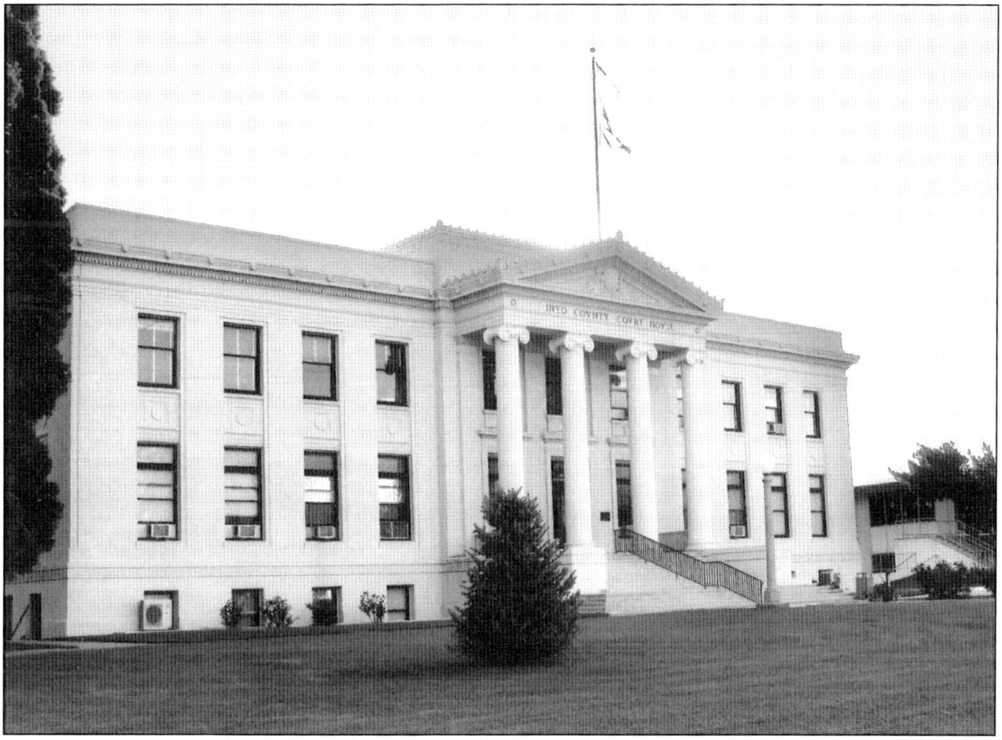


In Independence, California, is the courthouse where the films *Daft Punk's Electroma* (2006) and *Trial and Error* (1997), starring Jeff Daniels, Michael Richards, and Charlize Theron, were filmed. The photograph at right shows Daniels on the roof of the courthouse with the Eastern Sierras in the background.

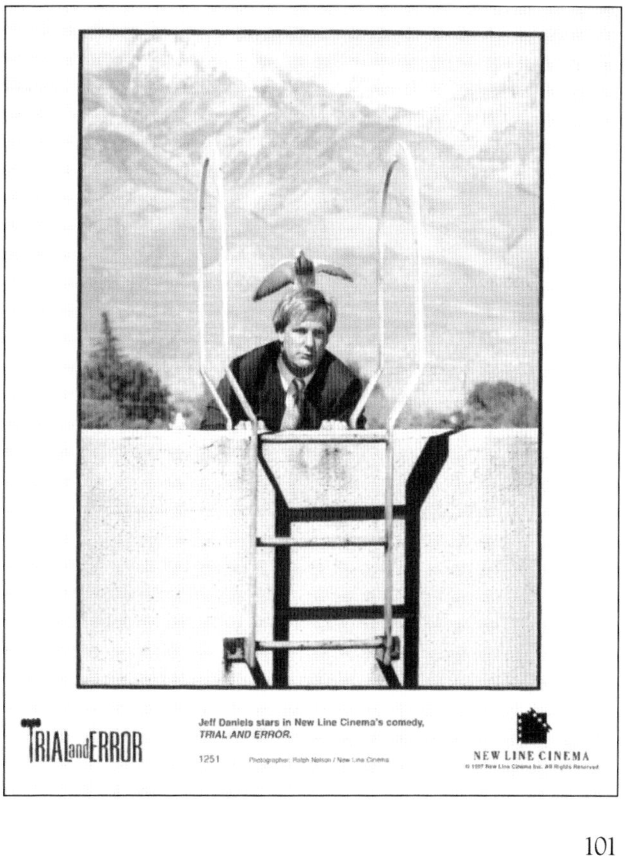

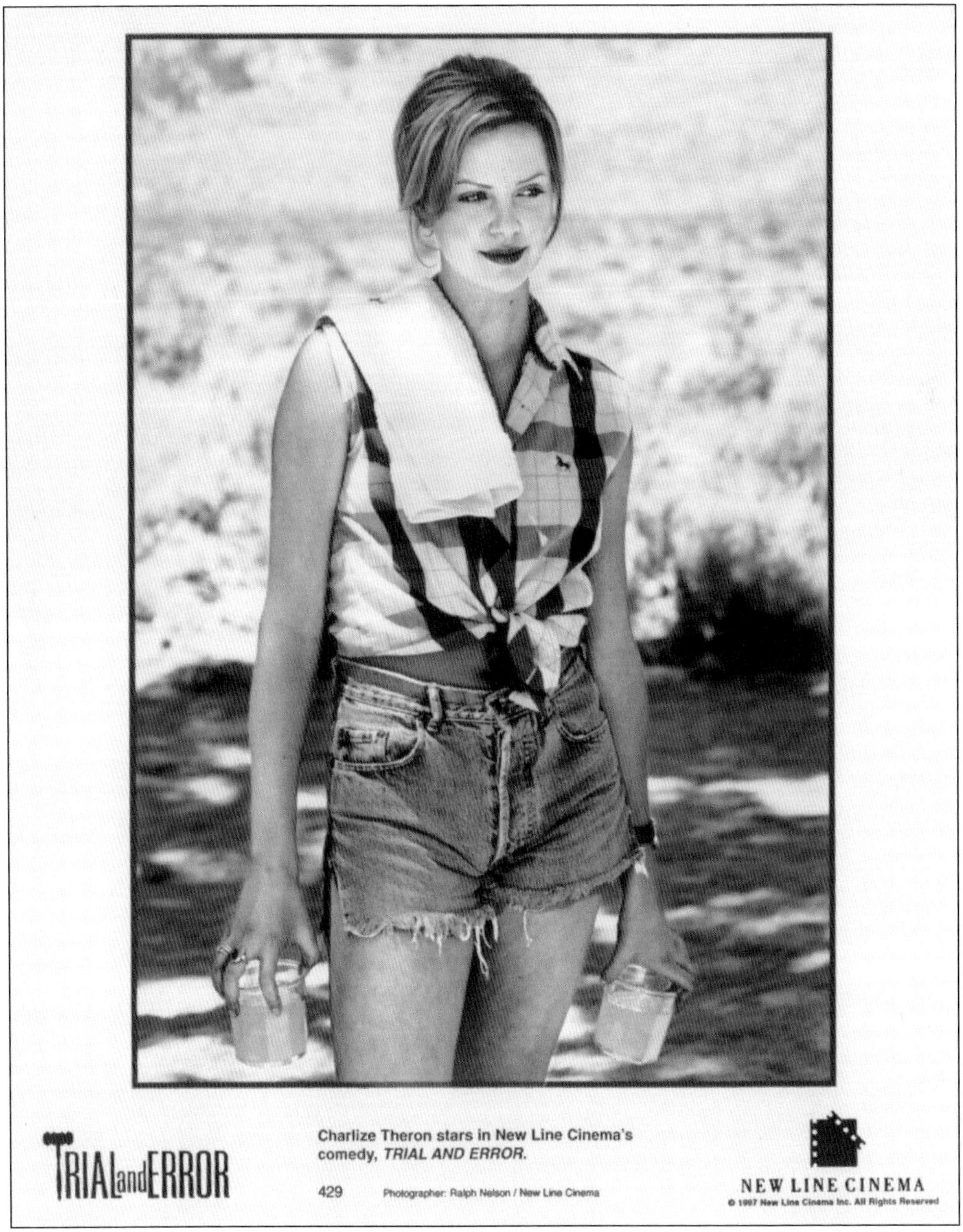


Charlize Theron plays a small-town waitress who becomes involved in the romantic-comedy courtroom story that is very entertaining. Local residents were used as extras in the *Trial and Error.*

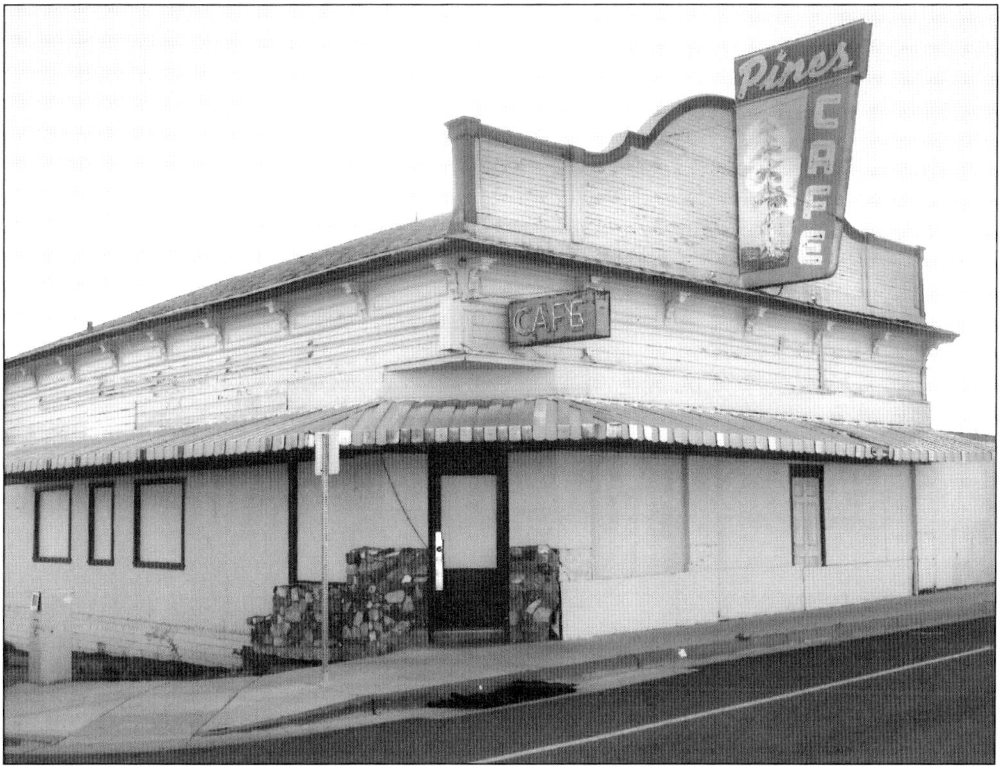


The Pines Café, the café that Charlize Theron worked at in the movie and where she confronts Jeff Daniels with a paper bag, is an old structure that has been used in other films. Near the café is where Nicholas Cage, in *Gone in 60 Seconds*, was a teacher of a little boys' racing school.

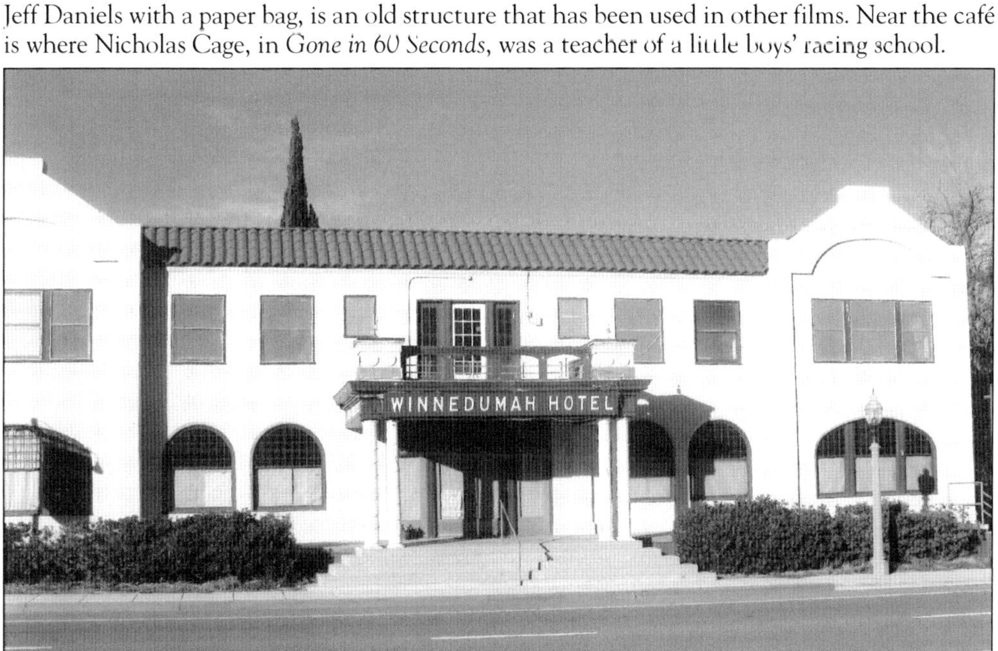


The Winnedumah Hotel was owned by the Dow family. Famous stars stayed there, and the building can be seen in old Westerns.

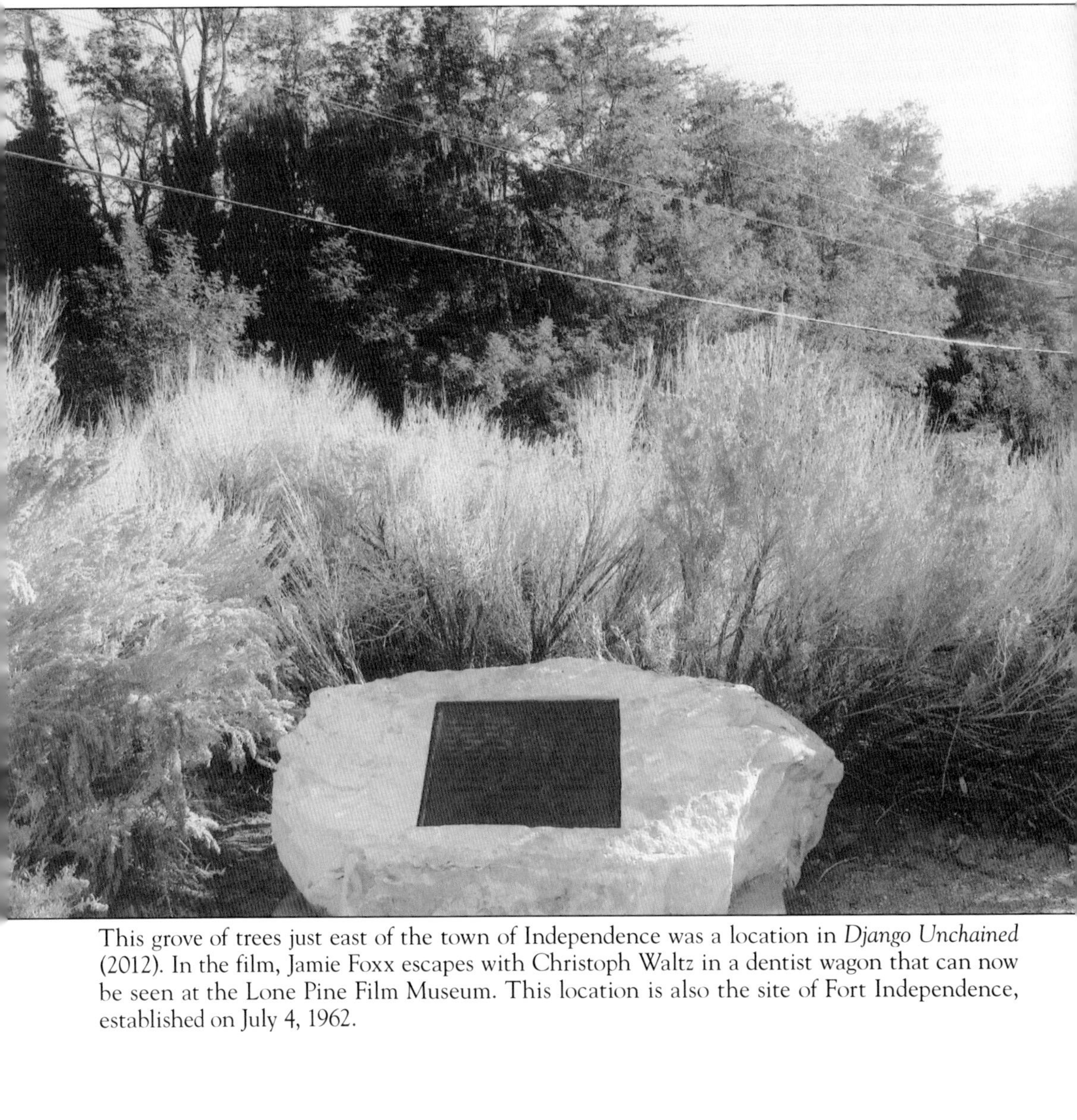

This grove of trees just east of the town of Independence was a location in *Django Unchained* (2012). In the film, Jamie Foxx escapes with Christoph Waltz in a dentist wagon that can now be seen at the Lone Pine Film Museum. This location is also the site of Fort Independence, established on July 4, 1962.

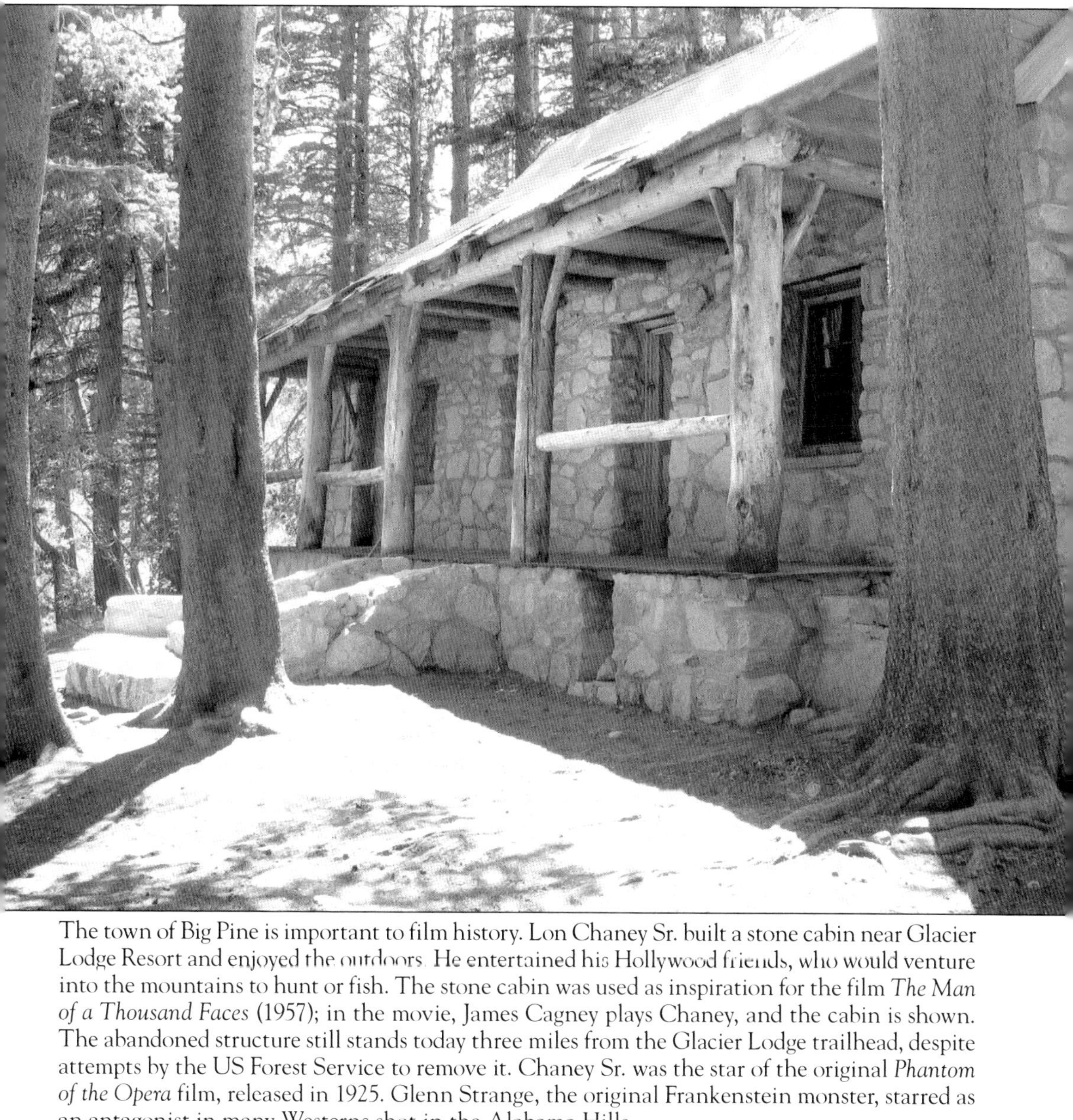

The town of Big Pine is important to film history. Lon Chaney Sr. built a stone cabin near Glacier Lodge Resort and enjoyed the outdoors. He entertained his Hollywood friends, who would venture into the mountains to hunt or fish. The stone cabin was used as inspiration for the film *The Man of a Thousand Faces* (1957); in the movie, James Cagney plays Chaney, and the cabin is shown. The abandoned structure still stands today three miles from the Glacier Lodge trailhead, despite attempts by the US Forest Service to remove it. Chaney Sr. was the star of the original *Phantom of the Opera* film, released in 1925. Glenn Strange, the original Frankenstein monster, starred as an antagonist in many Westerns shot in the Alabama Hills.

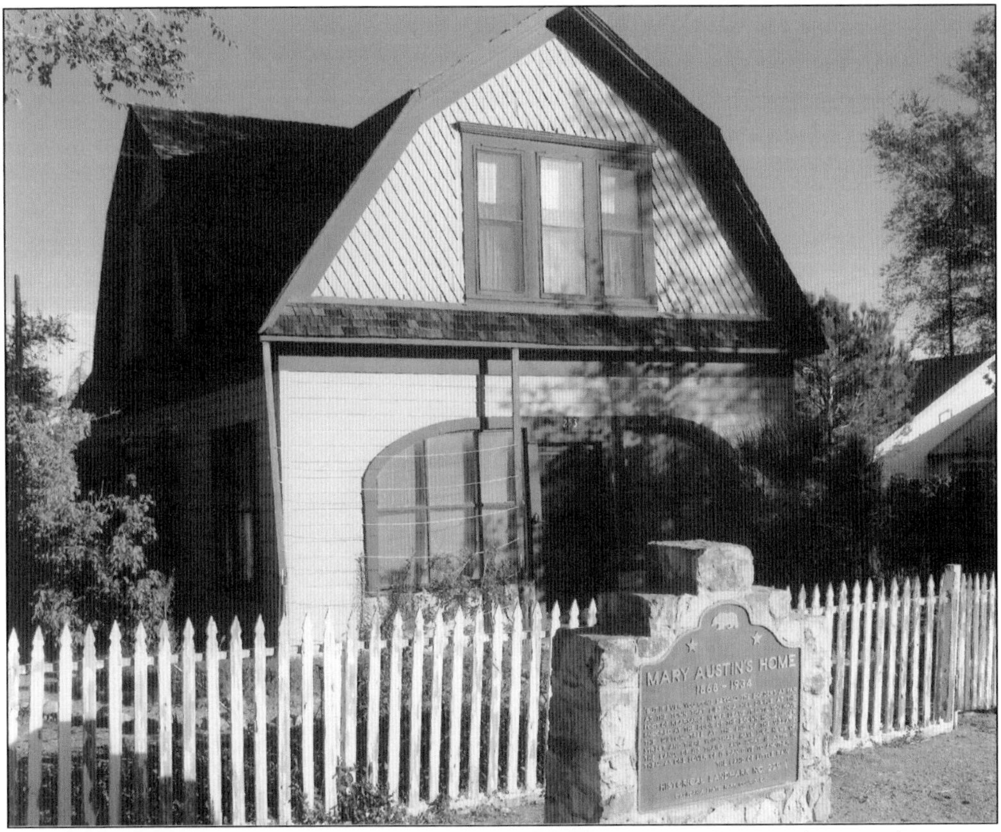


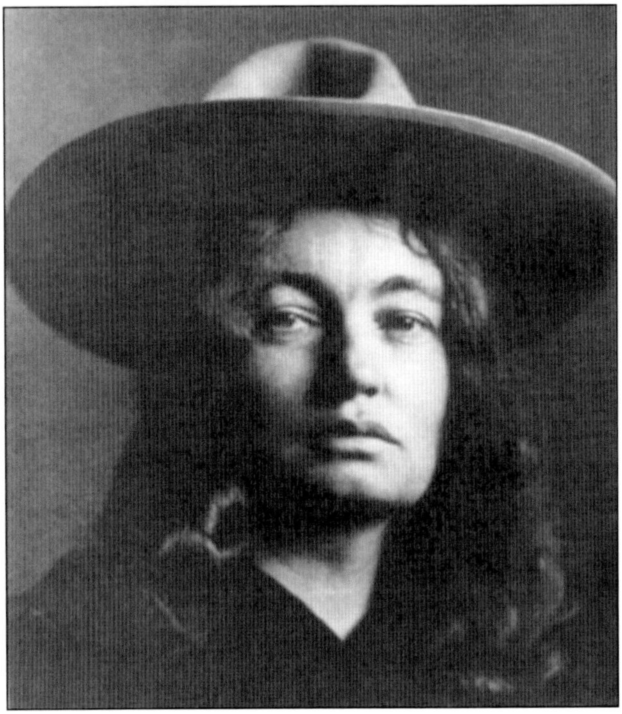

Mary Hunter Austin, whose home in Independence, California, is seen above, wrote nice poems about the Sierras. It is rumored that on this street is where the 1920 film *Pollyanna* with Mary Pickford was filmed.

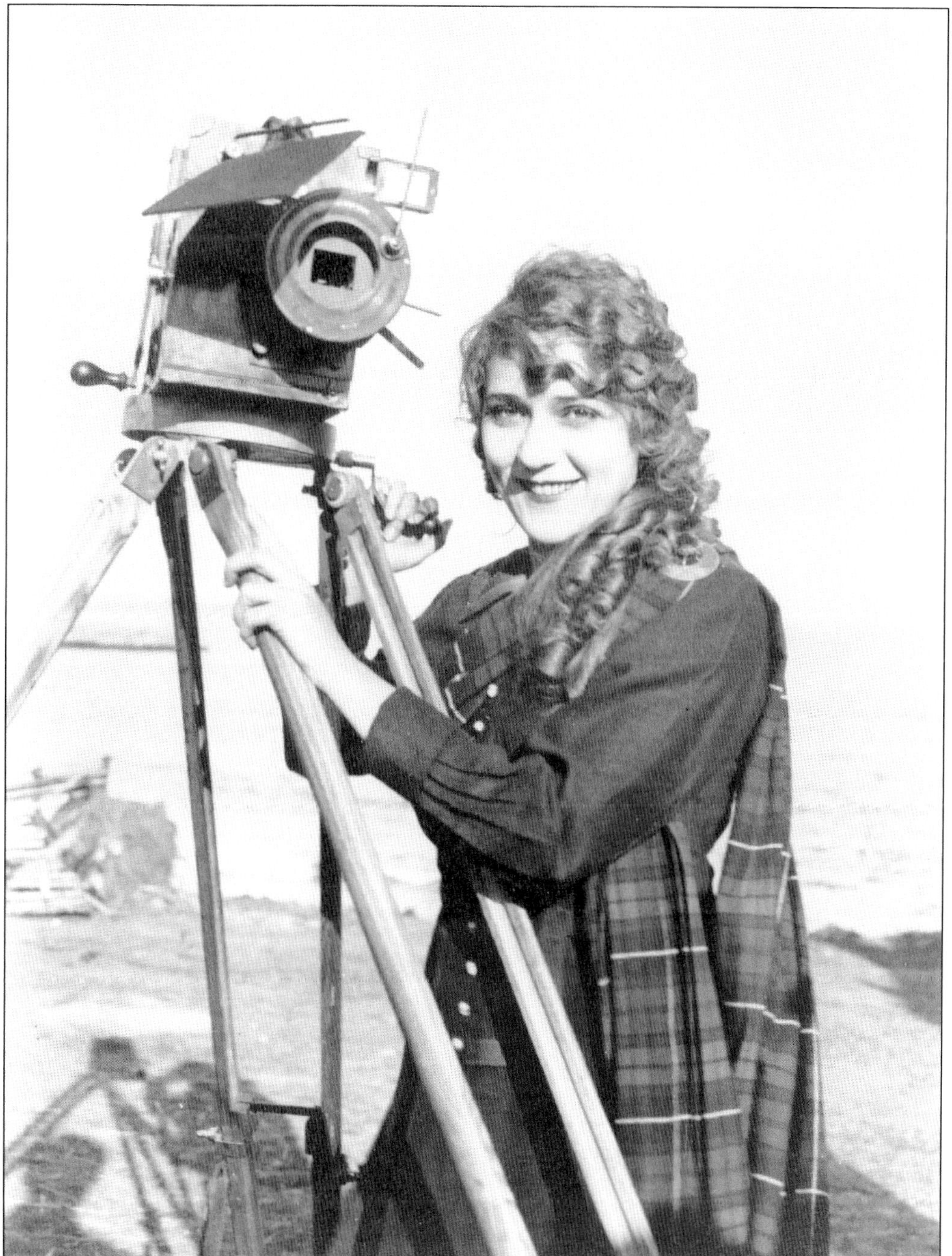

Mary Pickford is seen here in her role as a director. After starring in *Pollyanna* as a young girl, she went on to be a very successful movie-maker. (Courtesy of Library of Congress.)

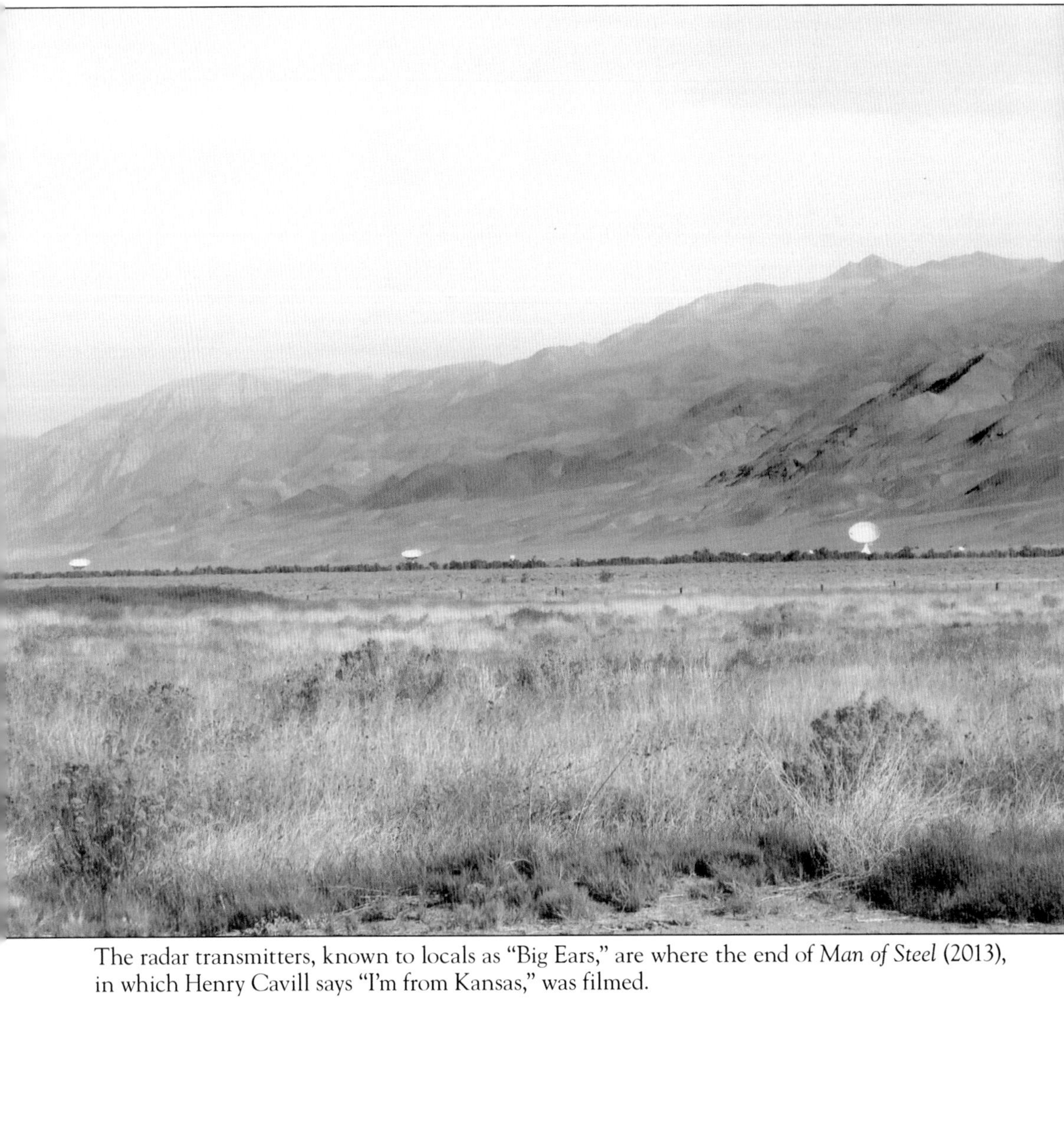

The radar transmitters, known to locals as "Big Ears," are where the end of *Man of Steel* (2013), in which Henry Cavill says "I'm from Kansas," was filmed.

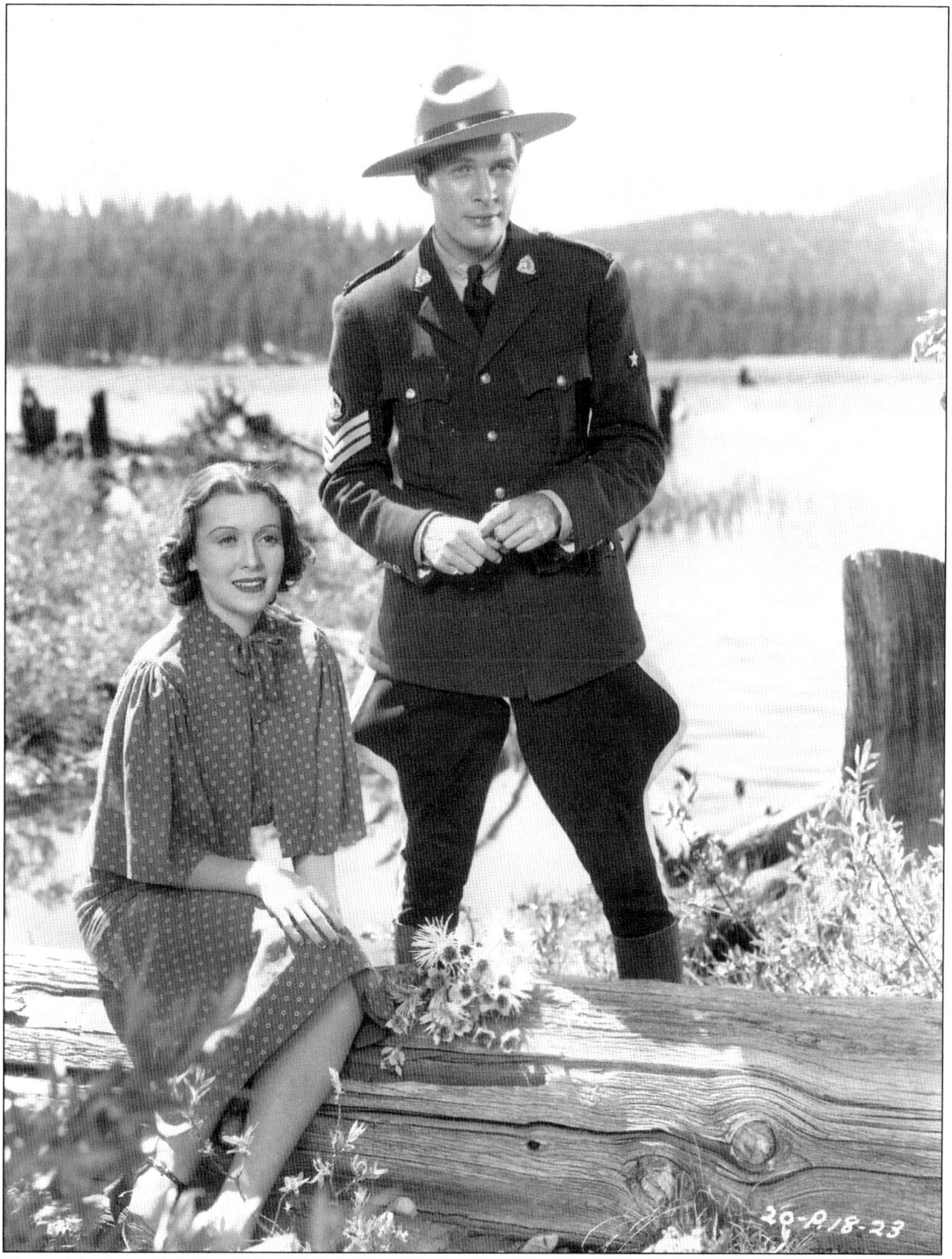


*King of the Royal Mounted* (1936) was filmed near the ski resort of Mammoth. *The Golden Child* and *Indiana Jones and the Temple of Doom* were other films shot there. In the nearby town of Bishop, *Joe Kidd*, *High Plains Drifter*, and *G.I. Joe: The Rise of Cobra* were filmed along Highway 395. The Rock Creek Lake area was also an early filming location for *The Golden Princess* (1925).

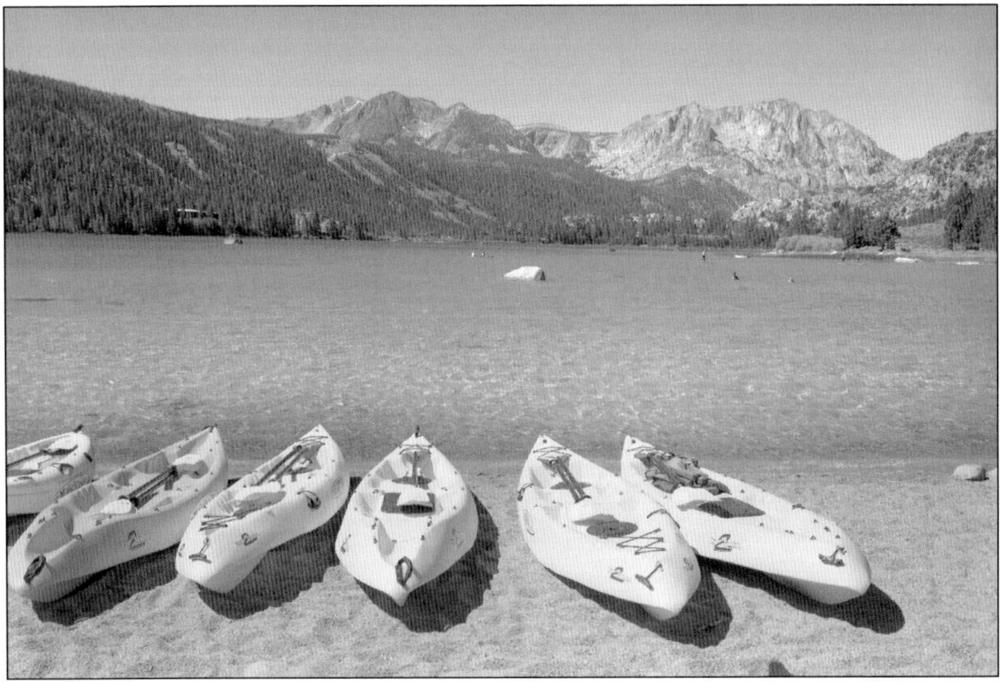

Continuing along Highway 395, one will come to June Lake Loop, where *Oblivion* (2013), starring Tom Cruise, was filmed. Most of this film was shot in Iceland and Maui, but the lake and meadow scene was filmed on June Lake. The site is a popular spot for kayaking and other recreational activities. (Courtesy of Library of Congress.)

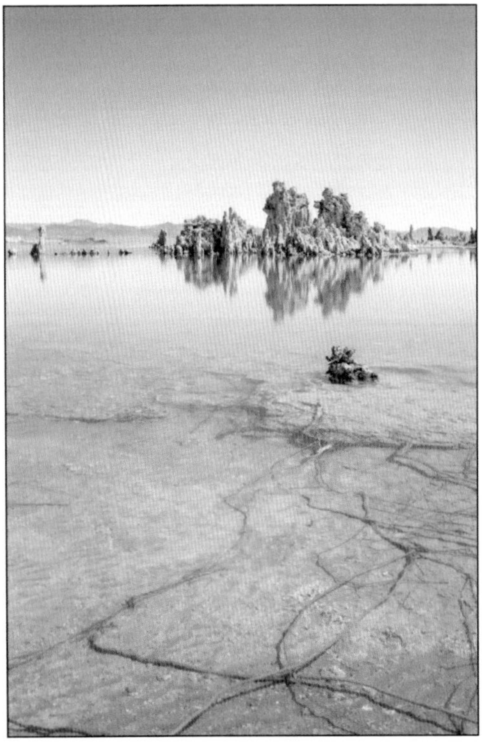

Mono Lake, which sits near the town of Lee Vining, gateway to Yosemite, featured a scaled model of a volcano from the film *Fair Winds from Java*. It was built by the Lydecker brothers, and the remnants of the structure are still there. (Courtesy of Wikipedia Commons.)

The town of Bridgeport, north of Lee Vining on Highway 395, is the filming location of one of the best film noirs, *Out of the Past* (1947), starring Robert Mitchum. Look across the street for the Bridgeport Courthouse in the beginning of the film. The Western *Stampede* (1949) was also filmed near Bridgeport, California.

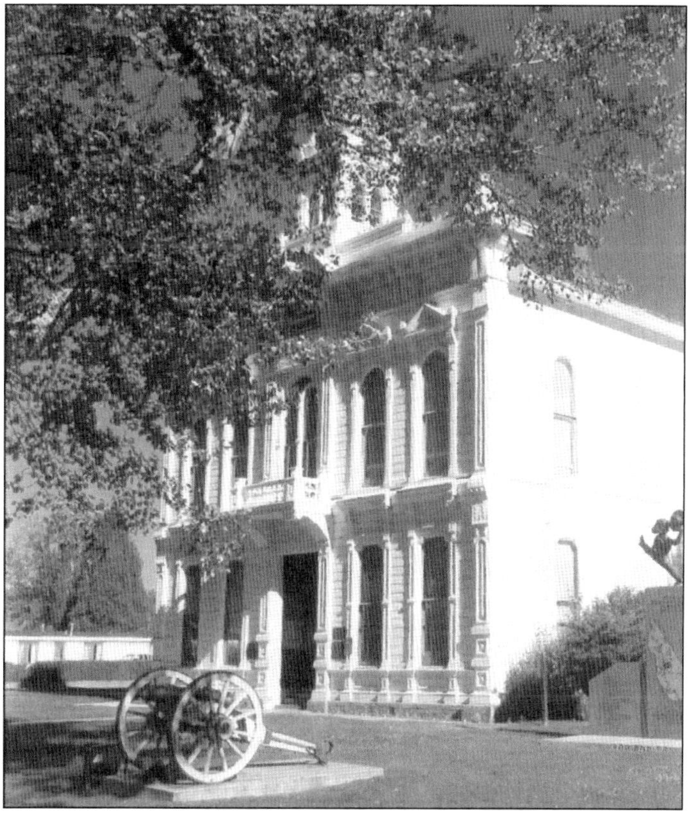

Pictured here are Mitchum and costar Jane Greer in *Out of the Past*. Mitchum also starred in two movies filmed in the Alabama Hills: *Nevada* (1944) and *West of the Pecos* (1945). (Courtesy of Wikipedia Commons.)

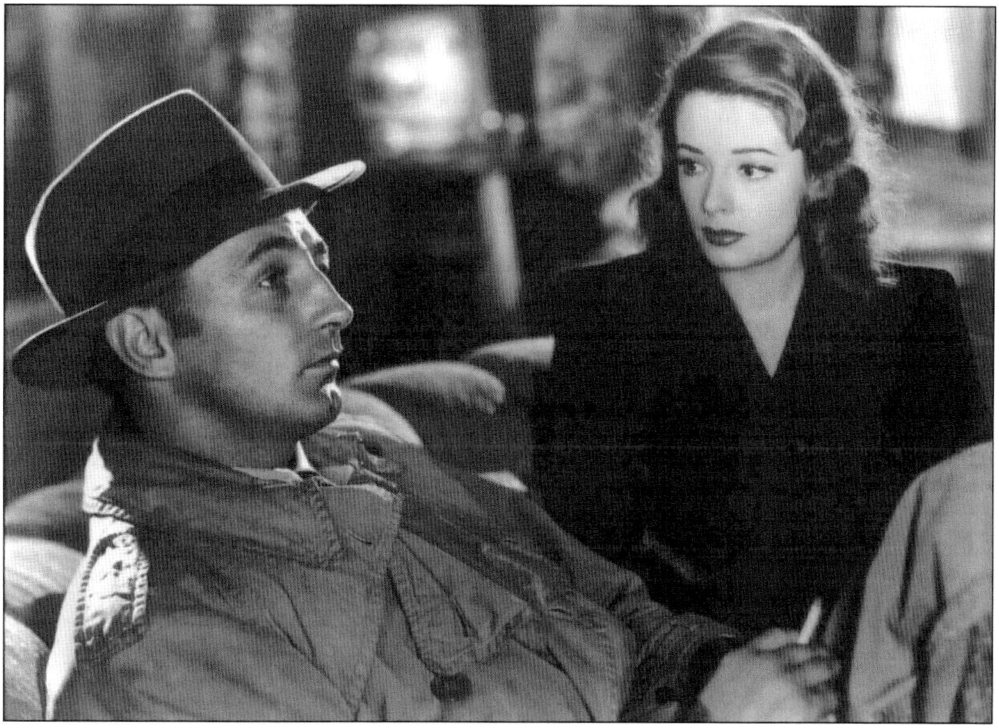

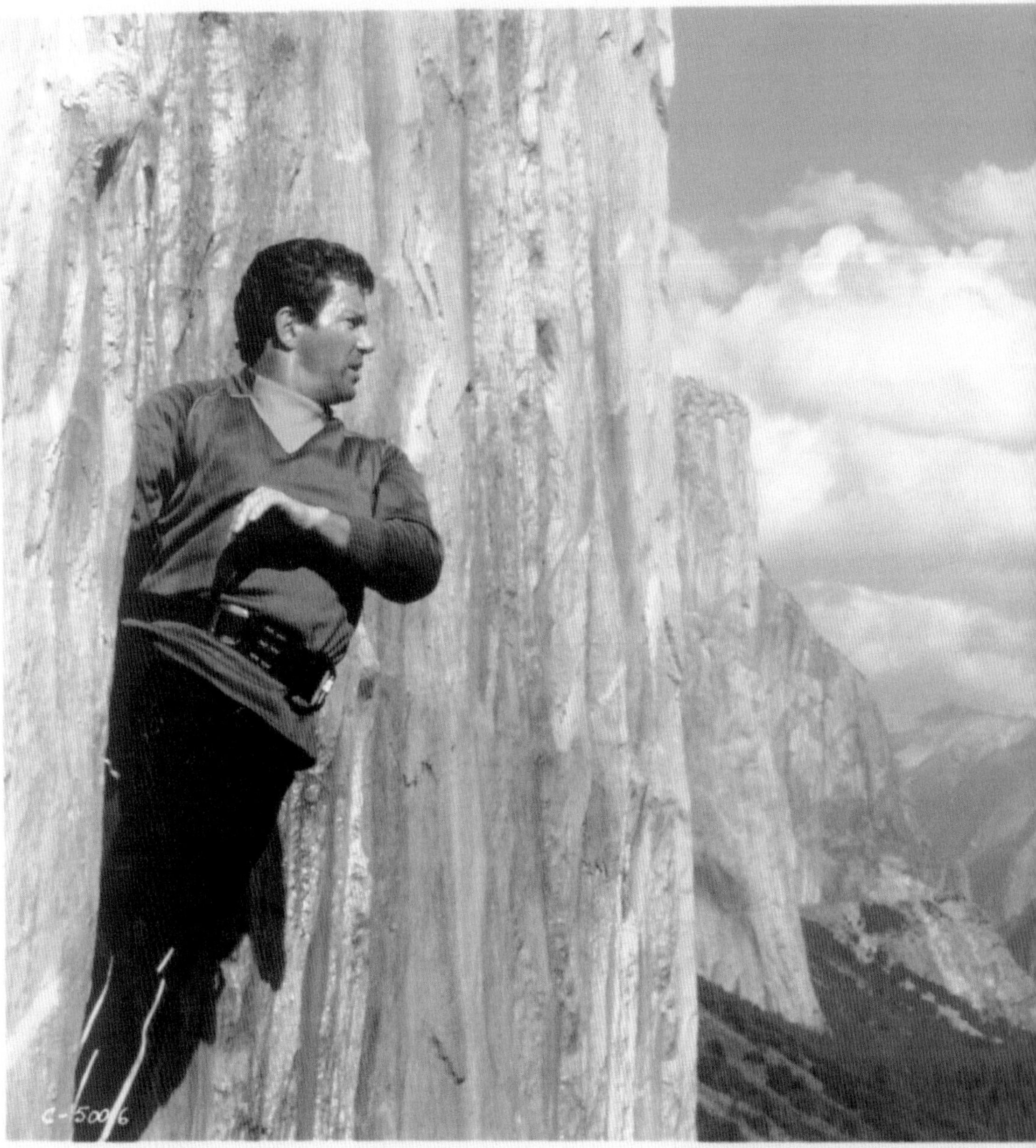


STAR TREK V
THE FINAL FRONTIER

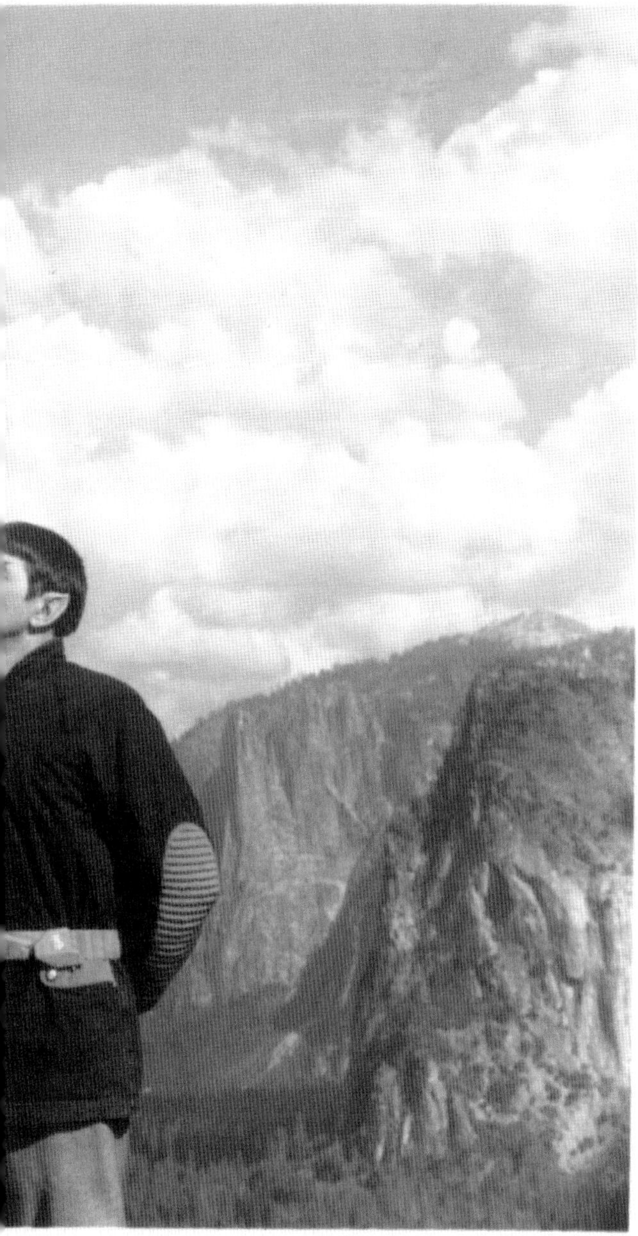

Photo by: Bruce Birmelin

ST5-CS-2 Before embarking on a mission that will take them on the most fantastic outer space adventure of all, Captain James T. Kirk (William Shatner, left) and Mr. Spock (Leonard Nimoy) take shore leave in Yosemite National Park in Paramount's "Star Trek V: The Final Frontier."

Yosemite Valley is most famous for three films: *The Long, Long Trailer* (1953), starring Lucille Ball and Desi Arnaz, *Star Trek V: The Final Frontier* (1989), and *The Caine Mutiny* (1954), starring Humphrey Bogart. This scene is from *Star Trek V*, in which Spock saves Captain Kirk from a fall off of Inspiration Point, doubling as El Capitan. *Maverick* (1994) was also filmed inside the park at Leidig Meadow and Washburn Point.

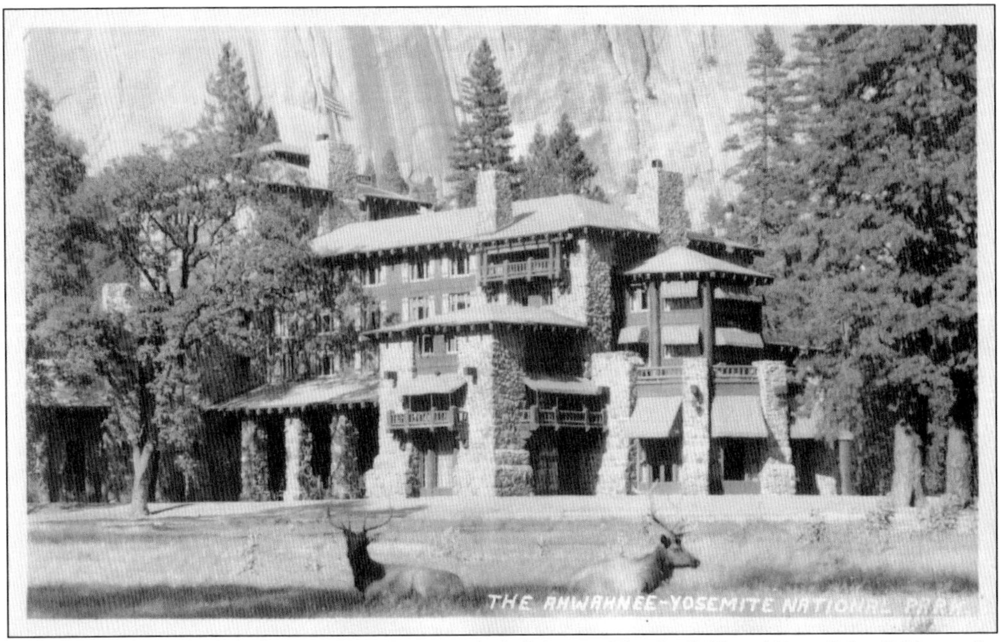


The Ahwahnee Hotel's notable guests have included Queen Elizabeth II and Pres. John F. Kennedy. The hotel, which is seen in *The Caine Mutiny*, served as a US Navy hospital during World War II. Some say the mezzanine floor is haunted.

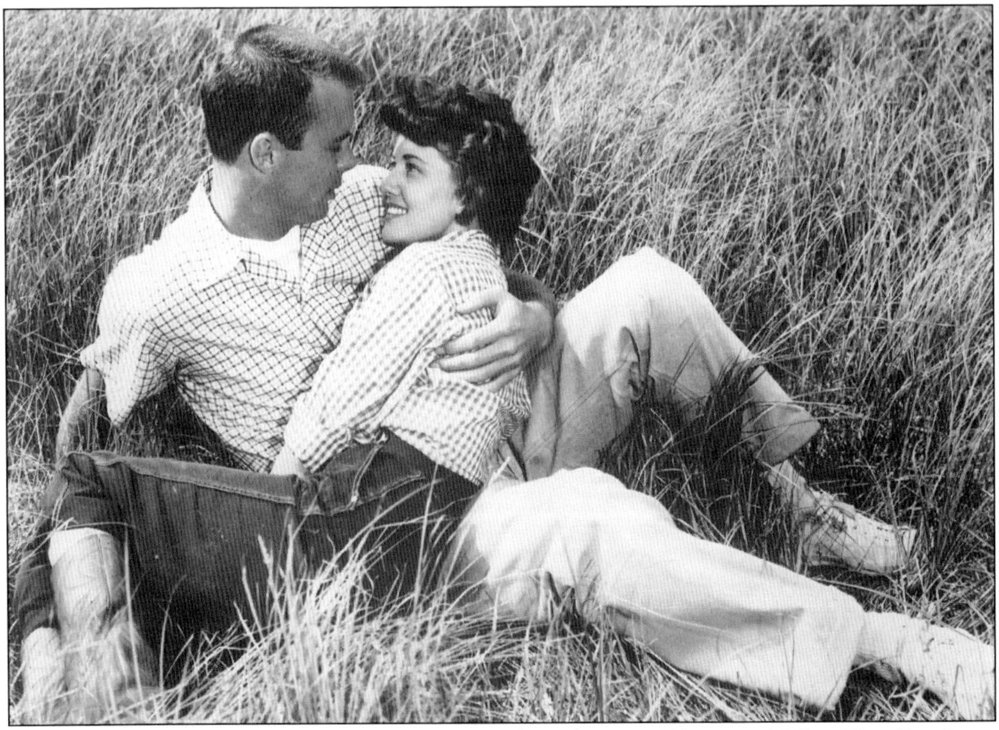

This scene from *The Caine Mutiny* shows one meadow of many in Yosemite Valley. The film shows one the best attractions Yosemite used to have—the Firefall—which was created when logs that were lit on fire were pushed over a steep cliff, resembling a waterfall of fire.

# *Seven*

# Exploring the Hills

The Alabama Hills, or "rocks" as some of the locals call them, are very special. It is a recreational area where residents may ride horses, and visitors can walk their dogs (on a leash) to explore the various filming locations discussed throughout this book.

Even though it can be viewed as a tourist destination, visitors should be cognizant of the fact that the Alabama Hills and the surrounding area are located in rough terrain. For example, the climate can be hot in the summer and incredibly cold in the winter. Rattlesnakes are prevalent, especially when venturing off-trail. When patrolling like the Light Brigade, visitors should dress in layered clothing, carry plenty of food of water, and wear comfortable shoes. Cellular phones may lose reception; thus, visiting in groups is advisable in the event that emergency medical attention is necessary. Further, visitors should use discretion in proximity of the boulders, as thousands of years of erosion have left the rocks brittle and unstable.

Feeding animals, disturbing plants, or taking artifacts as souvenirs is not permitted. If artifacts are located, visitors should contact the Beverly and Jim Rogers Museum of Lone Pine Film History.

When touring filming locations by vehicle, it is advisable to drive slowly, remain on designated roads, and stay close to the vehicle after exiting. Whitney Portal Road, which traces the route of Humphrey Bogart in *High Sierra* (1941), is closed in the winter. When open, visitors should exercise caution, as it is steep and winding. Overnight camping is allowed in authorized campsites.

If prepared, the Alabama Hills are truly worth exploring. Many visitors bring tangible photographs or digital images from a favorite movie scene and enjoy the hunt of finding the exact location where film stars once stood. Professional and amateur artists also frequent the area, especially at dusk, when the sunset alters the colors of the rocks to create jaw-dropping beauty.

The Alabama Hills can be equally enjoyable to those seeking picturesque landscapes and impeccable viewing locations to witness the grandeur of the Sierra Nevada.

To contribute to conservation efforts, such as "Don't Crush the Brush", visitors may obtain information from the Lone Pine Chamber of Commerce or the Alabama Hills Stewardship. Filmmakers seeking production permits or other necessary credentials should contact the Inyo County Film Commission and the Bureau of Land Management. Most importantly, visitors to the Alabama Hills should relaxingly enjoy the filming locations, have fun, and let the movies keep rolling along!

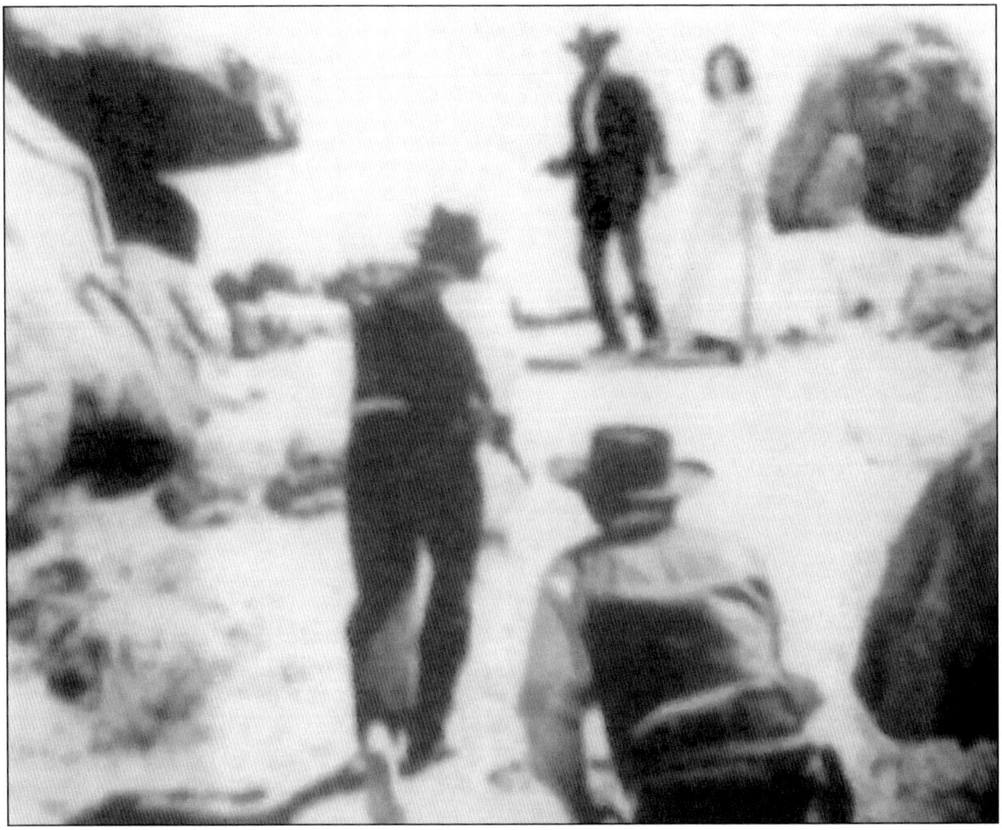

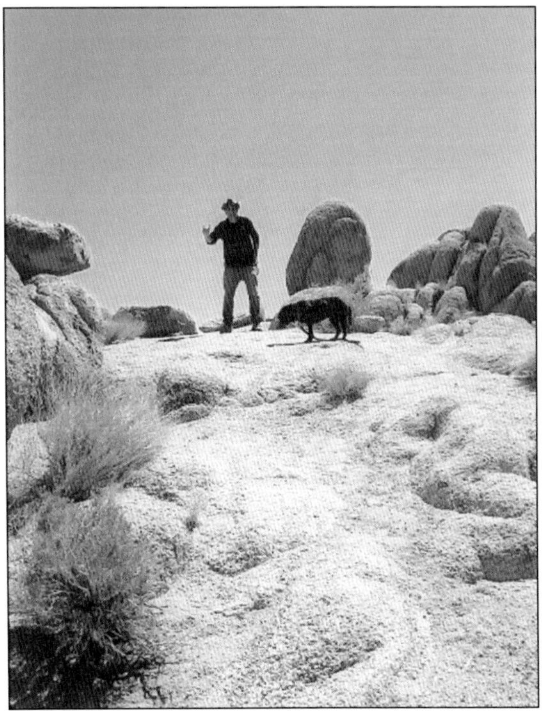

The image above is from *Hell Bent for Leather* with Audie Murphy and Felicia Farr. The image at left shows the author with his dog Doughgirl in same spot. Also pictured is Gary Cooper Rock, named after *Lives of a Bengal Lancer* was shot there in 1935.

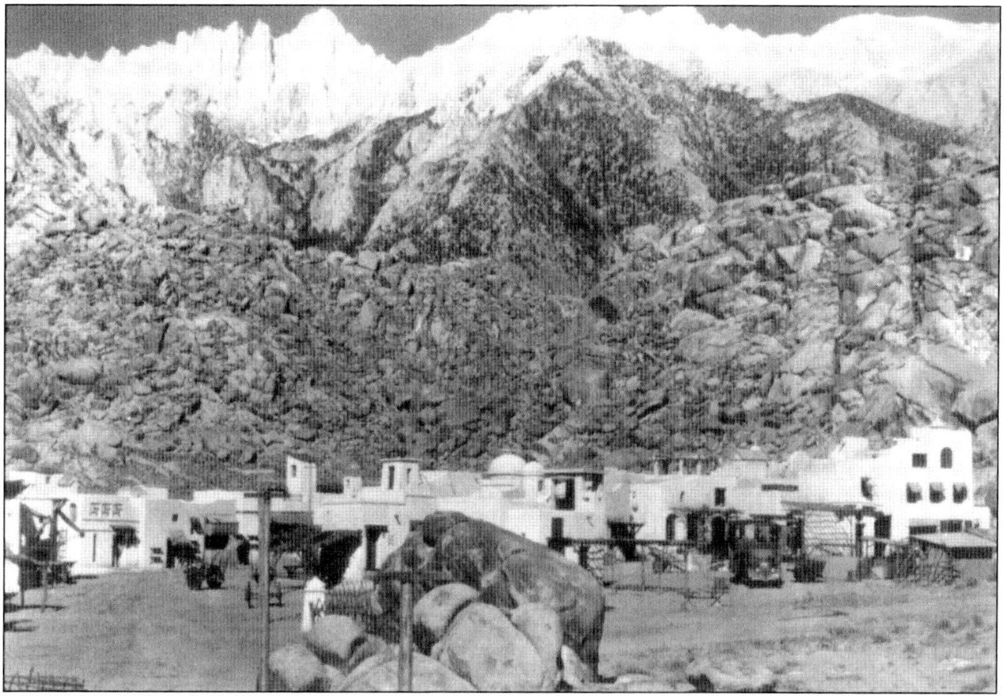

In the image above from *Gunga Din*, the town of Tantrapur is seen. Below, the author holds the *Gunga Din* DVD in the same spot where the town once stood.

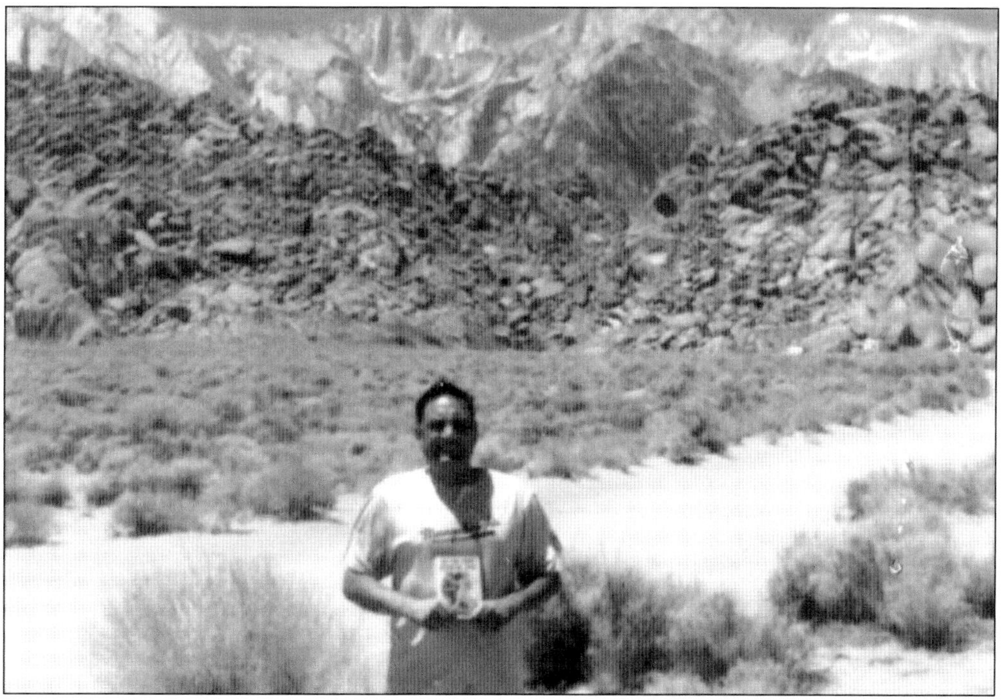

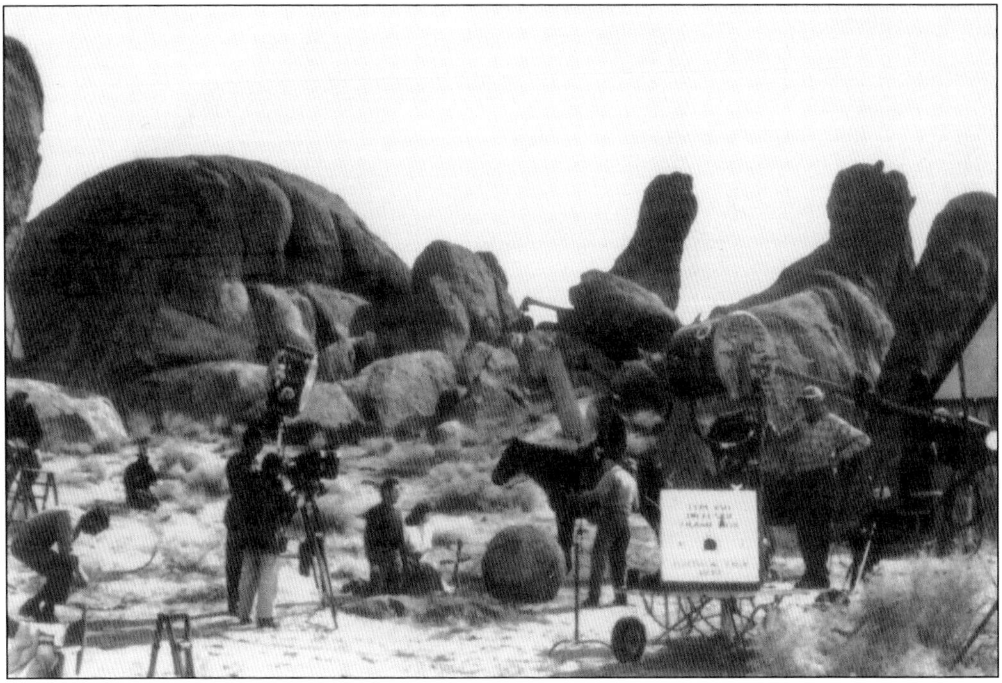

Pictured above is the *Rawhide* (1951) gravesite with filming crews. Below, the author is shown beside the same bowling ball rock, imitating the holding of the horse.

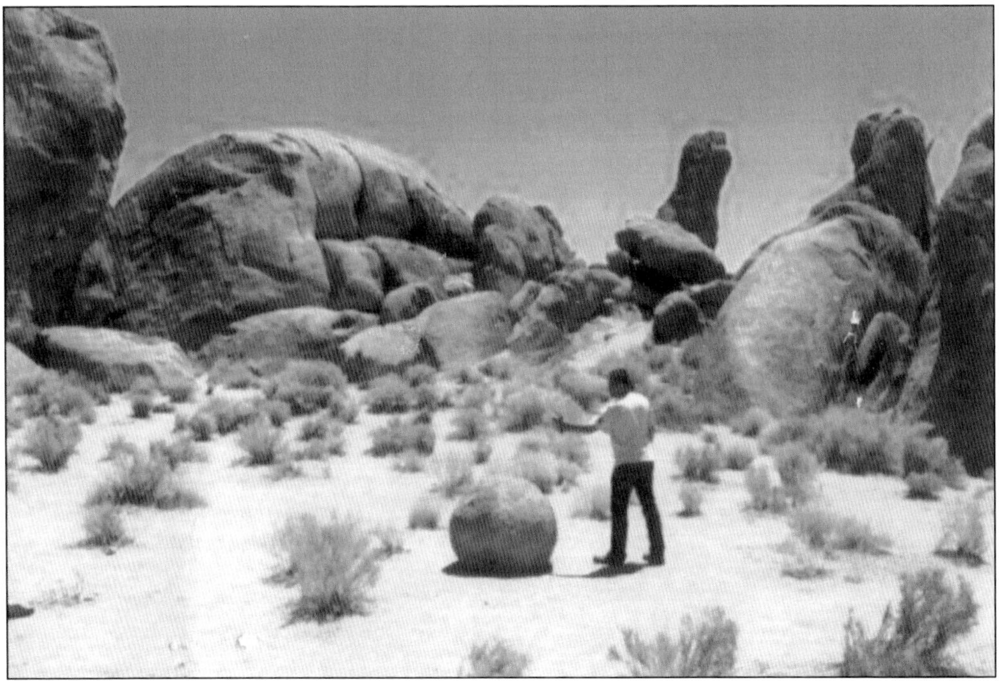

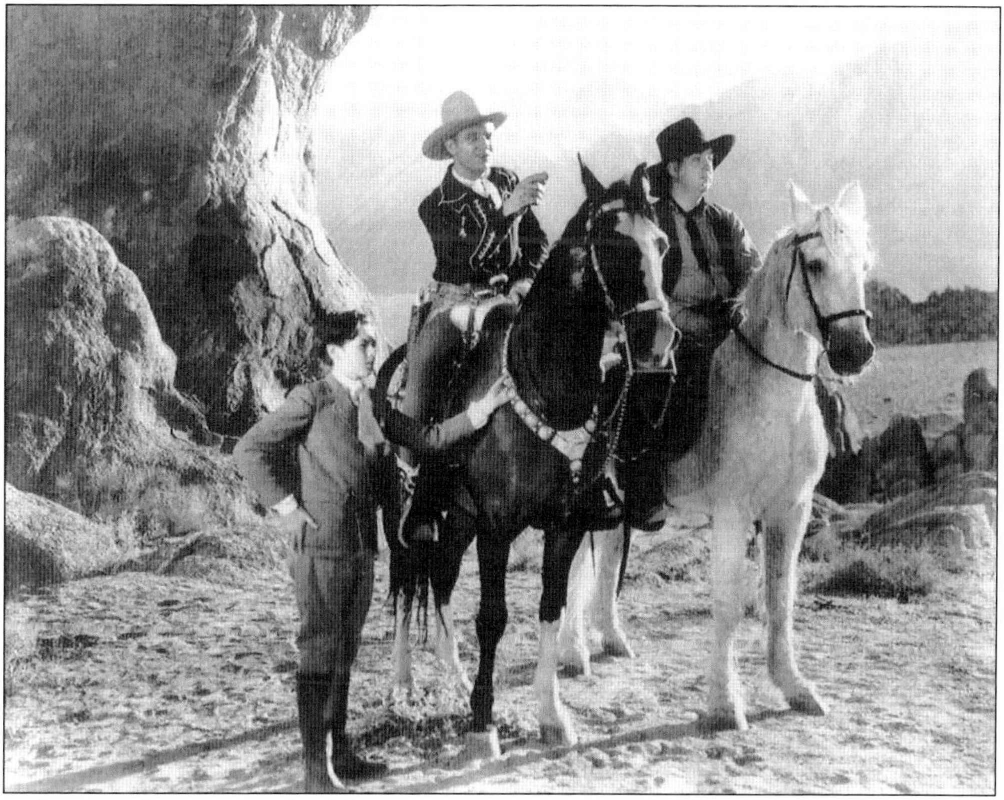

In this scene from *Boots and Saddles* (1937), Gene Autry is pictured at Gene Autry Rock. Shown below is Gene Autry Rock as it appears today.

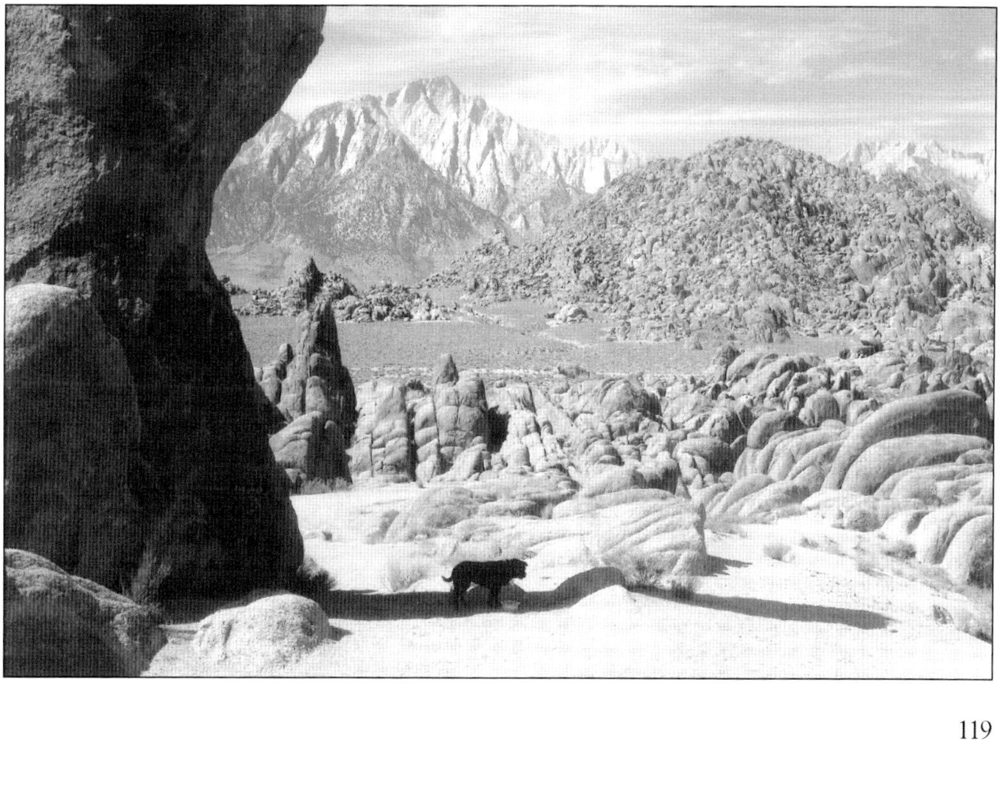

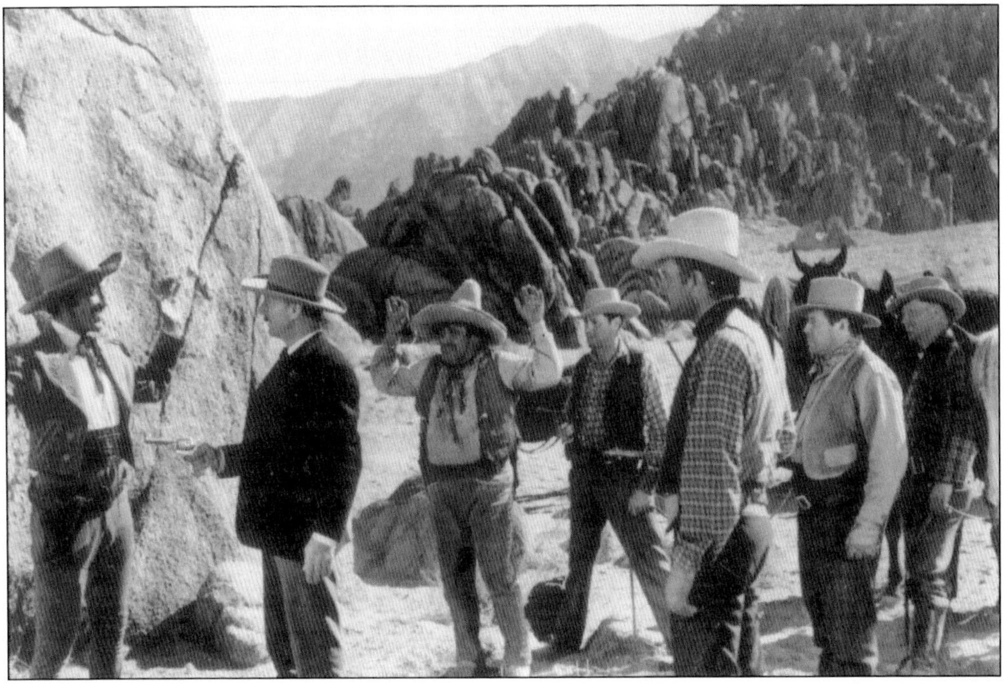

This still is from *The Cisco Kid and the Lady* (1939), which starred Cesar Romero, who was Tyrone Power's pallbearer. Below, the author imitates the same scene. This location is off Movie Road near the Gunga Din bridge site.

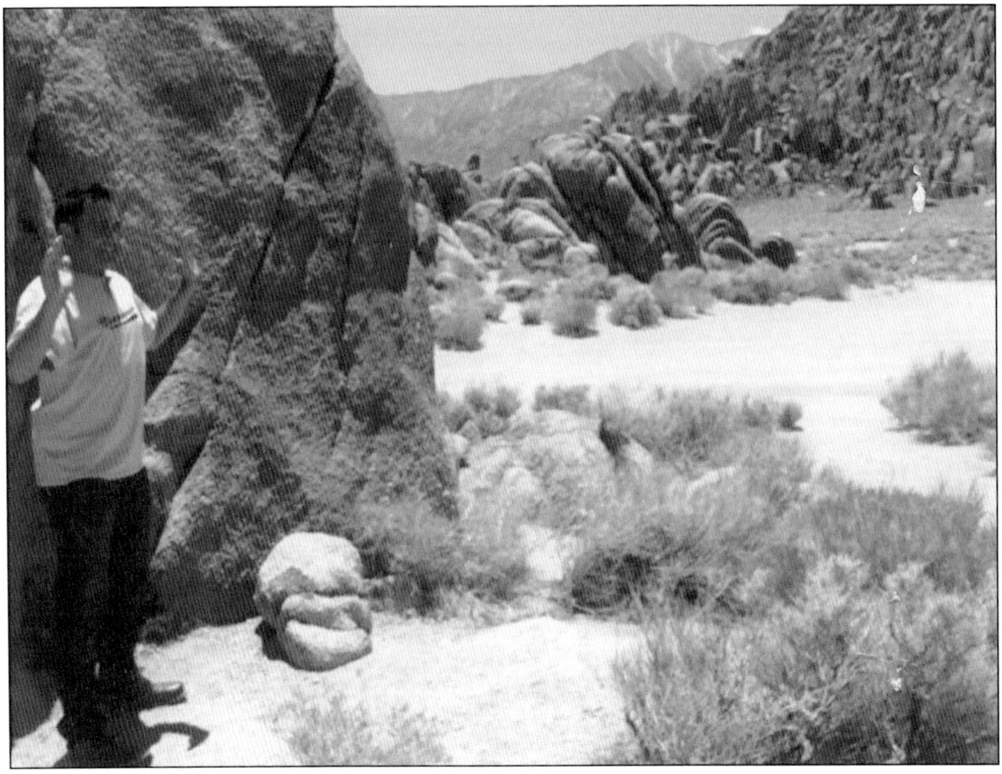

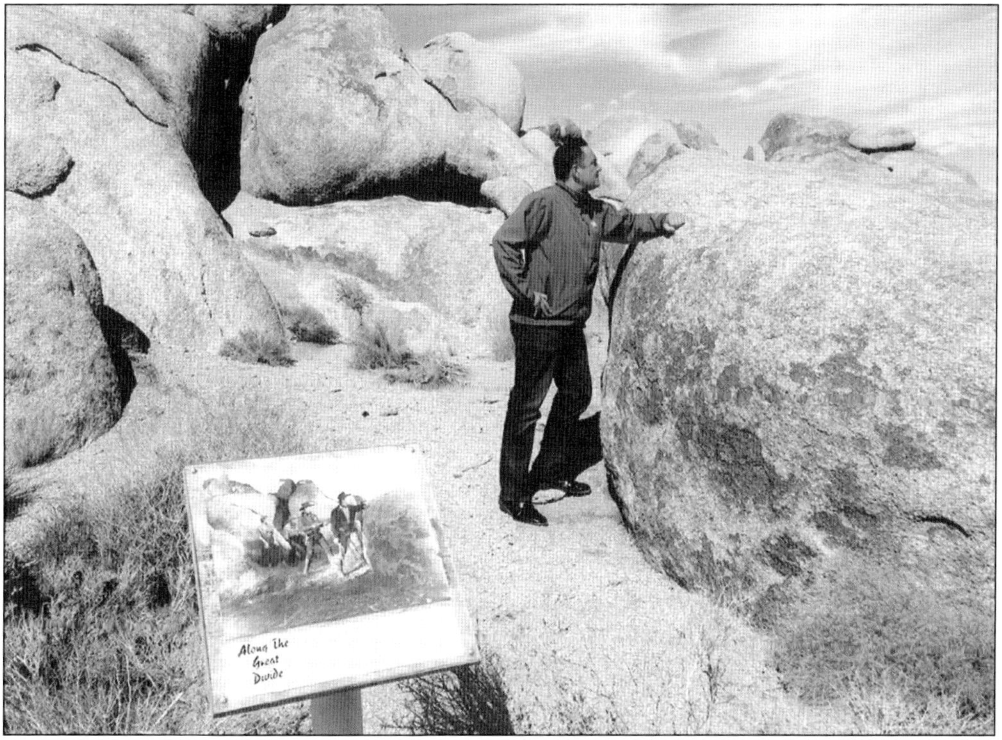


This filming location from *Along the Great Divide* can be found near Lone Ranger Canyon.

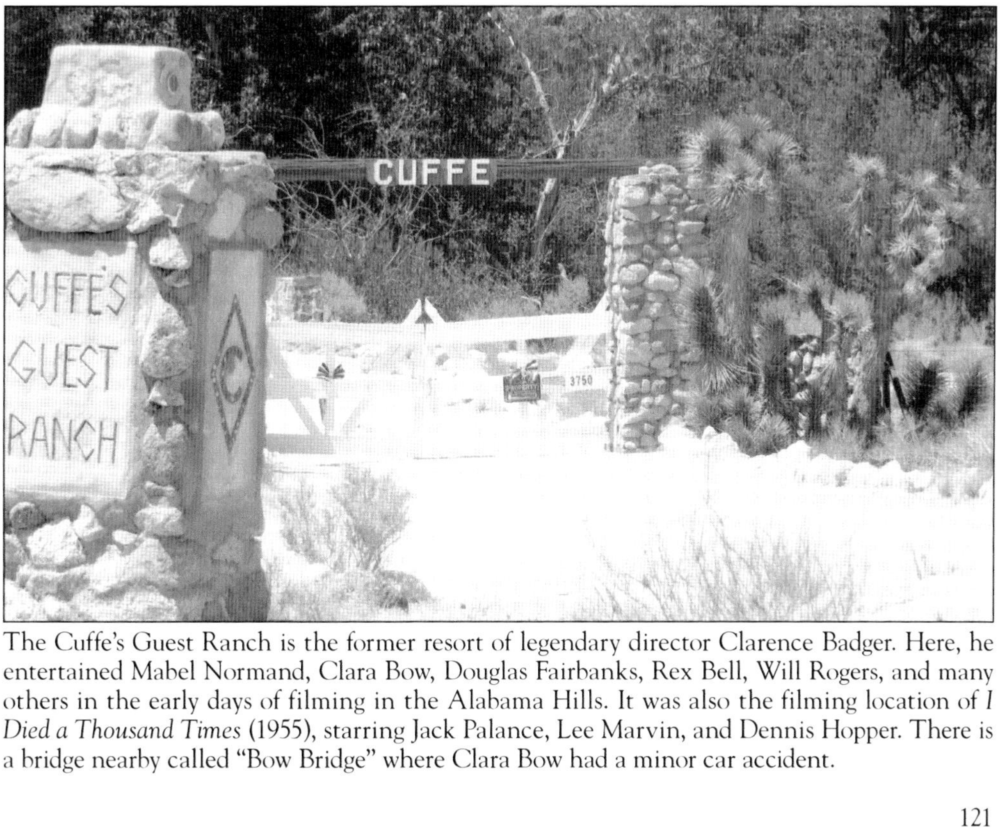


The Cuffe's Guest Ranch is the former resort of legendary director Clarence Badger. Here, he entertained Mabel Normand, Clara Bow, Douglas Fairbanks, Rex Bell, Will Rogers, and many others in the early days of filming in the Alabama Hills. It was also the filming location of *I Died a Thousand Times* (1955), starring Jack Palance, Lee Marvin, and Dennis Hopper. There is a bridge nearby called "Bow Bridge" where Clara Bow had a minor car accident.

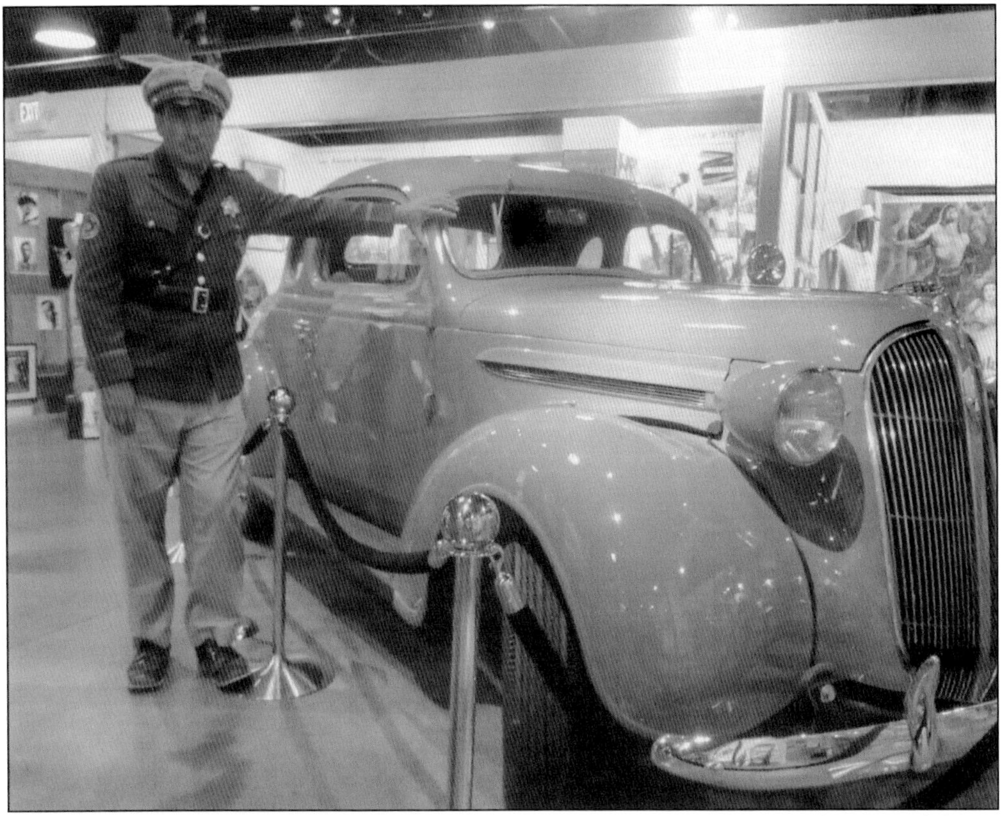

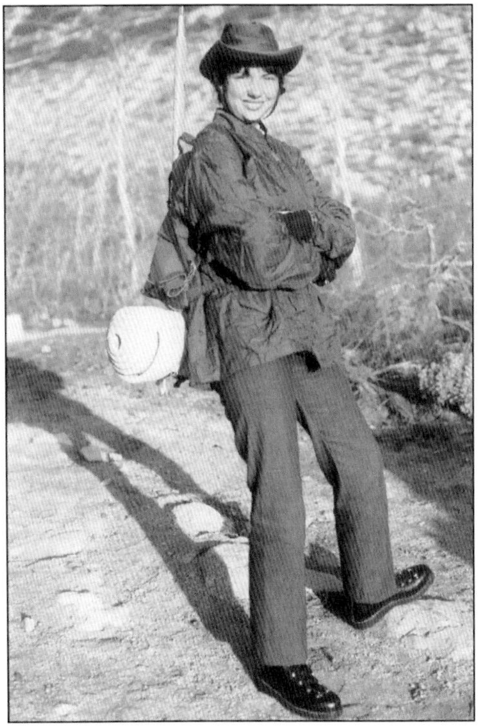

Here, the author wears an authentic California Highway Patrol uniform acquired from Byron Duncan. The car, a 1937 Plymouth Coupe, was driven by Bogart in a chase seen at the end of *High Sierra* (1941). The car can be viewed at the film museum in Lone Pine.

The author's mother, Jean-Marie Morfin, is shown here backpacking near the Alabama Hills. The area is popular for recreation and is administered by the Bureau of Land Management.

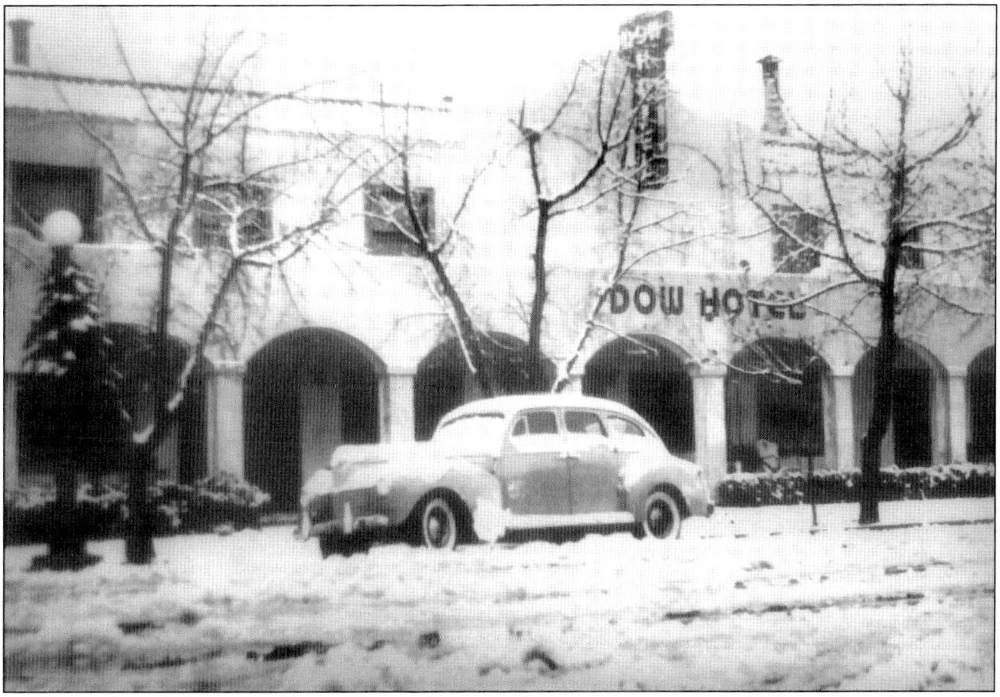


Above, the Dow Hotel is seen around the 1940s with a Plymouth Sedan similar to the one used in *Bad Day at Black Rock* (1955) and *Tycoon* (1947), starring John Wayne. Below, the Dow Villa, as it is now called, is pictured in 2013 after a complete restoration of its front facade. Wayne's room at the Dow Villa had the only in-room spa.

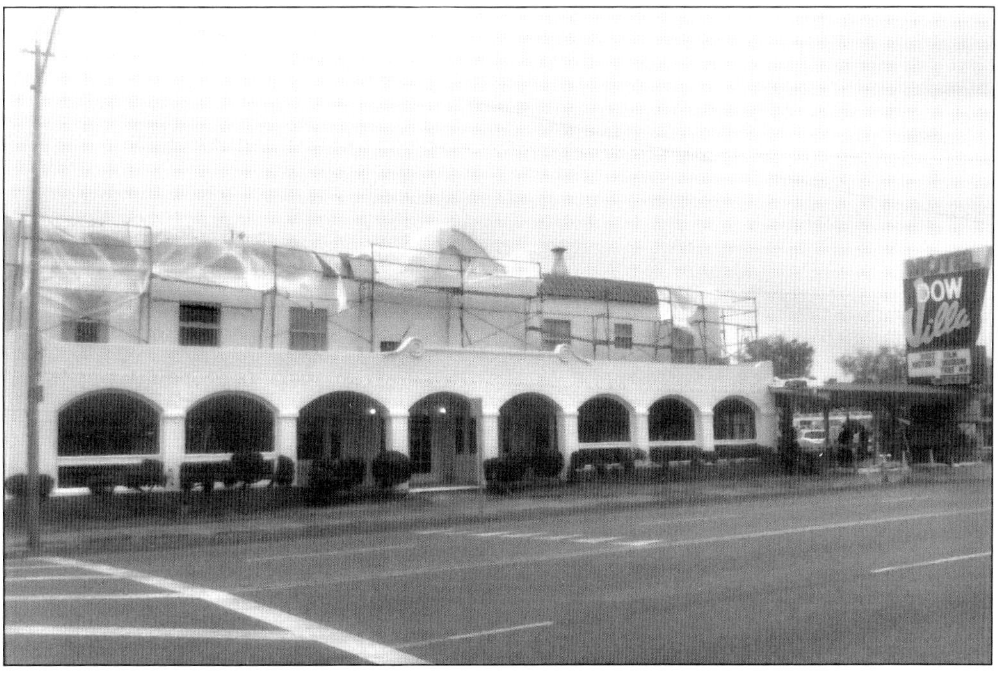

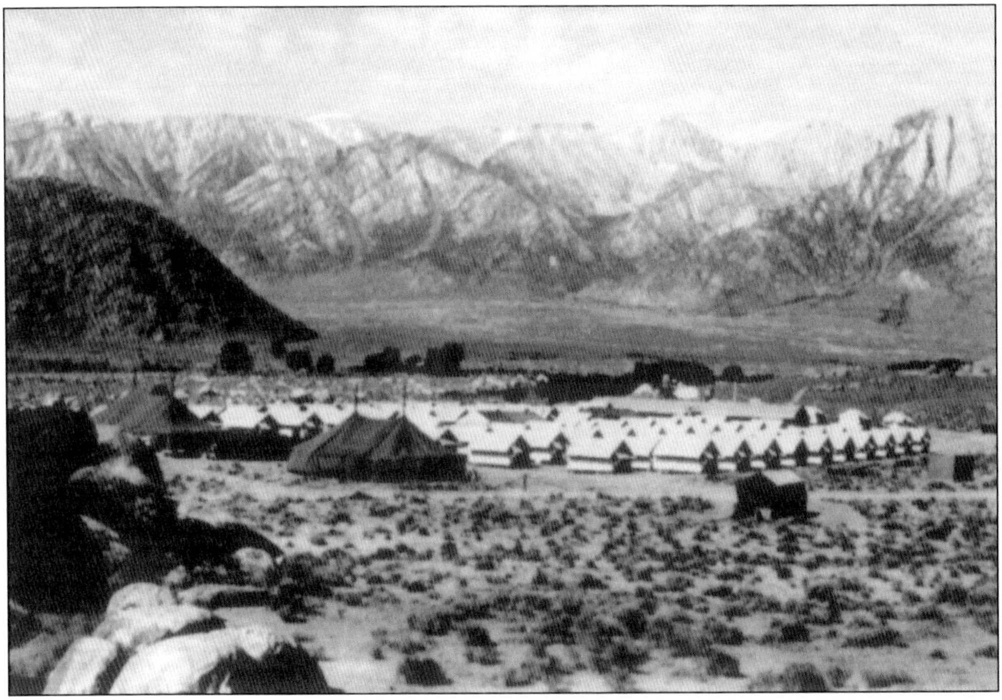

*Gunga Din* (1939) was the largest production to be filmed in the Alabama Hills. In the image below, the author shows where all the tents and crew were in 1939.

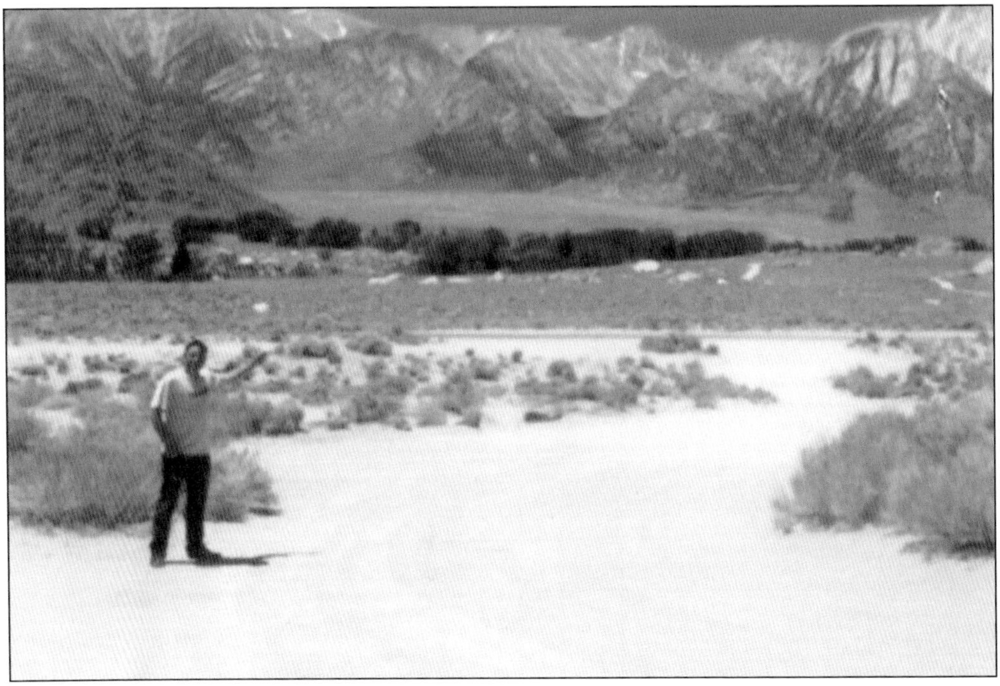

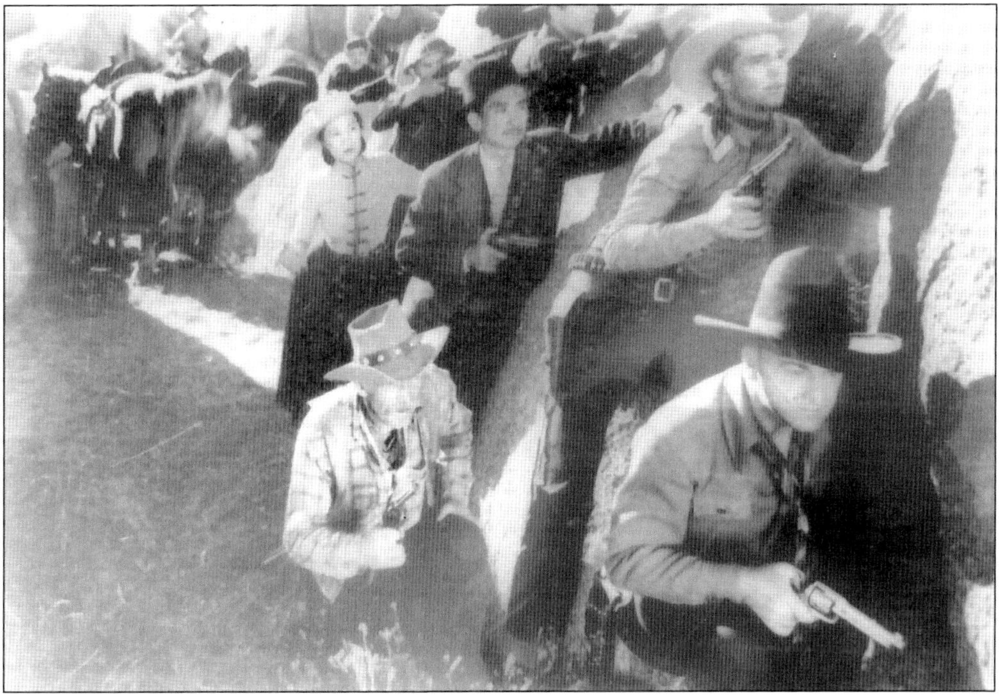

*Hopalong Cassidy* was one of the longest-running serials filmed in the Alabama Hills. The image above is from one of the 54 episodes and shows "Hoppy" crouching behind a rock. Below, the author poses in same location.

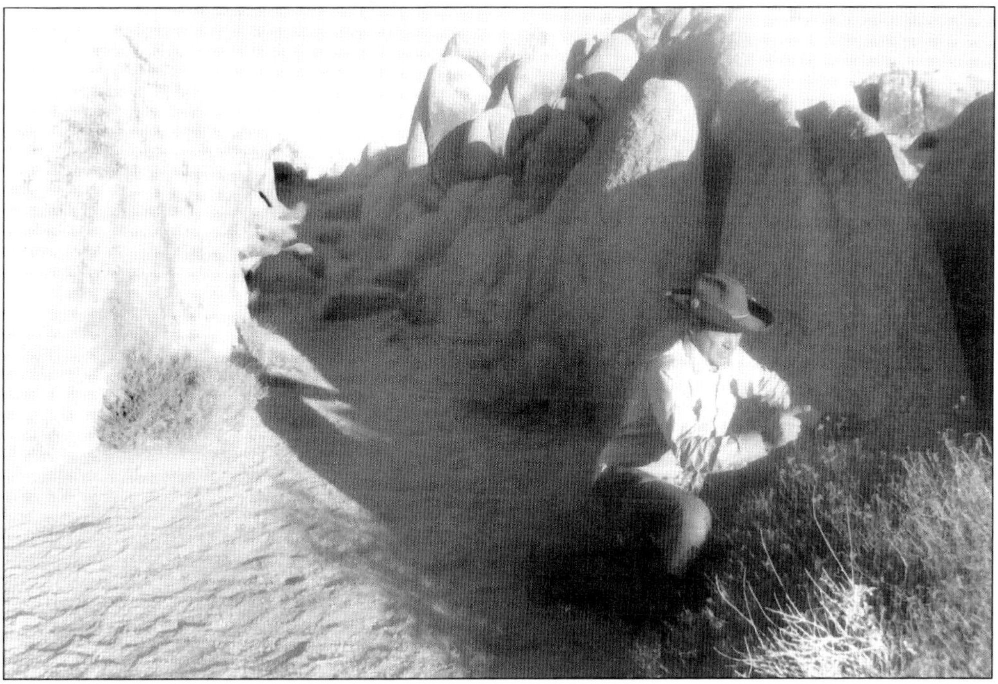

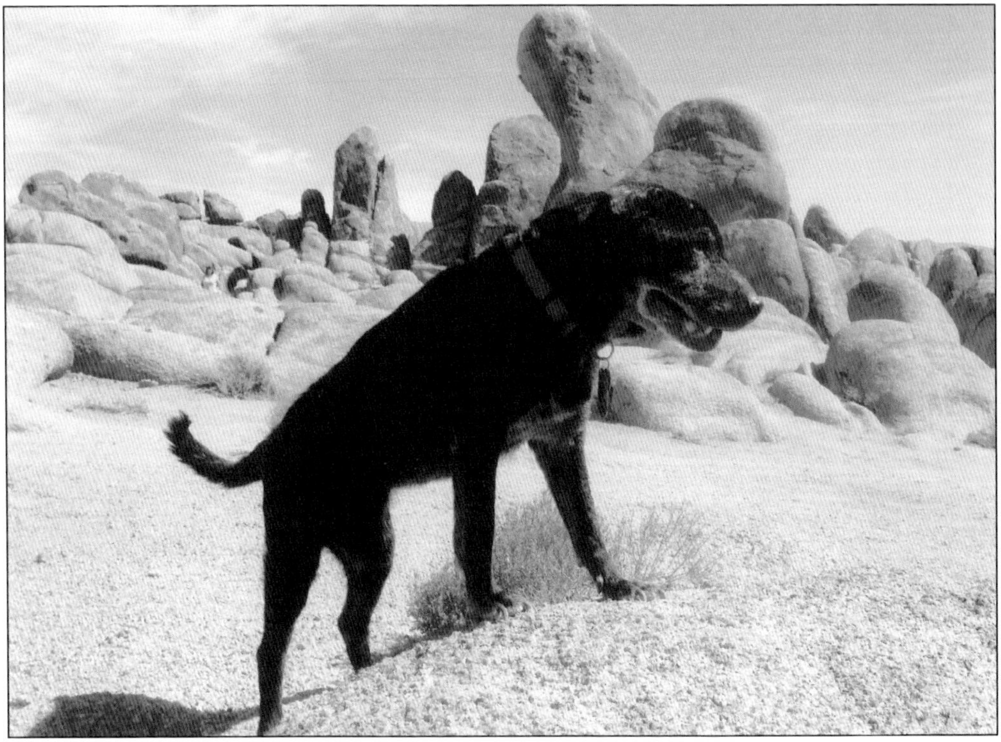

The author's dog Doughgirl is seen here in her favorite movie location. *Guns of Hate* (1948), *False Colors* (1943), *Lives of a Bengal Lancer* (1935), *Boots and Saddles* (1937), *Django Unchained* (2012), and many others were filmed this area.

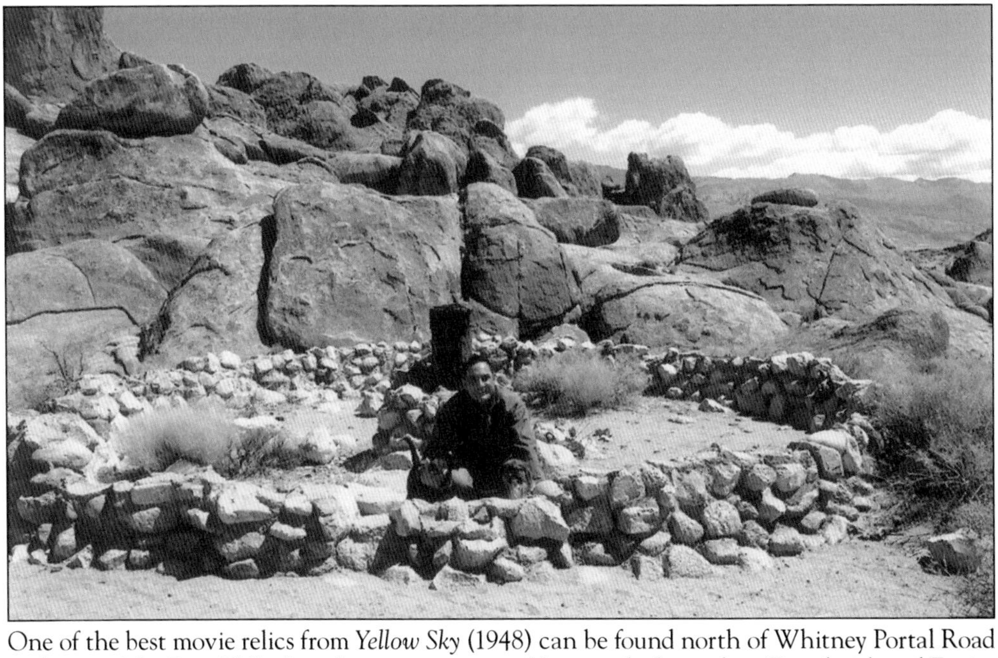

One of the best movie relics from *Yellow Sky* (1948) can be found north of Whitney Portal Road and west of the Ruiz Hills. It is the aristae, pictured here with the author, Doughgirl, and Ernies imitating Gregory Peck and others from the film.

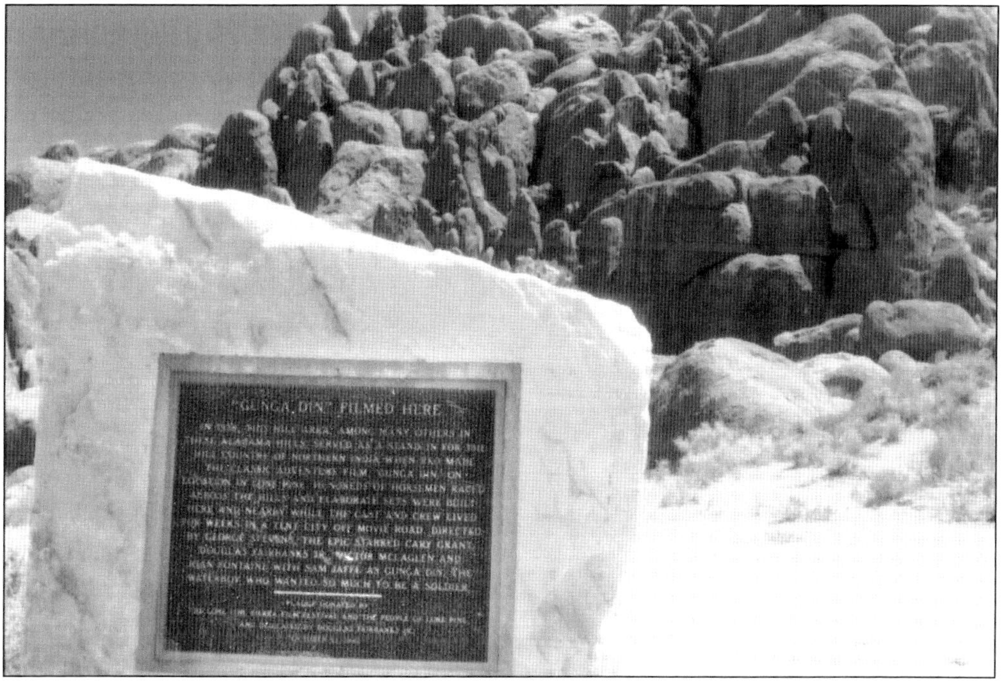


The monument to the temple from *Gunga Din* is located off Horseshoe Meadow Road from Whitney Portal Road.

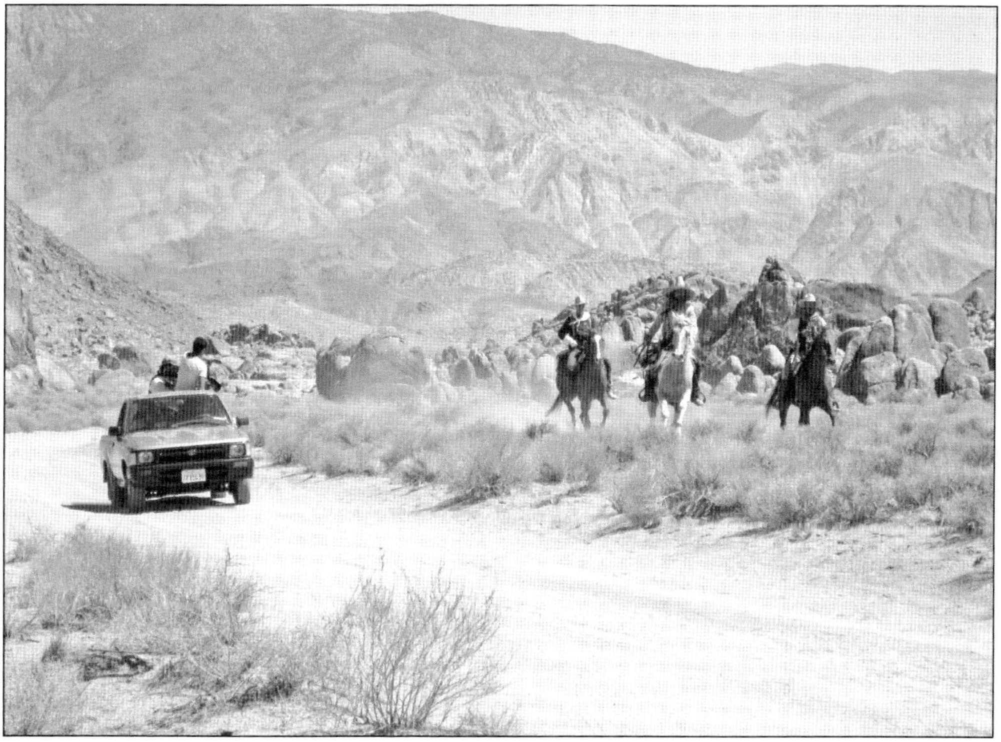

Modern filming crews may still be seen today in the rocks. Here is a crew form *Friend of the Devil* (2009), a Western short directed by Eric Heisner.

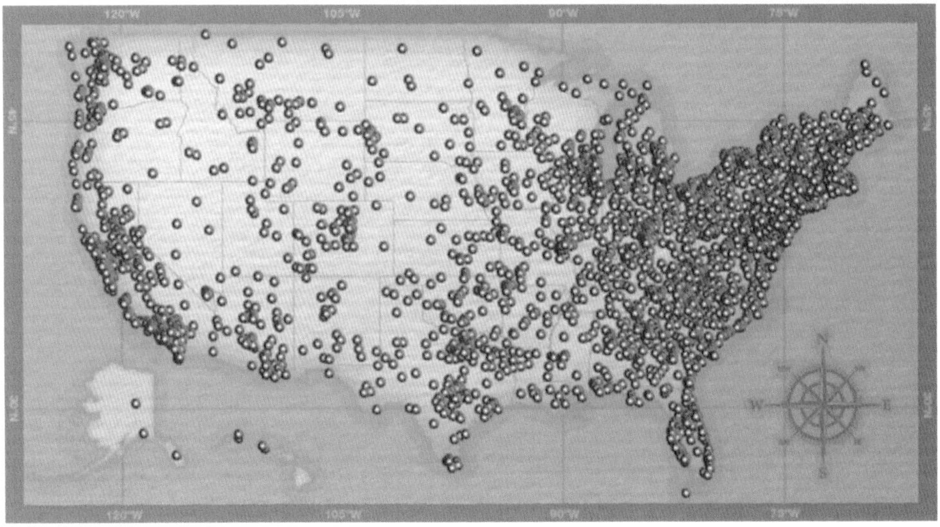